Choice, Expectation and Uncertainty

Choice, Expectation and Uncertainty

An Appraisal of G. L. S. Shackle's Theory

J. L. FORD

Martin Robertson · Oxford

First published in 1983 by Martin Robertson & Company Ltd.,
108 Cowley Road, Oxford OX4 1JF.

British Library Cataloguing in Publication Data

Ford, J.L.
Choice, expectation and uncertainty.
1. Decision-making in economics–Mathematical models
I. Title
330′.01′84 HC240

ISBN 0-85520-657-8

Typeset by
STYLESET LIMITED
Salisbury · Wiltshire
Printed and bound in Great Britain by
The Pitman Press, Bath

To my Mother
and
the loving memory of my Father

'And you cannot move at all in Time, you cannot get away from the present moment.'

'My dear sir, that is just where you are wrong. That is just where the whole world has gone wrong. We are always getting away from the present moment. Our mental existences, which are immaterial and have no dimensions, are passing along the Time-Dimension with a uniform velocity from the cradle to the grave. Just as we should travel *down* if we began our existence fifty miles above the earth's surface.'

'But the great difficulty is this', interrupted the Psychologist. 'You *can* move about in all directions of Space, but you cannot move about in Time.'

H. G. Wells *The Time Machine*

Contents

	List of Tables and Figures	ix
	Preface and Acknowledgements	xi
	Introduction Time and Uncertainty in Economics: A Perspective on Professor Shackle's Views	1
1	The Orthodox Approach and Portfolio Investment	15
2	An Outline of Professor Shackle's Theory	54
3	A Detailed Study of Portfolio Selection and the Shackle Theory	79
4	The Shackle Schema: A Critical Exegesis	96
5	The Critical Exegesis in Sum and An Axiomatic Treatment of the Shackle Model	135
6	Uncertainty and Choice: A Wider Perspective	157
7	Summary and Conclusions	177
	Notes	188
	Bibliography	204
	Index	209

List of Tables and Figures

TABLES

1.1 The states of nature pay-off matrix 17
2.1 An investment pay-off matrix 57
2.2 An investment pay-off matrix 59
4.1 The potential surprise pay-off matrix for three assets and three states of nature 119
4.2 The potential surprise pay-off matrix for two assets and two states of nature 120

FIGURES

1.1 Mean-variance frontier and correlation between asset yields 28
1.2 The optimum mean-variance combination 29
1.3 The effect of a change in asset yields on the optimal mean-variance combination 33
1.4 The optimum portfolio of assets 34
1.5 Marginal expected utilities and asset selection 40
1.6 The optimum holding of money in a two-asset model 42
1.7 The mean-variance frontier for money and two risky assets 42
1.8 The efficient investment frontier for one riskless and many risky assets 49
1.9 The method of derivation of the efficient investment frontier for one riskless and many risky assets 50
2.1 The ϕ-indifference map and the potential surprise function 63
2.2 The gambler-preference map 64
2.3 The ϕ-function 74
2.4 Wealth, the gambler-preference map and the attitude to risk 76
3.1 The gambler-preference map and the investment opportunity line 81
3.2 Investment opportunities with three financial assets 82
3.3 The investment opportunity frontier and constraints on asset choice 88
3.4 Marginal utilities and the selection of the optimum portfolio 89
3.5 An increase in wealth and the Shackle investment frontier 92

3.6 The investor's response to asset yields 93
3.7 Money and the investment frontier 94
3.8 The optimum mix of money and bonds 95
4.1 Primary and standardized focus gains 99
4.2 Potential surprise functions and focus gains 101
4.3 Primary and standardized focus gains and losses 104
4.4 The Shackle investment frontier with perfectly negative correlation between asset yields 122
4.5 The return-risk frontier of Domar and Musgrave 125
4.6 The selection of focus values and potential surprise 132
4.7 The selection of focus values and subjective probability 133
6.1 The Shackle scale opportunity line for investment in plant and machinery 159

Preface and Acknowledgements

Two publications more than any others enticed me for ever into the study of economics and, in particular, into the realm of economic theory. One of these was George Shackle's *Expectation in Economics*. The other was John Hicks' *Value and Capital*. I first read the latter as a schoolboy, and I cannot pretend that I understood more than a fraction of it. But the foundations were laid.

I came across George Shackle's book a year or so later at the beginning of my first year as an undergraduate at the University of Liverpool. Again, at that age and time much in the book mystified me, but it was fascinating and gripping material: I can still remember (to paraphrase George Shackle himself) the feeling of enjoyment by anticipation, that I experienced in just thumbing through the book and in effecting its purchase at the princely (second-hand) sum of 12s 6d. That feeling cannot be captured in words. But the intense pleasure was not dissipated by a deeper perusal of the book. In fact, it was heightened, despite my inability to grasp fully the novel and, therefore, somewhat alien framework that George Shackle was describing as a means of characterizing the way that individuals take decisions in a world of uncertainty. Later on, as a third year undergraduate, I was fortunate to learn about his theory from Professor Shackle himself.

Expectation in Economics is a highly original book and is a veritable *tour de force* as a theoretical work. Apart from a concentrated period of study of it in the 1950s, it has, however, received relatively scant discussion in the literature. This is despite Professor Shackle's restatements of his theory of choice in several articles and in a number of major books.

The purpose of this volume is to rectify that state of affairs. In the process, besides providing an exposition of Professor Shackle's theory, I will consider the criticisms that have been made of it in the literature (largely, as I have noted, in the 1950s), advance my own critique of the theory, and suggest an alternative theoretical framework that is very much in the spirit of Professor Shackle's theory but similar in the letter to the orthodox, probabilistic, approach to choice under uncertainty that he was challenging. I will evaluate the Shackle theory in the light of that orthodox approach.

I have endeavoured to describe this approach and to analyse the application of it to various situations involving choice of action, especially to that of portfolio selection (chapter 1), in a way that might make the material accessible to students, especially third-year undergraduates and post-graduate students. Such material is also presented in some length because every aspect of it provides a necessary backcloth to the presentation and evaluation of the Shackle paradigm.

Most of the contents of chapter 1 are well known. Those of the remaining chapters less so; and some of them, especially chapters 4, 5 and 6 (and in a small part chapter 2) contain new material. Hopefully, those chapters will have some appeal not only to academic economists but students and also to scholars in other disciplines.

The idea for this book first surfaced during 1969 when I had the pleasure of teaching in the Fall Semester at the University of California at Los Angeles. One of my duties was to lecture to graduate students on international trade theory; the other was to give a series of lectures on themes of my own choosing on a course with an aptly open-ended title: Issues in Economic Theory. It was for that course that I first prepared lectures on Shackle's theory of expectations, which gave me the idea of writing a book on that theme. But, thereafter, that idea receded into the background as other research work took priority. Apart from a six-month intensive spell of activity on it at the University of Sheffield in 1976, the majority of the manuscript was not started until mid-1981.

During the course of the preparation of the book I have benefited from the discussions I have had with my colleagues at the Universities of Sheffield and Birmingham, and from the comments I have received from undergraduate and post-graduate students at those Universities. To all of them I express my grateful thanks.

My greatest debt is, however, to Sir Charles Carter, John Hey and Stan Metcalfe, who read the first draft of the manuscript so painstakingly and with such a close attention to every detail.

Their comments have been more than perceptive: they have saved me from several errors and made numerous suggestions which have resulted in an improved presentation and a considerably wider perspective for the book. I offer them very special thanks, but at the same time I exonerate them from any errors of omission or commission that remain in the text.

I also owe a rather special thanks to my secretary, Marilyn Mansell. Without her remarkable productivity and efficiency the completion of this book would have been delayed considerably. The amazing turn-around of hand-written text into typed manuscript spurred me on to complete the writing. Also, throughout the several revisions of the manuscript her enthusiasm and cheerfulness never waned.

But my final acknowledgement must be reserved for my family: my wife Margaret and my three daughters, Alison, Elizabeth and Lynette. During the period of hectic activity on the manuscript in the Spring and Summer of 1982 they had to put up with my almost total absence from normal family life. They did so without complaint at the time. It is only afterwards when one emerges from the cocoon of the study that one realises what they were feeling and how much they have been neglected. For their forbearance and understanding at the time I say an inadequate 'thank you'.

J. L. Ford

Introduction

Time and Uncertainty in Economics: A Perspective on Professor Shackle's Views

Over a span of now nearly half a century, George Shackle has made numerous contributions to the economics literature, in the form of journal articles, monographs or texts-cum-treatises. There is hardly one of those publications that excludes a reference to or, indeed, a detailed – often exhaustive – discussion and analysis of the role of time and uncertainty in economics. Shackle has continually exhorted economists not to leave on one side the issues and difficulties raised by the existence of such factors. They are not merely metaphysical concepts, even if they have a psychological dimension. To ignore their existence, he has insisted, is to distort the frame of reference the economist should be using in order to produce his analysis of and remedies for the micro-economic and macroeconomic problems that exist in society. Whilst he has conceded that model-builders, for the unravelling of whatever issues they design the models, require to simplify as a necessary adjunct to the development of uncomplicated, transparent, analysis and findings, he has reminded us that decision-makers in markets, whether private individuals, enterprises, or governments, have to operate in those markets in conditions of uncertainty. The economy cannot be viewed as a static phenomenon, presenting a fixed image of an interconnected market with given prices and outputs of goods and services, and so on; in short, presenting a set kaleidoscopic picture. Neither can its evolution be viewed in terms of a steady growth path with variables that influence decisions, and hence economic phenomena, changing in a predictable way because it is assumed that economic agents have perfect foresight.

Shackle has reminded us that decisions have to be taken in

a world of less than perfect knowledge; indeed, on occasions in a world where the degree of ignorance is substantial. The outcomes of decisions, say, involving investment, wage bargaining, the setting of prices, and so on, are not known at the present moment (a solitary moment amongst the infinite number that will unfold from the present, when the relevant decisions have to be effected). The consequences of actions take time to reveal themselves. Knowledge cannot be gained before its time.[1]

Accordingly, throughout his writings Professor Shackle is highly critical of the major portion of economic theory, and he is especially severe on microeconomic theory and the general equilibrium (GE) paradigm which has evolved from that theory. Indeed, it is difficult to find a more powerful, coherent and imaginative demolition of GE theory than is provided, in the early chapters particularly, in his *Epistemics and Economics*.[2] There he lays bare the need for the GE model to be based on the possession of full information by any economic agent about the behaviour of all other economic agents: there has to be a pre-reconciliation of the needs of all market participants to produce the neat, clear-cut and aesthetically pleasing solution to economic problems which is the hallmark of the GE model. The entire contents of *Epistemics and Economics* are condemnatory of the value of the accepted body of knowledge in economics and of the predominant methodological approach to our subject which is to formalize ideas in a way that emulates the sciences and so favours the application of mathematical tools of analysis. The impression is gained, quite strongly in fact, that Professor Shackle would view the subject as glorifying in the use of such techniques.

He regards most of these developments as detrimental to the subject. They lead to an oversimplification of its analyses of economic problems and to a false sense of rightness in the conclusions of those analyses. To his mind the use of mathematics imparts an illusion of precisional exactitude to the exercise. It would seem that he holds this opinion even if the framework of analysis is dynamic and has moved away from the restrictive, self-assumed Utopia of the GE world, because, then, it is essential, at the very minimum, to be able to do three things:

(1) to portray adequately the time-dimension of the relevant variables, which themselves might have to be incorporated into the analysis on a discrete or a continuous time basis;

(2) to capture the expectations of, and the degree of uncertainty felt about, the set of 'future values' appropriate to the analysis being conducted;
(3) if the analysis is concerned with the behaviour in, say, a particular isolated market in the economy, which involves the interaction of the behaviour of many agents on both sides of the market, to aggregate their behaviour consistently.

In any 'model' that is devised to analyse the economic behaviour, in whatever context, of only one individual, it is clear that point (1) is the only problem; but then it is likely to be inconsequential; for the analysis and description of aggregate behaviour ineluctably brings us up against all three points; the first two of which are really nested within point (3).

Shackle's standpoint here seems to be this: aggregative economics is not feasible because it is not possible to devise scalar quantities, or scalar items, which will be the necessary outcome of any form of aggregation. These scalar quantities, no matter how sophisticated the index number constructs employed, will have emerged from the addition of variables that cannot be added. If we think of finding a global measure for output, this cannot be done because of the vast heterogeneity of goods in the economy. Like and unlike cannot be made homogeneous; inevitably the composition of output will alter, and so any claim of homogeneity is a figment.

More than this, Shackle would claim that the predilection towards aggregation in studying markets and top-level aggregation to consider macroeconomic policy rides roughshod over major obstacles to successful aggregation. Any realistic model, which pays full regard to expectations, finds itself in a quandary: unless the expectations of all economic agents are identical it cannot handle expected variables in any attempted aggregation.

Notwithstanding that fact, and, therefore, somewhat paradoxically, Shackle has placed great stress on the role of time and expectations in macroeconomic models and has, in a constant stream of major books, made significant and impressive contributions in that area and, in particular, to the understanding and development of Keynesian macroeconomics. Unfortunately, and one suspects that this is to the detriment of our subject, those last-mentioned contributions have passed relatively unnoticed.

Many reasons can be adduced to explain that situation. One obvious reason is that *reductio ad absurdum*, Shackle's writings produce a nihilist view of economics and of the role of its practitioners. They certainly offer no comfort to those seeking to devise and implement aggregate, macroeconomic policies that are of a quantitative nature; at the very best they offer only a qualitative evaluation of policy or of how the behaviour on markets will react to changes in data consequent on changes in government policy. Essentially, modelling of the economy is not feasible because it is not possible to model the collective and interactive behaviour of economic agents.

Here, however, there is a paradox in Shackle's work. His insistence on the need to take cognizance of uncertainty and expectations has led him to produce his own theory of decision-making under uncertainty. That theory, indeed, applies solely to the individual economic agent; which is consistent with Shackle's opinion that aggregation across individuals' behaviour is neither feasible nor meaningful. However, the theoretical apparatus that Shackle had advanced to explain the decision-making behaviour of individuals does constitute *a formal model.*

Many of use would take on board his strictures about GE and its total irrelevance (in any meaning of that word), and would also have more than passing sympathy with the points he has made concerning the construction of 'aggregate economics'. But we would not go as far as Shackle would take us. We would stand firm with him on the paramount necessity to set out analyses in a framework that, like the world around us, exists in real time and not in some artefact that, for all intents and purposes, means that we have abstracted from time and hypothesized a timeless world or one wherein there is only one moment – which is both the present and the future, since it has a 'unit' measurement of infinity. Also, we would surely agree, there must be a central place for uncertainty. Here too, there is likely to be a consensus that a serious alternative to the apodictic probability-based approach to decision-making under uncertainty is required: one alternative being embodied in Shackle's own theory of expectations and uncertainty.

There will remain intricate problems of aggregation but the objections that Professor Shackle has raised, apart from the difficulties posed by the possible divergencies in the expectations of individuals – as he himself has acknowledged in *Epistemics and Economics*, reduce to a statement that behavioural equations in markets will be stochastic. They cannot be regarded as deterministic any longer, for most of their parameters will be tending to alter over time, because they are compositional parameters.

That would accord with our own view that optimal economic policy, such as macro-monetary policy and international trade policy, has to be devised taking full account of the fact that the uncertainty which renders the implementation and consequence of that policy so difficult to unscramble, is present in the form of parameter instability. Indeed, a large part of our own recent research has been in that area.

In sum, therefore, whilst conceding that aspects of Professor Shackle's critique of existing economic doctrines and methodology do have both force and validity, we cannot accept all of his views. Yet we must bear in mind those latter views in constructing our models and theories, as either introducing caveats as to when our models/theories have validity or as factors we must take into account explicitly in choosing the way by which we formulate our study of key problems, especially of economic policy issues.

Unless some such stance is adopted it is hard to imagine, to recapitulate the point, what value there can be in attempts to institute any theory of rational individual behaviour under uncertainty. This is not to minimize the problems that exist in the transformation of individual into aggregate behaviour. The following pages of this book could be justified simply as constituting an investigatory exercise itself into Professor Shackle's own, innovative, theory of expectations. They do, nevertheless, concentrate solely upon the decision-making process of a single individual. This is not only to keep in line with the spirit of Professor Shackle's views but also to avoid the complexity and complications introduced by the application of Professor Shackle's theory to market behaviour. Such an application would obscure our main purpose, which is to concentrate on his own theory of decision-making under uncertainty; his major, novel, contribution to economic theory.

The extension to an analysis of aggregate behaviour and to an empirical evaluation of the theory requires a separate volume. So too does the consideration of Professor Shackle's views, inadequately summarized in the foregoing, on the broader question of the importance of time in economics. A volume on the latter theme would embrace the whole area of macroeconomic policy; and as an essential ingredient it would involve discussions of rational expectations and the relevance of active stabilization policy. Professor Shackle's general views on the nature of the expectations formation process, and the particular views expressed in his own theory, indicate that he will not accept that the uncertainty in the world can be characterized by a probability distribution. Thus modern macroeconomics now hypothesizes that the policy-maker has to choose his optimal policy in a world where doubt exists about the behaviour of the economic system only because of the presence of random errors (*à la* econometric model-building) with constant means of zero and known, constant, variances. Such a view is anathema to Professor Shackle. It is founded on the supposition that the future always mirrors the past. Why is this? Simply because the supposition is that there is a stationary stochastic process that generates the random errors, and the resulting distributions for the errors are, indeed, frequency distributions based upon past observations of the realizations of the errors. There is no room for *novelty*; no new realizations can occur. Apart from the obvious limitation (nonsense?) of such a position, it is scarcely tenable as an hypothesis because it requires for its truth that the observations on the random errors are of infinite number and are generated from a never-changing world.

The extreme form of the rational expectations hypothesis is the one that has dominated recent macroeconomic literature. It maintains that economic agents will know, or (since it will be of benefit for them to do so) they will soon discover, what the exact form of the economic model is that generates all the macro variables. Likewise it is assumed that those agents will know, or soon learn, what policy rules the authorities are pursuing and for what reasons. The upshot is that economic agents will be able to forecast all variables, of which they need an expectation in their decision-making processes, accurately: in effect, we should say on the average, because it is assumed that the economy is subject to random shocks, in its major sectors. Those shocks have the characteristics which we have ascribed to them previously; therefore, although it will be impossible for economic agents to forecast the actual value of any variable with exactitude, because they cannot, *ex definitione*, forecast the actual realization of all current shocks, it will be possible for them to form expectations which are correct on the average, in view of the fact that the expected value of all errors is zero. Economic agents thereby are blessed with what might be called stochastic perfect foresight. The real world is being placed in a strait-jacket which, for all intents and purposes, is equivalent to that imposed by the GE model.

For present needs these matters may be allowed to rest here with this rather inadequate *aperçu*. At the same time note that the general methodological issues raised by Professor Shackle have at last been the subject of analysis in the literature[3] as a consequence of the publication of his *Epistemics and Economics* (1972) and *Imagination and the Nature of Choice* (1979).[4] Previously, attention paid to it had been relatively scanty and had largely ceased by the end of the 1950s.[5] Finally I should draw attention to the fact that in previous *precis* I have not set out with the explicit intention of mapping out the full extent of Professor Shackle's contributions nor of providing an exhaustive bibliography. Far from it; those familiar with both of these areas can easily testify to the very limited scope of my observations on these two matters. More information on both counts, together with an evaluation and extension of Professor Shackle's own work, and topics of research firmly grounded in the area of expectations and uncertainty, can be found in the volume of essays on *Expectation and Uncertainty in Economics* (1972) produced as a *festschrift* for Professor Shackle.[6]

A position has now been reached, with this perspective in mind, where attention can be turned to Professor Shackle's own theory of expectations and uncertainty which is the concern of this particular volume. His theory of expectations and uncertainty is centred around the premise that the established theory, founded on the application of the probability calculus to choice of action-scheme under uncertainty, is inadequate – indeed, is misdirected. Decision-making takes place in a world where time is real and where ignorance rather than knowledge abounds. Individuals, in their endeavours to forecast the value of variables germane to their action-choice (such as anticipated profit streams over the life of a piece of machinery) are not confronted by a situation of risk. That is, they cannot rely on the relative frequencies of occurrence in the past of specified profit streams in order to make their own estimates. Such a situation, so it is contended, is tantamount to one wherein there is no uncertainty and, indeed, perfect knowledge. The application of a frequency distribution to action-choice requires that the individual believe the decision he is engaged in making (the 'experiment') is infinitely repeatable in unchanging conditions. If that is the case, the use of the distribution requires acceptance of the belief, the carrying-out of an infinite number of experiments, and hence it implies a known consequence for all of the experiments. Most decisions – certainly those made by individuals in, say, the capacity of speculator on financial markets or as entrepreneur – are *unique*, once-and-for-all, decisions. The 'experiment' cannot be repeated, the circumstances both of 'the world' and of the individual will have altered as the consequence of the impact of the initial 'experiment', be it a failure or a success. Shackle has maintained, therefore, that the probability calculus is not applicable to those, and to most, decisions taken in an economic and social context:

> Uncertainty is not present when the consequences of the action are actuarially certain. If the experiment or venture can be broken down into a long series of trials like the spinning of a coin . . . the relative frequencies of various contingencies can be established and the outcome of the series *as a whole* can be calculated as a 'mathematical expectation'. Such ideas are the basis of statistics, whose concern is with knowledge and not with true uncertainty.
>
> However, an experiment can be such as to destroy for ever the circumstances in which it was made. When he looks upon his action as a unique, non-repeatable experiment, the decision-maker must abandon the idea of frequency . . . and ask himself not what will happen in the long run but what can happen, at the best and at the worst, on this unique occasion.[7]

Shackle replaced the use of the probability distribution by what he called the *potential surprise function*, and he argued that the individual would employ that function to telescope his expectation into a 'worst' and a 'best' outcome for any given strategy as a replacement for the mathematical expectation of the outcome or in some instances for that expectation and other moments of the probability distribution of outcomes, as relevant. On that basis he constructed what appeared to be a radical and imaginative alternative to what is undoubtedly the apodictic doctrine on choice under 'uncertainty', paying due deference, as it were, to the humanity of man.

That theory has not found acceptance, however, let alone anything approaching a prominent place in the academic literature, although it was the subject of extensive and detailed scrutiny in the 1950s once Professor Shackle had returned to publishing academic papers and books on his theory immediately after the end of the Second World War.[8] The theory is barely referenced, let alone summarized or discussed.[9] It is never used as a vehicle for analysing portfolio investment decisions; with the exception of the book by Dr R. A. D. Egerton, it is almost invariably ignored in the analysis of the investment decision in real capital, for which it was primarily designed (but not exclusively, as will be noted).[10]

One possible reason for Shackle's theory of expectations and uncertainty as applied to portfolio choice, or to assets held for speculative gain, being given little consideration in the literature on his theory in the 1950s, when much attention was devoted to his theory *per* theory, was the implicit acceptance of the remark made by Dr J. Mars[11] in the first large-scale review of the theory. In referring to Professor Shackle's own analysis of 'Choice of assets held for speculative gain' (the title of chapter IV of his *Expectation in Economics*). He argues that:

> Shackle bases his analysis of speculative investment on a gambler (venturer's) indifference curve, and he arrives at the equilibrium situation by a point of tangency between the indifference curve which is a subjective phenomena [*sic*] and a 'gambler opportunity line' which is also a subjective element. This process of reaching equilibrium is wholly inadmissible. The essence of ordinary indifference curve analysis consists in explaining the process of adopting variable subjective rates of substitution to given objective rates of substitution. These objective rates may be price ratios or they may be marginal revenue ratios or marginal cost ratios (the latter two in imperfect competition). The indifference analysis must not be used to explain the adaptation of one subjective rate of substitution to another, but this is exactly what Shackle does. It is because his analysis exhibits this basic defect that it does not seem worth while to enter into a detailed criticism of it.[12]

Two comments can be made on that contention. The first is that Dr Mars devotes a substantial proportion of his two-part, monograph-length review article on *Expectation in Economics* to an exposition and evaluation of Professor Shackle's theory in the context of the choice by an investor of an optimal policy for investment in real capital, machinery or plant or whatever. That choice requires the individual investor to maximize a subjective preference ordering over the prospects of the returns from investment, gains balanced against losses, subject to an efficient investment locus, over the prospects of returns, which itself is a subjective phenomenon, peculiar to the individual and devised by him. Such a procedure, logically, cannot be adjudged to be correct for analysing investment in physical assets and to be inadmissible for evaluating investment in financial assets.

The second comment that can be made is of a general nature. It is clearly fallacious to postulate that an optimization problem cannot have any intrinsic meaning if the constraint on the individual's choice is not an exogenous one. A great deal of the theory of the optimizing behaviour of commodity-producing firms, of financial firms and of individuals, would have to be declared otiose; namely, all of it that attempts to model behaviour in an uncertain world. For example, the orthodox approach to the analysis of the portfolio choice of the individual, which plays such a major part in the theoretical and econometric literature on monetary and financial modelling, and which has a long history in the subject (predating Dr Mars's review of Shackle's monograph), would have to be declared null and void if Dr Mars's views held sway.

One other possible reason why Professor Shackle's theory has tended to be dismissed in the academic literature is the comment made by Sir John Hicks[13] which can be interpreted to state that Professor Shackle's theory offers no avenue for the exploration of the analysis of portfolio choice because, as it stands, the theory does not permit asset diversification over more than two assets. The argument, then, is this: in the real world multi-asset diversification by individuals and by firms is seen to occur; since the Shackle theory cannot predict asset diversification of such an extent, it is of no value and must be ignored. This is a false syllogism. It confuses statements about normative behaviour with those about positive behaviour. What individuals are observed to do need not be consistent with what they ought to do. Thus, should the theory that Shackle has constructed be correct it will be rational for an individual investor to hold a portfolio that does consist of only two assets.

Naturally there are several wider reasons for the comparative lack of discussion, and for the almost total lack of utilization of Shackle's theory, just as there are for the lack of impact of his more general, critical appraisal of 'time in economics'. Perhaps there are three main factors here.

The first is that the orthodox, traditional conceptualization of the decision-making process under uncertainty (despite the vehement strictures of those such as Frank Knight who had preceded Professor Shackle in expressing their dissatisfaction with its view that 'uncertainty' was 'risk') has gained a total domination of the subject. It is a simpler theoretical approach which offers the possibility of empirical testing of its hypotheses, particularly for investment decisions, and especially for investment in financial assets.[14]

The second point, which is really a corollary of the first point, is that the Shackle theory is that much harder to grasp because of the new pieces of theoretical apparatus it has introduced, but particularly because those pieces are based on psychological factors. They emphasize the subjective, personal nature of the expectations-formation process and of the resultant choice of action-scheme. Thereby the feasibility of producing representations of the *aggregate* behaviour of investors in specified financial markets, for which the appetence is so strong in the nature of our subject, is reduced quite considerably: indeed, Shackle would almost certainly say: 'reduced to zero'.

The third reason why Shackle's theory *per theory*, as opposed to the paradigm it offers of the choice of investment strategy, has gained little ascendancy, is that it has attempted to do too much. In effect Shackle has claimed that his theory of decision-making uncer uncertainty is a universal theory that can be applied to most areas where such decision-making is necessary, in economics or in social matters in general. Indeed, the examples that he cites to illustrate his theory, throughout his numerous writings, suggest that any unique decision can be handled by his new schema; so that all kinds of situations which include the formulation of strategies, including such things as the design of military strategy, come under the umbrella of his theory.[15]

Most of the attention that has been paid to Shackle's theory has been in terms of its application to the analysis of the decision by an entrepreneur whether or not to invest in this or that piece of capital equipment. That decision is often seen by Shackle to embrace the decision to purchase 'plant' and not just items of 'machinery'. The analysis concentrates on a comparison of the gains and losses promised by the relevant piece of equipment: it then considers the scale of investment that should be undertaken in the best piece of equipment. It does not assume that the entrepreneur has a given level of resources at his command which he might use either to diversify over items of equipment or to diversify over plants producing in different industries. Basically, the possibility of diversification only appears in the analysis of choice of financial investment. Nevertheless, it is feasible to extend any analysis of the investment decision to embrace diversification across types of equipment or industries, even though the analysis is complex.

In studying the investment-decision within his frame of reference, Shackle has used the net present value as the means by which any project can be assessed. We now know that is not always the best criterion by which to rank projects, since it can produce results that differ from a ranking by the internal rate of return. Also, in instances where the businessman aims to maximize the net wealth of shareholders in a world where borrowing and lending rates differ, the use of the net present value criterion produces a range of indeterminancy over which it is not possible to state whether investment should be undertaken. I shall partly sidestep these issues by assuming, along with Professor Shackle, that the businessman is an entrepreneur in the Schumpeterian fashion, whenever we have occasion to refer to the decision to invest in real capital.

The material in this book will indeed be related solely to Shackle's own theory, or model, of decision-making under uncertainty. To recapitulate, consideration of Shackle's contribution to the whole role of 'time in economics' would involve too wide a canvas for one volume; it needs separate treatment. In any case, Shackle's critique of economic theory and his strictures against model-building are *more* widely known – even if not widely known – than are the main elements of his own theory; and his general views on economics, it has to be reiterated, really lead us into a cul-de-sac.

In discussing Shackle's own theory the main vehicle we have used is the example of portfolio selection by an individual. This is a topic in which the probabilistic approach is deep-rooted and has a long history; and it is a topic wherein the Shackle theory is alleged to have no role to play, as we have noted. However, in chapter 6 we consider the optimal choice of physical, rather than financial, investment. More importantly, in that chapter, the coverage of the decision-process is extended out of the field of investment so that some intimation can be provided on the possible consequences of applying the Shackle theory to a few of the numerous other areas of action-choice under uncertainty to which the probabilistic approach has been applied. The kinds of models considered are: the consumption-saving decision of the individual in a two-period model; a consumer search model (and by analogy a labour search model); a labour supply model for an individual; and the output decision of an entrepreneur in a world where the price of his product is uncertain.

A requisite of any critical assessment of Shackle's approach (or the one that we shall develop from it in chapter 5) is a comparison of it with the conventional wisdom. Consequently, the orthodox (probability) approach, founded on the work of Von Neumann and Morgenstern on the *expected utility theorem*, is summarized in chapter 1. It is done so explicitly for portfolio selection or asset choice: but the presentation there can readily be adopted by the reader to encompass other situations in the text where we rely on that theorem. In chapter 1 the implications for the description of the portfolio choice of individuals are drawn out so that it can be seen clearly what the Shackle theory must be capable of if it is to match the orthodox approach.

Chapter 2 provides an outline of Shackle's objections to the use of the probability calculus to decision-making under uncertainty, together with a summary of his own theory of expectations and uncertainty set out in a form allowing direct comparison between its main characteristics and those of the probabilistic approach. The development of the theory for portfolio selection, however, has been kept separate from descriptions of the theory *per se*, and becomes the subject-matter of chapter 3.

Chapters 2 and 3, besides offering a picture of the Shackle schema and of the method of applying it, will have provided some early indication of the ambiguities contained in the schema, and the difficulties that arise in using it to analyse choice of action in the way Shackle himself has advocated it should be. Therefore, prior to any further application of the Shackle schema to other decisions under uncertainty, it seemed sensible and appropriate to provide a detailed and critical exegisis of the main elements in Shackle's new schema, which is the subject of chapter 4. In that chapter, literature critical of the schema is presented and evaluated. Criticisms of my own, both of that literature and of Professor Shackle's schema, are advanced.

Chapter 5 offers a summary of the deficiencies and apparent inconsistencies in Shackle's new framework. It then attempts to remedy those defects to produce a coherent, rational, model for asset choice under uncertainty, taking account of some of Shackle's views.[16] However, the two models developed there have a framework that is similar to that of the orthodox approach. In the one case the only difference between the approaches is that Shackle's insistence that, for any project, gains and losses will be viewed separately (and not collectively in a combination such as the expected value of profit) by the investor, is retained. In the second model, so too is his concept of potential surprise, albeit in a slightly modified form.

Chapter 6, to reiterate, provides a wider perspective on the Shackle framework and the analysis of decision-taking under uncertainty. In that chapter it is demonstrated that, if we disregard the logical inconsistencies in the Shackle paradigm, it is able to produce solutions to the appropriate choice of action an individual should adopt under conditions of uncertainty in a variety of models hitherto only tackled by the orthodox approach based on the probability calculus. So the Shackle schema *per se* is more versatile and flexible than has been thought, despite the fact that, as we shall discover in chapter 3, it does have limited appeal when used as a means of describing portfolio choice. If the critique of Shackle's theory is accepted then the Shacklesque models developed in chapter 5 have to be used as a feasible alternative to the orthodox model. It is shown that on occasions the two models can lead to the same optimal action-choice; but that it is possible for them to produce divergent results. A summary of the arguments of this book, and its main findings, then follow in chapter 7.

1

The Orthodox Approach and Portfolio Investment

Let us consider the following simple situation. An investor has at his disposal a given level of wealth – financial capital. He intends to invest this wealth for a given period – say a year. There are just two assets in which he could invest his wealth, which we may label simply as 'money' and 'bonds'.

The question now arises: *a priori*, how can we model the way in which the investor will allocate his wealth across the two assets, perhaps on occasion holding just one or other of the available assets? The answer to this question requires an analysis of choice under uncertainty, since the chosen portfolio of assets is still to be held for a specified length of time; the presence of time introduces uncertainty about the capital values of the assets over the investment period and hence about the yields on the assets.

The main orthodox approach to this analysis is based on the application of probability theory. It is argued, similar to the theory of consumer behaviour under certainty, that the individual investor has an actual utility U function which (here, however) depends exclusively upon the actual, realized, return R on the chosen portfolio, that is on his wealth W. The supposition is that, in the way described by Keynes in *The General Theory*, individuals decide how much of their income to allocate to consumption and how much, therefore, to save. The latter is the addition to wealth, of course; they then decide how to allocate their inherited and additional wealth across the available financial assets. Such a supposition is not, however, necessary; models have been developed to handle jointly[1] the consumption-saving-optimum portfolio decision. For my purposes in this book, however, it is sufficient to remain within the Keynesian approach.

If the investor had full knowledge about the returns per £1 invested in each of the assets, he would select an asset which had a higher return (in general the asset with the highest return). In that way his utility would be maximized for the given level of wealth, on the usual assumption that utility is an increasing function of return; although it is posited that the utility function exhibits diminishing marginal utility. His more conventional utility will be maximized also, because the whole of this approach hypothesizes, implicitly, that utility (*per* 'satisfaction' or ophelimity) depends upon the goods and services that the individual can consume now and in the future. That consumption depends upon current and future earned income, and current and future returns on wealth.

The basic problem, naturally, is that the investor is *uncertain* about the returns that the assets will yield over the investment period. For an asset such as a government bond the yield per £1 invested, or the percentage yield, depends upon two elements: the one element is the coupon payment on the bond, which is known (usually provided the bond is held for six months and a day) at the outset of the investment period; the second element is the capital gains or loss that can arise because of a change in the value of the bond, which change is *not* known at the point when the portfolio has to be selected.

The probabilistic approach, which had its first formal application to asset choice theory/portfolio selection in the early work of Professor Sir John Hicks,[2] argues that the investor portrays that uncertainty in this way. He lists the possible 'states of nature' or 'eventualities' that could occur; he then specifies the yield he believes he would obtain if any designated state of nature did materialize; finally, he assigns to each state of nature a probability that it will occur.

It is assumed that the states of nature exhaust what in statistical theory is referred to as 'the universe of discourse'. In other words, the set of states of nature includes all the states of nature that could possibly occur. Those states of nature refer to possible configurations of the economy influenced in part, of course, by political considerations. It need *not* be assumed that in each state of nature there is only *one* yield on each asset that will materialize should that state of nature turn out to be the true state of the world. The orthodox approach to choice under uncertainty can accommodate quite straightforwardly[3] the possibility that, in the investor's opinion, there can be several feasible yields on a particular asset in any state of nature. All that that possibility implies is that in each state of nature there will be a probability distribution for the yields on each of the assets; the probability of each distribution, of course, being equal to the probability of occurrence of the relevant state of nature. (We shall proceed on the supposition that for a specified asset, in a given state of nature, the investor believes with certainty that *a* particular yield will emerge for any asset.)

The probabilities attached to the state of nature are often regarded as objective probabilities, but they can, equally well, be thought of as subjective probabilities. Sometimes, however, the explicit reference to states of nature is omitted and the orthodox analysis is often viewed as one based on objective probabilities. Thus, to be specific: we can imagine the investor attempting to form a picture of the possible range of yields on each asset. To each yield he thinks is feasible he then attaches a probability of occurrence; that probability is usually considered to be one derived from the relative frequency of past occurrences of each of the feasible yields within the set of all past yields. In that situation the probabilities are objective probabilities. Alternatively we might argue that the investor merely attaches to each of the potential yields his estimate of the likelihood that it will, in fact, materialize. Such an estimate would entail the probabilities being subjective probabilities. The formation of the latter might well be based, of course, on information that the investor has at his disposal about the past yields on the assets.

If we think of the investor as utilizing a states of nature approach then the situation, as he sees it, will be epitomized by the information contained in table 1.1. Here the states of nature α_i have prob-

Table 1.1
The states of nature pay-off matrix

States of nature (α)	$\alpha = 1$	$\alpha = 2$	...	...	$\alpha = n$
Asset 1 (money)	a_{11}	a_{21}	...	...	a_{n1}
Asset 2 (bond)	a_{12}	a_{22}	...	...	a_{n2}
Π	Π_1	Π_2	...	...	Π_n

abilities Π_i, with $\Sigma\Pi_i = 1$; and a_{ij} is the yield per £1 invested in asset j in the ith state of nature.

It follows immediately that for *any given* allocation of his wealth across assets 1 and 2, say x_1^* and x_2^* (which denote the *value* of holdings), there will be a probability distribution for R, the actual return on the given level of wealth. Thus, if state 1 materializes, the actual return in that state R_1 will be:

$$R_1 = a_{11}x_1^* + a_{12}x_2^* \qquad (1.1)$$

which will have a probability of Π_1.

Therefore, in general:

$$R_i \mid_{x^*} = f(\alpha_i); \quad i = 1, 2, \ldots, n \qquad (1.2)$$

where x^* denotes the vector of asset placings; and in terms of our matrix the probability density function for R_i is discrete, but can, of course, be continuous.

The investor's objective is to choose the best, the optimum, values of x^*. He is faced, then, with a choice over probability distributions of R; since R *is* stochastic he cannot simply maximize his utility function over (actual) R. Following the work of Von Neumann and Morgenstern[4] it is accepted that the investor will be making a *rational choice* over the distribution of R_i if he maximizes the *expected value* of his utility from his given wealth (and subject to any other constraints that might impinge upon his choice of assets).

This expected utility theorem of Von Neumann and Morgenstern is deduced from a set of axioms concerning choice of probability distributions. I shall specify those axioms by direct reference to the selection of an optimum portfolio of assets. A particular choice of portfolio P_i available to the investor will be indicated by:

$$P_i = [(R_1, \Pi_1), (R_2, \Pi_2), \ldots, (R_n, \Pi_n)] \qquad (1.3)$$

where, as hitherto, $\Pi_i \geqslant 0$ and $\Sigma_{i=1}^{n} \Pi_i = 1$.

The outcomes R_i, in the state of nature i to n, are thus mutually exclusive. When ordering the choices P_i confronting the investor we shall use standard notation. Thus: $P_i \succ P_j$, means that portfolio choice P_i is preferred to portfolio P_j; $P_i \sim P_j$ means that the investor is indifferent between portfolios i and j.

Axiom 1: Ordering of the outcomes (portfolio returns, R_i)

Either $R_i \succsim R_j$ or $R_j \succsim R_i$, for all $i, j = 1, \ldots, n$.

Axiom 2: Transitivity of portfolios (hence transitivity of portfolio returns)

If $P_i \gtrsim P_j$ and $P_j \gtrsim P_k$ then $P_i \gtrsim P_k$

Axiom 3: Continuity

With R_1 the most and R_n the least preferred outcome there exists some number u_i where $0 \leqslant u_i \leqslant 1$:

$$R_i \sim [(u_i, R_1), (1 - u_i, R_n)]; \quad \text{for all } i = 1, \ldots, n$$

Axiom 4: Substitutability of outcomes and portfolios

If $R_i \sim Q_i$ then $\lambda_1 \sim \lambda_2$ where:

$$\lambda_1 = [(R_1, \Pi_1), (R_2, \Pi_2), \ldots, (R_i, \Pi_i), \ldots, (R_n, \Pi_n)]$$

$$\lambda_2 = [(R_1, \Pi_1), (R_2, \Pi_2), \ldots, (Q_i, \Pi_i), \ldots, (R_n, \Pi_n)]$$

Axiom 5: Monotonicity

If (via Axiom 1) $R_i \gtrsim R_j$ and if $P_1 = [(R_i, \Pi_0), (R_j, 1 - \Pi_0)]$ and $P_2 = [(R_i, \Pi_1), (R_j, (1 - \Pi_1))]$ then:

$$P_1 \gtrsim P_2 \text{ iff } \Pi_0 \geqslant \Pi_1$$

It is assumed that the investor has a known probability distribution for the possible states of nature. That is, if the investor believes that two states of nature, i and j, are the only two feasible states that could occur over a portfolio investment period it is supposed that the investor attaches a *certain* probability to those states, Π_i and Π_j, with their sum equal to unity. It is perfectly possible, as intimated previously, for each of the states of nature themselves to have probability distributions. Then, for example, the probability of the state of nature i will be conditional upon the set of events the investor feels will influence the occurrence of state i. That set again must be seen as an exhaustive one; in that case, by the laws of probability, Π_i will equal the sum of the probability of state i for each given 'causal event' for i multiplied by the causal event's probability of occurrence.

It follows, therefore, if there is a probability distribution for each (or at least one) state of nature, the portfolio decision can still be envisaged as one where a choice of portfolio is made when each of the states of nature is (felt to be) known with certainty. An additional axiom states that position.

Axiom 6: The axiom of combining

If $P_j = [(R_i, \Pi_{ij}), i = 1, \ldots, n]$ for $j = 1, \ldots, m$

and if $\lambda_1 = [(P_j, \alpha_j), j = 1, \ldots, m]$ then:

$$\lambda_1 \sim \lambda_2 \text{ where } \lambda_2 = [(R_i, \Pi_i), i = 1, \ldots, n]$$

$$\text{and} \quad \Pi_i = \sum_{j=1}^{m} \Pi_{ij}\alpha_j, \quad \text{for } i = 1, \ldots, n.$$

These axioms have produced extensive discussions in the literature and continue to do so.[5] The controversial axioms have been axioms 3 and 4. In an application to portfolio selection there is less force in the objectives that are conventionally levelled at axiom 3 since all of the variables R_i, R_1 and R_n are outcomes/returns on a particular portfolio and hence are fully comparable.

Axiom 3, in fact, states that for each of the possible outcomes R_i (and hence for any portfolio choice where the outcomes are independent of the states of nature, and hence *known*) a combination of outcomes, and hence a portfolio choice, can be found which is indifferent to R_i. That choice is based upon the best and the worst outcomes, such that there is some probability (which has been labelled u_i) that the best outcome will occur *or* that the worst outcome will materialize with probability $1 - u_i$, which will just make that choice equivalent to the certain outcome R_i. As we shall confirm later it is to be expected that the probabilities here, the u_i, will depend upon the utility function of the investor over R_i and thus on his attitude to risk; hence the use of u_i (for *u*tility) rather than the continued use of Π_i or α_i for probabilities.

Axiom 4 is usually known as the axiom of independence of irrelevant alternatives. Thus if an outcome in a portfolio is replaced by another outcome (occurring with the same probability) that is equivalent to it in the investor's preference ordering, then the two portfolios themselves will be equivalent in his portfolio preference ordering.

Axiom 5 is perfectly acceptable. It states that the investor will prefer to choose a portfolio that contains the same outcomes as another portfolio if, and only if, the probabilities of the higher outcomes (returns) in the one portfolio exceed the probabilities of these outcomes in another portfolio. Then the probabilities of occurrence of the lower returns in the one portfolio are less than those in the other portfolio.

Axiom 5 can be cast in an alternative form which is often used in the literature and is labelled the axiom of stochastic dominance or absolute preference; in essence this is a corollary of axiom 5 as it now stands.[6] It can be stated as follows:

Axiom 5(a): Stochastic dominance or absolute preference

If for at least one $i = j$, $R_i \succ R_{n+i}$ and for $i \neq j$, $R_i \succcurlyeq R_{n+i}$, for $i = 1, \ldots, n$, then $P_1 \succ P_2$, where:

$$P_1 = [(R_1, \Pi_1), (R_2, \Pi_2), \ldots, (R_n, \Pi_n)];$$

$$P_2 = [(R_{n+1}, \Pi_1), (R_{n+2}, \Pi_2), \ldots, (R_{n+n}, \Pi_n)]$$

Thus, in words, axiom 5(a) hypothesizes that the investor will prefer a portfolio (P_1) that promises him a preferred outcome in at least one particular state of nature and an equivalent or more preferred outcome in another state of nature than any other portfolio can (P_2). Since it is not known which one of the states of nature will materialize, the outcomes R_n are stochastic but the stochastic outcomes offered by P_1 dominate those promised by P_2: hence the nomenclature 'stochastic dominance'. In general, we might expect that $R_i \succ R_j$ if $R_i > R_j$, therefore axiom 5(a) states that P_1 will be preferred to P_2 if in at least one state of nature it promises a higher return, and at least the same return in all other states of nature.

Axiom 6 is useful in translating preferences over choices into a cardinal utility measure for selection of the optimal portfolio; but it is readily apparent that it indicates how it is possible to consider a situation where at least one state of nature has a probability distribution of occurrence – a situation referred to earlier in this chapter.

These axioms lead to the *theorem* that an individual will be acting rationally when choosing between probability distributions of outcomes (the P_i) if he acts by maximizing the value of the utility function, U, where U is defined by:

$$U(P) = \sum_{i=1}^{n} \Pi_i u_i; \quad P = [(R_i, \Pi_i), i = 1, \ldots, n] \qquad (1.4)$$

It will then follow that:

$$u_i = U(R_i) \qquad (1.5)$$

with the values of u_i implied by axiom 3. In effect, of course: $0 \leqslant u_i \leqslant 1$. Thus $u_n = 0$ since R_n is the least-preferred outcome and $u_1 = 1$ since R_1 is the most-preferred outcome. Then if $\Pi_1 = 1, P = R_1$ and:

$$U(P) = U(R_1) = u_1 \tag{1.6}$$

Therefore:

$$U(P) = \sum_{i=1}^{n} \Pi_i U(R_i) \tag{1.7}$$

Hence the notion that the investor should select that portfolio, P_i, which maximizes his 'expected utility'. The assumptions necessary to move from the set of preferences over the outcomes and the portfolio choices to the selection of the optimal portfolio are that some cardinal measure of the 'utility' can be assigned to each and every outcome, and that that utility level is represented by the u_i (in axiom 3) which indicate the risk-aversion of the investor.

The utility function must be consistent with the preferences stated in the axioms. Thus:

$$U(P_1) > U(P_2) \quad \text{iff} \quad P_1 \succ P_2 \tag{1.8}$$

That the conditions specified in (1.8) hold can be proved by the following. Suppose that:

$$P_1 = [(R_i, \Pi_i); \quad i = 1, \ldots, n]; \quad P_2 = (R_i, q_i); \quad i = 1, \ldots, n \tag{1.9}$$

Axioms 3 and 6 permit us to re-write P_1 and P_2 as:

$$P_1 = [(R_1, \alpha), (R_n, 1 - \alpha)]; \quad \alpha = \sum_{i=1}^{n} \Pi_i u_i \tag{1.10}$$

$$P_2 = [(R_1, \beta), (R_n, 1 - \beta)]; \quad \beta = \sum_{i=1}^{n} q_i u_i \tag{1.11}$$

It then follows from axiom 5, since $R_1 \succ R_n$ that:

$$P_1 \succ P_2 \quad \text{iff} \quad \alpha > \beta \tag{1.12}$$

Equation (1.7) informs us that $U(P_1) = \alpha$ and $U(P_2) = \beta$, therefore we conclude that (1.8) does hold.

THE EXPECTED UTILITY THEOREM AND PORTFOLIO SELECTION WITH TWO RISKY ASSETS

Once the investor has specified his utility function the choice of portfolio is straightforward. He chooses that set of placings of his wealth accross the available assets that produces the probability distribution of returns which maximizes the expected value of his utility. Thus, in each state of nature there is an outcome R_i for a particular portfolio, the utility therefrom, $U(R_i)$ is multiplied by Π_i; all such operations are summed over all of the possible states of nature to determine the expected utility from that portfolio.

Suppose that the investor's utility function is a quadratic in the actual outcomes on his portfolio being, therefore, a Tobinesque function[7]:

$$U = aR + bR^2 \tag{1.13}$$

His U function from equation (1.5) is now the expected value of (1.13):

$$E(U) = a\mu_R + b\mu_R^2 + b\sigma_R^2 \tag{1.14}$$

where μ_R and σ_R^2 denote, respectively, the mean value and the variance of the (random) return on a given portfolio. Given his wealth, W, and any other constraints that limit his choice of portfolio, the investor seeks to maximize the value of $E(U)$. If b is not zero, the investor is concerned about the risk of his portfolio. In effect, if $b < 0$ he is a risk-averter and he is a risk-lover if $b > 0$.

To ensure that the marginal utility of return is non-negative it is necessary to assume that $R \leqslant (-a/2b)$; for parameters consistent with that requirement and with, say, $b < 0$, the investor whose preferences are epitomized by equation (1.13) will choose that probability distribution for R_i which has the 'best' mean and variance. In those circumstances his constant expected utility indifference curves will be upward-sloping in mean, variance space: that is they will reflect the fact that the investor considers 'risk' *a* 'bad', but the curves can either be concave or convex.

Should the $U(.)$ function be a polynomial in R of higher than the second order it will follow naturally that moments of the probability distribution of R besides its mean and variance will affect the investor's choice of optimum portfolio or strategy unless R happens to possess a Normal probability density function. Also, as another example, if the investor's utility function should be exponential, say:

$$U = \alpha - ce^{-\beta R}; \quad \alpha \gtrless 0; \quad c, \beta > 0 \qquad (1.15)$$

then provided $R \sim N(\mu_R, \sigma_R^2)$, $E(U)$ will depend upon only the mean and variance of R; but the expected utility indifference curves will now be linear in (μ_R, σ_R^2) space.[8] This is because the risk-aversion properties of equations (1.13) and (1.15) differ.

With $b < 0$ in equation (1.13) and $\beta > 0$ in equation (1.15), both functions exhibit risk-aversion. The latter is usually assessed by two measured devised by Pratt and Arrow.[9] These are referred to as absolute risk-aversion (ARA) and relative risk-aversion (RRA) which are defined as follows:

$$ARA = \frac{-U''(R)}{U'(R)} \qquad (1.16)$$

$$RRA = \frac{-RU''(R)}{U'(R)} \qquad (1.17)$$

Therefore, the Tobinesque utility function exhibits decreasing absolute risk-aversion as R (return) increases whilst for the exponential function absolute risk-aversion is constant at β: both possess increasing relative risk-aversion as R increases.

It will be sufficient for our expositional purposes if we limit ourselves to working with the Tobinesque utility function. In that case the choice of portfolio, or investment project, will depend upon the combination of mean and variance the investor believes he can obtain with his wealth constraint, W.

The choice of the best mean–variance pair will depend upon the combinations of mean and variance that the investor can obtain with his budget constraint, W. In effect, there will be an equation which informs him of the terms upon which he can 'trade' mean and variance, given his wealth; doing so by altering the composition of his asset holdings, that is by adjusting his portfolio. In static consumer theory if we are considering a situation where an individual is choosing two commodities in order to maximize his utility we know that his utility is constrained by the fact that his income is limited, which itself means that for that given level of income and the prices of the commodities, there is an equation which indicates the terms upon which the individual can exchange the two commodities in his consumption.

For the investor the analogue of that budget line in consumer theory is the investment opportunity frontier. That frontier epitomizes the best mean–variance combinations from the infinite number that are available when the value of the holdings of the assets are completely divisible. The way in which the mean–variance pairs of all of the probability distributions of R (for all possible portfolios) are, in fact, sifted out to derive the frontier is as follows.

In essence the objective is to choose the optimum combination of the *assets*, and the selection of the best–variance pair is a means to that end. Suppose for the moment that there exist only two assets in which the investor can invest, as we stipulated in the introduction to this chapter (later we shall consider the presence of n assets). For any given mean value of return the investor will wish to select that combination of assets which produces the lowest variance since he is a risk-averter, given $E(U)$ in equation (1.14). Thus he should:

$$\textit{choose } x_1, x_2 \text{ to } \textit{min } \sigma_R^2, \text{ subject to } \mu_R \text{ and } W \tag{1.18}$$

Here

$$\mu_R = E(R) = E(r_1 x_1 + r_2 x_2) = e_1 x_1 + e_2 x_2 \tag{1.19}$$

where r_1 and r_2 represent the actual returns per £1 invested in assets 1 and 2, respectively; and e_1 and e_2 denote the expected value of those unit returns. In general:

$$E(r_i x_i) = E(r_i)E(x_i) + \sigma_{r_i x_i} \tag{1.20}$$

(where $\sigma_{r_i x_i}$ is the covariance between the holding of one asset and the unit return on that asset) but since the own-return covariance is assumed to be zero as it is posited that the investor is operating in a perfectly competitive capital market and the investor knows x_i because he is choosing its value, equation (1.20) reduces to (1.19). Also:

$$\sigma_R^2 = E[R - \mu_R]^2 = \sigma_1^2 x_1^2 + \sigma_2^2 x_2^2 + 2\sigma_{12} x_1 x_2; \; \sigma_{12} = \rho_{12}\sigma_1\sigma_2 \tag{1.21}$$

where: σ_i^2 is the variance of the return on asset i; σ_{ij} is the covariance between the returns on assets i and j; and ρ_{ij} is the degree of correlation between the returns on assets i and j. Given that $R = r_1 x_1 + r_2 x_2$ and the definition of μ_R from equation (1.19) it is easy to see that (1.21), which is nothing other than the standard definition of a variance, does hold. Finally:

$$W = x_1 + x_2 \tag{1.22}$$

The values of r for any asset depend upon the states of nature and so will in general consist of more than one possible value. In effect, the r for the assets will be summarized by a matrix such as that contained in table 1.1. Thus, in terms of that table where $r_i = a_i$ for each state of nature, α_j:

$$e_1 = \sum_{\alpha=1}^{n} a_1(\alpha) f(\alpha) \tag{1.23}$$

$$\sigma_1^2 = \sum_{\alpha=1}^{n} [a_1(\alpha) - e_1]^2 f(\alpha) \tag{1.24}$$

Here $f(\alpha)$ is the probability of occurrence of the relevant state.

If there exist only two assets then the operation defined in (1.18) is straightforward since the optimum values of x_1 and x_2 can be obtained from equations (1.19) and (1.22). Thus:

$$x_1 = \frac{\mu_R - e_2 W}{e_1 - e_2}; \quad x_2 = \frac{e_1 W - \mu_R}{e_1 - e_2} \tag{1.25}$$

Upon substitution of (1.25) into (1.21) we have the mean–variance frontier

$$\begin{aligned} &\sigma_R^2 (e_1 - e_2)^2 - \mu_R^2 (\sigma_1^2 + \sigma_2^2 - 2\sigma_{12}) \\ &\quad + 2\mu_R W(\sigma_1^2 e_2 + \sigma_2^2 e_1 - \sigma_{12}(e_2 + e_1)) \\ &\quad - W^2(\sigma_1^2 e_2^2 + \sigma_2^2 e_1^2 - 2\sigma_{12} e_1 e_2) = 0 \end{aligned} \tag{1.26}$$

If we replace σ_{12} by $\rho_{12}\sigma_1\sigma_2$ in equation (1.26) we can trace out the effect that the value of ρ_{12} has on the shape of the frontier. We consider the three limiting cases where $\rho_{12} = -1$, $\rho_{12} = 0$ and $\rho_{12} = 1$, under the assumption that $e_1 < e_2$ but $\sigma_1^2 < \sigma_2^2$ (so that a *choice* of portfolio becomes a real choice). For $\rho_{12} = -1$ we discover that:

$$\frac{d(\sigma_R^2)}{d\mu_R} = \frac{-2W(\sigma_1 e_2 + \sigma_2 e_1 + 2\sigma_1\sigma_2(e_2 + e_1))}{(e_1 - e_2)^2} + \frac{2\mu_R(\sigma_1 + \sigma_2)^2}{(e_1 - e_2)^2} \tag{1.27}$$

$$= \delta + \gamma\mu_R; \quad \delta < 0; \quad \gamma > 0 \tag{1.28}$$

Thus, the frontier is curvilinear, and it bends back upon itself since at a value of μ_R equal to or less than δ/γ, equation (1.28) becomes zero or negative, respectively. The frontier, in fact, bends at a σ_R^2 of zero; from equation (1.21) we discover that when $\rho_{12} = -1$, the minimum value of σ_R^2 occurs when $x_1/x_2 = \sigma_2/\sigma_1$. Furthermore, when the assets are held in that proportion, σ_R^2 becomes zero.[10] Thus the minimum risk does not occur when all of the investor's wealth is placed in the least risky asset.

Similarly, when $\rho_{12} = 0$ we can see from differentiation of equation (1.26) that the frontier is curvilinear and bends back upon itself. To be exact, the minimum risk occurs when the assets are held in inverse proportion to their variances, rather than to their standard deviations as was the case for $\rho_{12} = -1$. In the current situation, the minimum value of total risk becomes equal to $W(\sigma_1\sigma_2)^2(\sigma_1^2 + \sigma_2^2)^{-1}$; so once again the minimum value of risk cannot be achieved by holding all of wealth in the safer asset.[11]

When $\rho = 1$, it is again seen readily from differentiation of equation (1.26) that the mean–variance frontier is curvilinear. Now, however, in contrast to the two previous cases, the frontier does not bend back on itself since the minimum level of risk is incurred when all of the wealth is held in the safer asset; and as wealth is transferred out of that asset and into the riskier asset, total risk rises continually.[12]

The relative positions of the frontier for the three limiting situations are delineated by their minimum risk points and the value of μ_R at those points. In that respect it is necessary to compare the value of μ_R for the instances where the correlation is minus unity and zero. Employing the values of the minimum risk for the respective frontiers in equation (1.26) we discover that:[13]

$$\mu_R \mid_{\rho_{12}=0} \gtreqless \mu_R \mid_{\rho_{12}=-1}$$

as: (1.29)

$$\sigma_1^2 \gtreqless \sigma_2^2$$

With asset 1 posited to be the safer asset it follows from (1.29) that the expected value of the yield on the portfolio at the minimum-risk point for zero correlation between the asset returns will be lower than that for perfectly negatively correlated asset returns. The mean–variance frontier confronting the investor in the three limiting cases will then assume the forms depicted in figure 1.1 (where negative asset holdings are excluded). On the figure, point A represents the position when all of the investor's wealth is held in the safer asset; so that $\mu_R = e_1 W$ and $\sigma_R^2 = \sigma_1^2 W^2$; similarly, point B refers to the holding of the whole of wealth in the riskier asset. With the mean–variance frontier for $\rho = -1$ it is thus possible for the investor to transfer some of his wealth from position A,

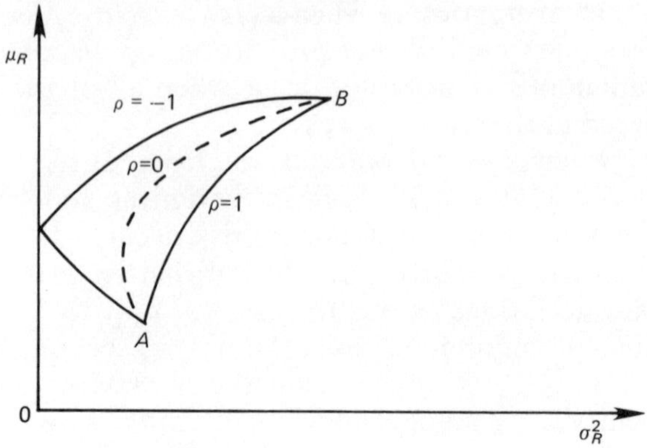

Figure 1.1 Mean-variance frontier and correlation between asset yields

out of the less risky asset 1 into the more risky asset 2 and yet reduce the total risk of the portfolio, since the asset returns move (perfectly) in opposite directions. A mixed portfolio in those circumstances can produce a variance of zero on the whole portfolio.

Whatever the degree of correlation between the asset returns happens to be, the investor will be faced by an efficient investment frontier given by equation (1.26). For any given level of risk that equation will indicate the maximum value of expected return that the investor can expect from his given wealth and his expectations (probability distribution) of returns on the available assets. The investor will maximize his expected utility, which is dependent upon the mean and variance of portfolio return (equation (1.14)), subject to the mean–variance frontier. The best mean–variance combination will be located at the point of tangency of the frontier with a constant expected utility (indifference) curve.

In the introductory remarks it was noted that Tobinesque utility function produced indifference curves in mean–variance space that sloped in a north-east direction. In effect, we derive the slope of any constant expected utility curve by setting the total derivative of equation (1.14) equal to zero, from which process we deduce that:

$$\frac{\mathrm{d}\sigma^2}{\mathrm{d}\mu} = \frac{-(a + 2b\mu)}{b} > 0; \quad \frac{\mathrm{d}}{\mathrm{d}\mu}\left(\frac{\mathrm{d}\sigma^2}{\mathrm{d}\mu}\right) < 0; \quad a + 2b\mu > 0, b < 0 \tag{1.30}$$

The indifference curves in $E(U)$, therefore, are convex and they will assume the same form as the curves portrayed on figure 1.2. To persuade him to take on more risk (a 'bad') the investor needs to be compensated by more expected returns.

The mean–variance frontier is represented generally by AB. Hence, as drawn, the investor's optimum position is at Z so that the mean–variance combination he should select is μ^* and $(\sigma^2)^*$. At those values there will be a *unique* combination of the assets, *ex definitione*, given the means by which the frontier is obtained. In the two-asset model that we have assumed so far, that is appreciated easily since, from equation (1.19), to each μ_R there is one, and only one, value of the holding of each asset, provided $e_1 \neq e_2$.

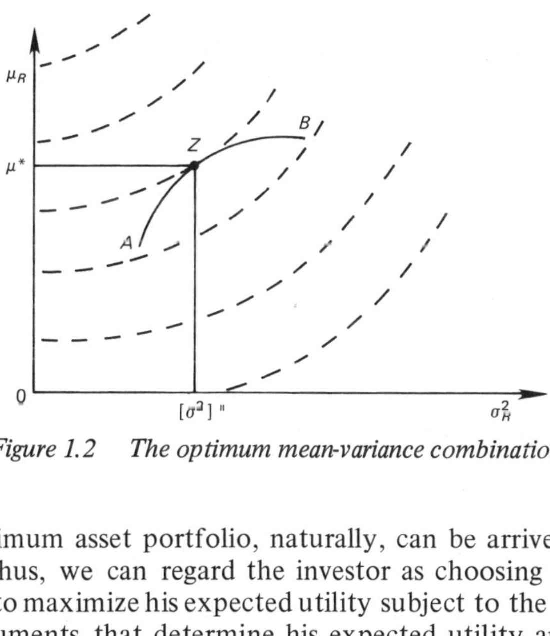

Figure 1.2 The optimum mean-variance combination

The optimum asset portfolio, naturally, can be arrived at more directly. Thus, we can regard the investor as choosing the values x_1 and x_2 to maximize his expected utility subject to the definition of the arguments that determine his expected utility and subject to his wealth constraint (together with any other constraint that inhibits his choice of asset portfolio).

The method of direct, immediate, solution for the optimum asset holdings is one by which we solve for the *demand equations* for the assets, in the analogous way to that adopted in static consumer choice theory. Suppose, then, that the expected value of the investor's utility function permits us to write his expected utility (which for ease of notation we shall now refer to as U rather than as $E(U)$) as a function exclusively of mean and variance:

$$U = U(\mu_R, \sigma_R^2); \quad U'_\mu > 0; \quad U'_{\sigma_R^2} < 0 \tag{1.31}$$

Let the variance σ_R^2 be denoted by V, and μ_R by μ, for simplicity. One specific form of equation (1.31) will be the Tobinesque utility function, but for our purposes it is best if we use this general specification and then translate it later on into a specific form.

The decision process is now:

$$\text{choose } x_1 \text{ and } x_2 \text{ to max } U = U(\mu, V) \tag{1.32}$$

$$\text{subject to:} \quad \mu = e_1 x_1 + e_2 x_2 \tag{1.33}$$

$$V = \sigma_1^2 x_1^2 + \sigma_2^2 x_2^2 + 2\sigma_{12} x_1 x_2 \tag{1.34}$$

$$W = x_1 + x_2 \tag{1.35}$$

Performing the operation defined in (1.32) subject to (1.35), with λ the Lagrange multiplier on that constraint, allows us to write these first-order conditions:

$$\frac{\partial U}{\partial x_1} = \frac{\partial U}{\partial \mu_R}\frac{\partial \mu_R}{\partial x_1} + \frac{\partial U}{\partial V}\frac{\partial V}{\partial x_1} + \lambda = 0 \tag{1.36}$$

$$\frac{\partial U}{\partial x_2} = \frac{\partial U}{\partial \mu_R}\frac{\partial \mu_R}{\partial x_2} + \frac{\partial U}{\partial V}\frac{\partial V}{\partial x_2} + \lambda = 0 \tag{1.37}$$

$$\frac{\partial U}{\partial \lambda} = x_1 + x_2 \qquad = W \tag{1.38}$$

Equations (1.36) and (1.37) are the wealth-constrained *marginal (expected) utility equations* for the assets. Insertion of the partial derivatives of (1.33) and (1.34) into (1.36)–(1.38) provides us with the equations for the holding of the two assets:

$$\begin{bmatrix} 2\dfrac{\partial U}{\partial V}\sigma_1^2 & 2\dfrac{\partial U}{\partial V}\sigma_{12} & 1 \\ 2\dfrac{\partial U}{\partial V}\sigma_{12} & 2\dfrac{\partial U}{\partial V}\sigma_2^2 & 1 \\ 1 & 1 & 0 \end{bmatrix} \begin{bmatrix} x_1 \\ x_2 \\ \lambda \end{bmatrix} = \begin{bmatrix} -\dfrac{\partial U}{\partial \mu} e_1 \\ -\dfrac{\partial U}{\partial \mu} e_2 \\ W \end{bmatrix} \tag{1.39}$$

Solving by Cramer's Rule:

$$x_1 = (\alpha\beta)e_1 - (\alpha\beta)e_2 + (\gamma\beta)W \tag{1.40}$$

$$x_2 = -(\alpha\beta)e_1 + (\alpha\beta)e_2 + (\delta\beta)W \tag{1.41}$$

where:

$$\alpha = \frac{\partial U}{\partial \mu_R} \bigg/ \frac{\partial U}{\partial V}\,; \quad \beta = (2\sigma_{12} - \sigma_1^2 - \sigma_2^2)^{-1}; \quad \gamma = \sigma_{12} - \sigma_2^2;$$

$$\text{and} \quad \delta = \sigma_{12} - \sigma_1^2 \tag{1.42}$$

Inspection of equations (1.40)–(1.42) reveals that:

$$\sum_{i=1}^{2} \frac{\partial x_i}{\partial W} = 1 \tag{1.43}$$

$$\sum_{i=1}^{2} \frac{\partial x_i}{\partial e_1} = \sum_{i=1}^{2} \frac{\partial x_i}{\partial e_2} = 0; \quad i = 1, 2 \tag{1.44}$$

These are two familiar aggregation conditions, the former being the Engel condition, the latter being the Cournot condition. The Cournot follows trivially from the existence of a budget (W) constraint, the Engel also follows self-evidently from the fact that if only the investor's level of wealth changes, the total change in that wealth has to be apportioned across the two assets. We also perceive that the coefficients on the expected yields on the assets are *symmetric*; and as they must be in a two-asset model, the assets are *gross substitutes* for each other. This last result follows from the fact that in equations (1.40)–(1.42), $\alpha < 0$, *ex definitione*, but so too is β, for the maximum value of β, defined in (1.42), will occur when $\sigma_{12} = \sigma_1 \sigma_2$, that is when $\rho_{12} = 1$. However that maximum value then equals $-(\sigma_1 - \sigma_2)^2$ which must be negative. Hence, for example, as the expected yield on asset 2 increases, *ceteris paribus*, there is a fall in the demand for, holding of, asset 1; likewise, when the expected yield on asset 1 increases the holding of asset 2 falls. These two effects are equal in absolute value, therefore we have symmetry.

Ceteris paribus effects on the asset holdings of an alteration of the expectation of yields on the assets can only be seen as *gross* effects. The changes in asset yields will generate an implicit wealth effect and it is possible, for example, in the general case, that the wealth effect that arises out of an increase in the yield on asset 2, the more lucrative investment, might be zero or negative in regard to that asset. The *pure substitution* (net effect) must work in favour of an increase in the holding of asset 2 by the assumption made that the investor is a risk-averter. Thus, at the margin the terms upon which he will be rewarded in terms of extra yield from taking on additional risk will increase.[14] In essence, for a *given* expected utility indifference curve the new mean–variance frontier will be tangential to that curve at a higher value of both mean and variance. This pure 'substitution' effect which will induce the investor to take on more risk can be dominated in the general case, however, by the *implicit wealth effect* that the increase in the expected yield on asset 2 generates. In the specific case given by equation (1.41), however, the substitution effect dominates the implicit wealth effect since $\alpha\beta > 0$. That implicit wealth effect is analogous to the implicit income effect in consumer choice theory which is engendered by a *ceteris paribus* reduction in the prices of one of the commodities the consumer is purchasing.

In general then, if e_2 increases, as we can appreciate from equation (1.26) for the efficient investment frontier, for any given value of the variance on the portfolio, except that where all of the wealth is held in the form of the safer asset, the mean value of the return on the portfolio is higher than it was previously. Had there been an *explicit* increase in the investor's wealth then the new mean–variance frontier, naturally, would have lain completely outside the original frontier, assuming that the investor's expectation of returns and risks on the individual assets remained constant. The implicit wealth effect carries with it the same implication as would an explicit increase in wealth. In effect, for any given value of the variance of return on the portfolio the investor can now have a higher expected value of return from the two assets. Or, alternatively, to obtain a given mean return the investor need not subject himself to as much risk as he needed to do hitherto. That consideration might induce him to assume less risk now; whether he does so or not depends, of course, upon his preference ordering over mean and variance. Should risk be an 'inferior good' in that preference ordering then he will reduce the total amount of risk he takes on now that his assessment of the expected yield e_2 on the riskier asset is more sanguine. In that case the wealth effect could dominate the 'substitution' effect; if it should do so, the investor will now hold a lower risk portfolio.

Thus, let us consider the situation depicted in figure 1.3. There the old mean, variance frontier is AB; the new is AB'. The original optimum position is Z. The *ceteris paribus* increase in e_2 shifts the frontier to AB', where the maximum total risk that can be assumed is the same as hitherto. The new optimum position is at M: this indicates that the total amount of risk undertaken is the same as on AB. The reason for this is that the 'wealth' effect, *represented*

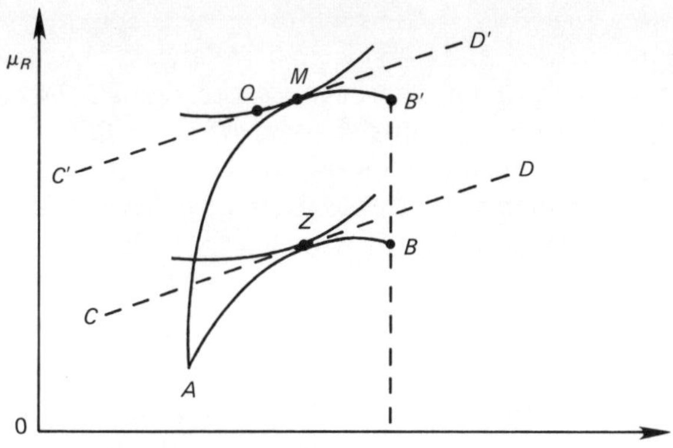

Figure 1.3 *The effect of a change in asset yields on the optimal mean-variance combination*

by the move from Z to Q, counterbalances completely the 'substitution' effect from Q to M. The two effects are illustrated in an analogous manner to that utilized in the Hicksian indifference curve analysis of consumer theory: therefore CD indicates the 'trade-off' between mean and variance at the original set of expected yields and wealth. $C'D'$ is parallel to that trade-off line and is tangential at Q to the new level of (expected) utility at the new optimum position M. The (positive) difference between the slope of AB' at M, and of $C'D'$, induces the substitution effect. The observed move, naturally, is a direct one from Z to M.

The impact that, for example, a *ceteris paribus* change in the expected yield on the riskier asset does have upon the total risk undertaken by the investor depends upon his preference ordering over mean, variance or whatever from his expected utility function. As far as the riskier asset is concerned, however, the substitution effect dominates the wealth effect, and the coefficient on e_2 in the demand equation for x_2 is positive; whilst that, of necessity therefore, for x_1 is negative – see equations (1.40) and (1.41). The fact that this of itself does not necessarily mean that the total risk assumed is increased can readily be demonstrated. In effect there is not a one-to-one, positive relationship between total risk and the holding of the riskier asset, or vice-versa. From equations (1.34) and (1.35) we discover that:

$$\frac{\partial x_2}{\partial \sigma_R^2} = [2x_2(\sigma_1^2 + \sigma_2^2 - 2\sigma_{12}) + 2W(\sigma_{12} - \sigma_1^2)]^{-1} \qquad (1.45)$$

and, of course, $\partial\sigma_R^2/\partial x_2$ is the reciprocal of this expression. The first term in parentheses in (1.45) is positive always; but the second can be positive, zero or negative. Hence the sign of the reciprocal of (1.45) depends upon the initial share of the riskier asset in the portfolio and the correlation between the returns on the asset. Therefore, even though x_2 increases with a *ceteris paribus* increase in e_2, σ_R^2 will remain constant provided:

$$\frac{x_2}{W} = \frac{\sigma_1^2 - \sigma_{12}}{\sigma_1^2 + \sigma_2^2 - 2\sigma_{12}} \tag{1.46}$$

Since x_2/W must be non-negative, this itself means that it is necessary that:

$$\sigma_1 \geqslant \rho_{12}\sigma_2 \tag{1.47}$$

With $\sigma_1 < \sigma_2$ holding *ex hypothesi*, it follows that (1.47) will be guaranteed only if the correlation between the returns on the assets is non-positive. Expression (1.46) provides the conditions for minimum total risk when $\rho_{12} = 0$. If we assume that the correlation coefficient is zero we can construct figure 1.4 which illustrates the holding of the assets as well as the choice of mean–variance. Although the individual assets are required only indirectly because

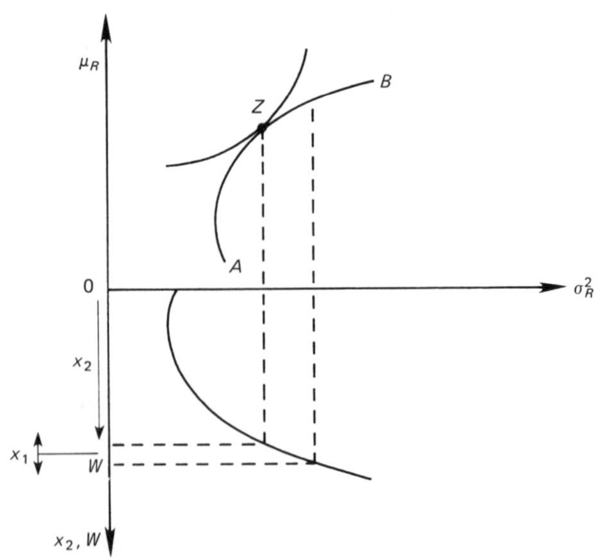

Figure 1.4 The optimum portfolio of assets

of the characteristics such as their mean and variance of yield they bring with them when they are part of a portfolio, and so help determine the characteristics of the total portfolio on which the investor's utility is based, the focus of concern in econometric/applied studies of behaviour in financial markets of individual investors, of banks and non-bank financial intermediaries, is the demand equation (and where relevant the supply/liability equations) of the particular investor. Analysis is often undertaken, however, of the effect on risk-taking of, say, changes in taxation which affect the (after-tax) yields on assets. The main subject for attention even for policy purposes, however, is the effect on the asset holdings themselves of changes in the circumstances surrounding the investor's choice of portfolio. That effect, naturally, will embody the preferences of the investor and the direct choice he makes of the variables that order those preferences, as he responds to changes in his investment circumstances, such as an increase in the expected yield on the riskier asset. The same preference ordering and the same set of information are used in both cases; in choosing the best mean–variance pair the information is used in a modified form from the way it is used to unscramble the asset demands.

The asset demand equations for an expected utility function that only encompasses the mean and variance of portfolio yields willl take on the general format portrayed in equations (1.40) and (1.41), with their concomitant Cournot and Engel Aggregation conditions. Those equations can be generalized for the case where there are n assets available for selection. Also the two-asset and the n-asset models can be particularized for the case where one of the assets is a safe asset, 'money'.

PORTFOLIO SELECTION AND n RISKY ASSETS

Consider then first of all the situation when there are many assets in which the investor could hold his portfolio. Suppose still that his expected utility is dependent upon just the first two moments of the probability distributions of the possible yields on his wealth. To obtain the efficient investment frontier the procedure is:

$$\text{choose } \mathbf{x} \text{ to } \textit{min}: \quad \sigma_R^2 = \mathbf{x}'\Omega\mathbf{x} \tag{1.48}$$

$$\textit{subject to}: \quad \mu_R = \mathbf{x}'\mathbf{e} \tag{1.49}$$

$$W = \mathrm{i}'\mathbf{x} \tag{1.50}$$

where we have now had to resort to matrix algebra to simplify matters, so that:

$$\mathbf{x}' = [x_1 x_2 \ldots x_n] = x' \tag{1.51}$$

$$\mathbf{e}' = [e_1 e_2 \ldots e_n] = e' \tag{1.52}$$

$$\mathbf{i}' = [1\ 1\ \ldots 1] = i' \tag{1.53}$$

and

$$\Omega = \begin{bmatrix} \sigma_1^2 & \sigma_{12} & \ldots & \sigma_{1n} \\ \sigma_{21} & \sigma_2^2 & \ldots & \\ \cdot & & \cdot & \cdot \\ \cdot & & \cdot & \cdot \\ \cdot & & \cdot & \cdot \\ \sigma_{n1} & & \ldots & \sigma_n^2 \end{bmatrix} \tag{1.54}$$

so that Ω is the variance–covariance matrix for the asset returns. The result of the operation defined in equations (1.48)–(1.50) is this expression for the n-asset mean–variance frontier (see appendix A):

$$\sigma_R^2 [(e'\Omega^{-1}e)(i'\Omega^{-1}i) - (e'\Omega^{-1}i)(i'\Omega^{-1}e)] - \mu_R^2 (i'\Omega^{-1}i) + 2\mu_R W(i'\Omega^{-1}e) - W^2(e'\Omega^{-1}e) = 0 \tag{1.55}$$

When $n = 2$, this equation reduces to equation (1.26) already derived as the mean–variance two-asset investment frontier.

Along the frontier the holding of the vector of assets **x** (which results from the execution of the operations described in (1.48)–(1.50) and from which the n-asset frontier is derived) is described by this equation:

$$x = \Omega^{-1}(\lambda_1 e + \lambda_2 i) \tag{1.56}$$

where:

$$\lambda_1 = \frac{\mu_R (i'\Omega^{-1}i) - W(i'\Omega^{-1}e)}{D}; \quad \lambda_2 = \frac{W(e'\Omega^{-1}e) - \mu_R (e'\Omega^{-1}i)}{D} \tag{1.57}$$

and:

$$D = (e'\Omega^{-1}e)(i'\Omega^{-1}i) - (e'\Omega^{-1}i)(i'\Omega^{-1}e) \tag{1.58}$$

Therefore, as in the two-asset world, once the investor has located his preferred position – along his mean–variance frontier – this will prescribe automatically a value of the mean which can be slotted into equations (1.56)–(1.58) to yield the optimum x vector.

We note one major difference, however, between the two-asset and the n-asset models. In the two-asset model the feasible set of asset holdings is also the efficient set; this is simply because only two assets are available. In that situation a given holding of the one asset must imply a unique holding of the other asset, when the investor has a specified value of wealth. Therefore, a given mean value of portfolio yield must be accompanied by a particular, unique, value of the variance of portfolio yield. Thus the set of mean–variance pairs is specified uniquely; for any given mean it is not possible to locate a lower variance. But, alternatively, consider the n-asset case in the limiting situation of three assets. Select a particular mean value of portfolio yield; then there will be an infinite number of combinations of the asset holdings that will be compatible with it (not just one value for each asset holding) and to a *given* μ_R there will be just one combination of x_1, x_2 and x_3 that will provide *the lowest variance*. It is that combination which is the efficient set for the given μ_R; and that set is not co-terminal with the feasible set quite self-evidently. In terms of the mean–variance frontier this informs us that that frontier really is a frontier or a boundary; within the frontier, that is beneath it in (σ_R^2, μ_R) space (that is as we have drawn it), is the attainable but inefficient set. The mean–variance frontier is the boundary of that feasible set.

Now, what about asset demands in the n-asset model? The answer is that if we suppose that the investor still wishes to maximize this expected utility function:

$$U = U(\mu, V) \tag{1.59}$$

then he chooses the x vector to maximize U subject to the definitions of μ, V and wealth provided in equations (1.48)–(1.54). The procedure is exactly the same as that followed in (1.32)–(1.39) above; so with λ the Lagrange multiplier on the wealth constraint, the set of wealth-constrained marginal (expected) utility curves produce these equations from which we can deduce the optimum holdings of the assets and hence their demand equations:

$$\begin{bmatrix} x \\ \lambda \end{bmatrix} = \begin{bmatrix} \dfrac{\partial U}{\partial V}\Omega & i \\ i' & 0 \end{bmatrix}^{-1} \begin{bmatrix} -\dfrac{\partial U}{\partial \mu}e \\ W \end{bmatrix} \tag{1.60}$$

In equation (1.61), $(\partial U/\partial V)\Omega$ is an $n \times n$ matrix; i is an $n \times 1$ vector; i' is an $1 \times n$ vector; 0 is a scalar; $-(\partial U/\partial \mu)e$ is an $n \times 1$ vector, and W, of course, is the scalar variable wealth.

Now, let:

$$\begin{bmatrix} \frac{\partial U}{\partial V}\Omega & i \\ i' & 0 \end{bmatrix}^{-1} = \begin{bmatrix} A_1 & A_2 \\ A_3 & A_4 \end{bmatrix} \tag{1.61}$$

so that:

$$\begin{bmatrix} \frac{\partial U}{\partial V}\Omega & i \\ i' & 0 \end{bmatrix} \begin{bmatrix} A_1 & A_2 \\ A_3 & A_4 \end{bmatrix} = \begin{bmatrix} I & 0 \\ 0' & 1 \end{bmatrix} \tag{1.62}$$

In the identity matrix on the right-hand side of equation (1.62): I is $n \times n$; 0 is an $n \times 1$ null vector; $0'$ is a $1 \times n$ null vector; and 1 is a unit vector.

We can deduce from equation (1.62) that:

$$i'A_1 = 0' \tag{1.63}$$

$$i'A_2 = 1 \tag{1.64}$$

Therefore, given the definition of the matrices/vectors in equations (1.63) and (1.64) these two equations inform us that: A_1 must have all of its columns summing to zero; and the elements of A_2 (which is $1 \times n$) must sum to unity. The former is the Cournot aggregation condition and the latter is the Engel aggregation condition, because from (1.60) and (1.61) we have that the x vector is:

$$x = A_1 \left(-\frac{\partial U}{\partial \mu}\right) e + A_2 W \tag{1.66}$$

Additionally, the matrix A_1 will be *symmetric*, so that *ceteris paribus* changes in the expected asset yields will have symmetric effects across the asset holdings, as they did in the two-asset model. To be precise:[15]

$$A_1 = \left(\frac{\partial U}{\partial V}\Omega\right)^{-1} \left[I - i\left[i'\left(\frac{\partial U}{\partial V}\Omega\right)^{-1} i\right] i'\left(\frac{\partial U}{\partial V}\Omega\right)^{-1}\right] \tag{1.66}$$

If we evaluate the transpose of the right-hand side of (1.66) we discover that it is equal to the expression for A_1 given in (1.66);

therefore, A_1 is symmetric.[16] As in the two-asset world it incorporates the variances–covariances of asset returns and the risk-aversion properties of the investor's utility function.

MONEY, A RISKY ASSET AND PORTFOLIO CHOICE

We may now turn our attention to the situation where *a riskless asset*, say, 'money', exists. In that case, if we exclude inflationary considerations, there will be no variance of the yield on money and in general only a zero expected yield. For near-money assets, of course, that yield will be positive; and for money *per se* in a world of expected price deflation it will be positive. Suppose, then, that the yield on money is zero; and consider first of all the situation when the only alternative to investing in money is to purchase a risky asset ('bonds' or 'equities'). Call money asset 0; and the risky asset, asset 2.

Then, from our earlier deliberations in equations (1.32)–(1.39), the wealth-constrained marginal (expected) utility (MU) of the two assets will be:

$$\frac{\partial U}{\partial x_0} = MU_0 = \lambda \tag{1.67}$$

$$\frac{\partial U}{\partial x_2} = MU_2 = \frac{\partial U}{\partial \mu} e_2 + 2\frac{\partial U}{\partial V}(\sigma_2^2 x_2) + \lambda \tag{1.68}$$

Here λ is the marginal (expected) utility of wealth and the latter equals the sum of x_0 and x_2. It follows from (1.67) and (1.68), since MU_0 is zero, that utility is maximized when the marginal utility of wealth is zero and the holding of asset 2 is such as to reduce MU_2 also to zero. The equilibrium portfolio (Z) is portrayed on figure 1.5 for given, at-the-optimum values of $\partial U/\partial\mu$ and $\partial U/\partial V$. The marginal utility curve for money coincides with the horizontal axis.

Should $\partial U/\partial\mu$ and $\partial U/\partial V$ be constants then as wealth alone alters the intercept and slope of the MU_2 curve will not change. Thus, a *ceteris paribus* increase in wealth would then imply that all of the extra wealth would be allocated to the safer asset. A *ceteris paribus* increase in e_2 would increase the value of x_2 and hence lower that of x_0; a *ceteris paribus* reduction in σ_2^2 would have similar consequences.

In general, $\partial U/\partial\mu$ and $\partial U/\partial V$ will alter with the attainment of

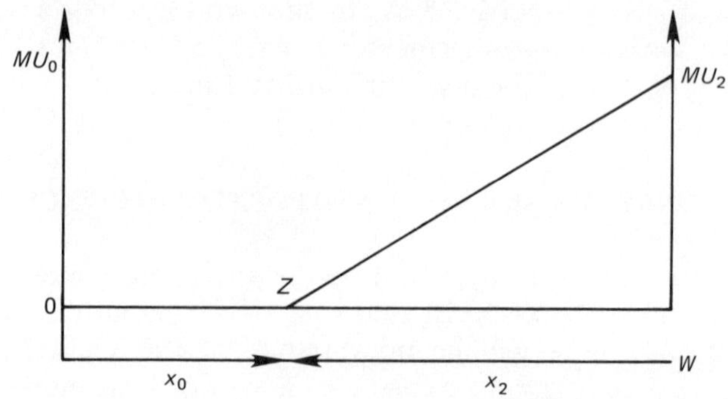

Figure 1.5 Marginal expected utilities and asset selection

each optimum portfolio. This is the case, for example, with the Tobinesque expected utility function (1.13) above.[17] However, setting equation (1.68) to zero enables us to solve explicitly for the optimum holding and demand equation for x_2, and for x_0 via the wealth constraint. We can then deduce, given the *signs* of $\partial U/\partial \mu$ and $\partial U/\partial V$, the *qualitative* effects on the optimum portfolio of adjustments in asset expected yields and their variances and of alterations in wealth. For a specific form of the expected utility function, such as (1.13) above, we could quantify those effects:

Thus, in general:

$$x_2 = \frac{-(\partial U/\partial \mu)}{2(\partial U/\partial V)}\left(\frac{e_2}{\sigma_2^2}\right) \tag{1.69}$$

and

$$x_0 = W + \frac{(\partial U/\partial \mu)}{2(\partial U/\partial V)}\left(\frac{e_2}{\sigma_2^2}\right) \tag{1.70}$$

Therefore, naturally, at the optimum point (and at all such points no matter how $\partial U/\partial \mu$ and $\partial U/\partial V$ change) both the Cournot and Engel Aggregation conditions are satisfied.

In general, as wealth, for example, changes, $(\partial U/\partial \mu)/(\partial U/\partial V)$ will change, from the one optimum position to the other. It is necessary to posit the exact form the expected utility function takes in order to convert equations (1.69) and (1.70) into demand equations that will enable us to sign the wealth effects and the *ceteris paribus* effect of changes in e_2, σ_2 on the optimum holding of the assets. All this again, of course, is identical with the findings for the two-risky-asset model.

As a particular example then we consider the Tobinesque utility function given in equations (1.13) and (1.14). Then equations (1.69) and (1.70) become:

$$x_2 = \frac{ae_2}{-2b(\sigma_2^2 + e_2^2)}\,; \quad a > 0, b < 0 \tag{1.71}$$

$$x_0 = \frac{ae_2}{2b(\sigma_2^2 + e_2^2)} + W \tag{1.72}$$

A *ceteris paribus* increase in wealth will be absorbed completely in the holding of money, the safe asset. An increase in e_2 alone will increase x_2 (and reduce x_0) provided $e_2 < \sigma_2$. In that situation if we regard asset 2 as bonds, make the further assumption that the expected capital gain/loss per £1 invested in bonds is zero, so that e_2 is 'the' rate of interest on bonds for the unit investment period, we have a 'speculative' demand for money with the Keynesian properties: an increase in the rate of interest reduces the demand for/holding of money, *ceteris paribus*.

When there exist only two assets and one of them has no mean or variance of yield the mean–variance frontier can be derived in trivial fashion. Also it is a simple matter to portray the choice of (μ_R, σ_R^2) and of x_0, x_2 on one picture. Thus since:

$$\sigma_R^2 = \sigma_2^2 x_2^2 \quad \text{and} \quad \mu_R^2 = e_2^2 x_2^2 \tag{1.73}$$

and

$$\mu_R = \left(\frac{e_2}{\sigma_2}\right)\sigma_R\,; \quad \sigma_R = \sigma_2 x_2 \tag{1.74}$$

Hence figure 1.6.

MONEY, RISKY ASSETS, PORTFOLIO SELECTION AND THE SEPARATION THEOREM

We now turn our attention to a model in which there exist several risky assets and one riskless asset – money. In that situation we know that the mean–variance frontier will take on the kind of form and shape shown in figure 1.7. Its exact form depends upon the risk-return characteristics of the assets and the covariances between asset returns, for given wealth. We have investigated this for the case of two risky assets previously and for n such assets

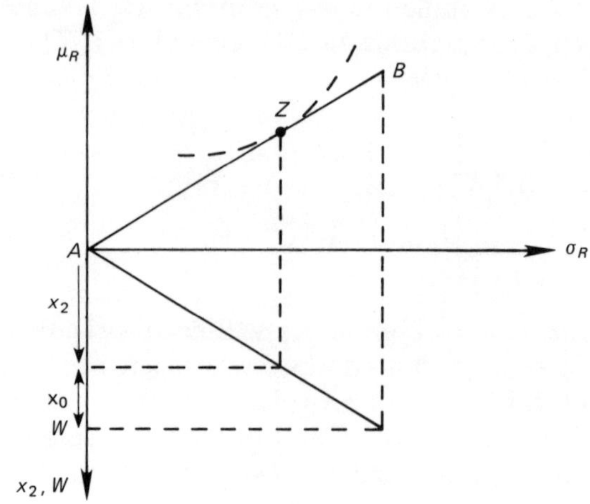

Figure 1.6 *The optimum holding of money in a two-asset model*

the situation is similar, as can be deduced from equation (1.55) for the n-asset investment frontier. But we do not need to develop those points further.

We have only to note that at any point along the efficient mean–variance frontier there will be an optimum vector for the asset holdings given by equation (1.56). We can suppose, for the sake of our argument, that there are two risky assets only. Then equation (1.56) is replaced by equation (1.26). Let the frontier be that portrayed by AB in figure 1.7.

Now, suppose that a riskless, no-return, asset is available for inclusion in the optimum portfolio. Then there will exist a multi-

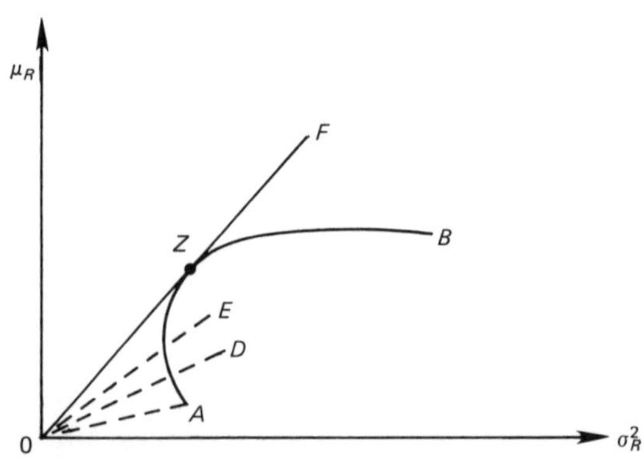

Figure 1.7 *The mean-variance frontier for money and two risky assets*

tude of possible investment frontiers which include the holding of three assets. Thus one such frontier is given by the line *OA* which involves the trading of money, asset 0, for the less risky asset, asset 1. Likewise, *OD* will indicate the terms upon which wealth can be moved out of asset 0 into some combination of assets 1 and 2. The *best* such trading line is provided by *OZF* which is tangential to the risky asset investment frontier. *OZF dominates* all the feasible trading lines such as *OA, OD* and *OE* because for any given level of risk it promises higher yield. It represents, in fact, the efficient set of riskless–risky assets being on the boundary of the feasible set of such combinations. At *Z* all of the available wealth is held in risky assets.

The efficient investment frontier *OZ*, for combinations of risky–riskless assets, is linear because the 'bundle' of risky assets at *Z* can be envisaged as one (a composite) asset, with its own risk and return characteristics. With that composite asset being traded for a riskless, no-return, asset we have a situation that, effectively, amounts to having one risky and one riskless asset; the case we have just considered.

At *Z* the assets will be held in a fixed proportion to wealth. In effect, let:

$$\frac{x_1}{W} = \alpha; \quad \frac{x_2}{W} = \beta \tag{1.75}$$

Then, at *Z* we may write these expressions:

$$\sigma_R^2 = \sigma_1^2\alpha^2 W^2 + \sigma_2^2\beta^2 W^2 + 2\sigma_{12}\alpha\beta W^2 \tag{1.76}$$

$$\mu_R = e_1\alpha W + e_2\beta W \tag{1.77}$$

$$W = x_1 + x_2 \tag{1.78}$$

Therefore, the risk per £1 invested in the composite asset ${}_1\sigma_2^2$ is:

$${}_1\sigma_2^2 = \sigma_1^2\alpha^2 + \sigma_2^2\beta^2 + 2\sigma_{12}\alpha\beta \tag{1.79}$$

and the expected yield:

$${}_1e_2 = e_1\alpha + e_2\beta \tag{1.80}$$

In general, along *OZ*:

$$\sigma_R^2 = {}_1\sigma_2^2(x_1 + x_2)^2 \tag{1.81}$$

$$\mu_R = {}_1e_2(x_1 + x_2) \tag{1.82}$$

$$W = x_0 + x_1 + x_2 \tag{1.83}$$

Hence:

$$\mu_R = \left(\frac{{}_1e_2}{{}_1\sigma_2}\right)\sigma_R \tag{1.84}$$

The investor's utility function will determine whether or not he does choose a portfolio along (1.84) and if so, what value of wealth will be allocated to the riskless asset and what will be allocated to the two risky assets. We note two important points about the allocation of wealth across the riskless and the risky assets. These constitute the major *Separation theorem* in portfolio selection discovered by Tobin then restated in more explicit form by Lintner, Sharpe and Sir John Hicks.[18] The two elements in the theorem are as follows.

(1) The *shares* of the risky assets in the total portfolio are *independent* of the holding of the riskless asset (hence they are independent of the share of the riskless asset); and they are independent of the individual investor's (expected) utility function.

(2) The holding and share of the riskless asset in the investor's portfolio is not independent of the shares of the risky assets. Hence the asymmetry and the name Separation theorem.

It is a straightforward matter to prove this theorem. Thus, suppose the investor does decide to select a mean–variance (standard deviation) pair along OZ; as we allow the point chosen to shift then x_0 changes *but* the shares of x_1 and x_2 cannot alter; they are fixed, *ex hypothesi*, at α and β respectively. Alternatively, for a given set of constant expected utility indifference curves let the trading line between the riskless and risky assets be OE on figure 1.7. Then the holding of money, x_0, and its share must alter; but it only alters because α and β, the shares of the risky assets, have altered.

So it is perfectly possible for a riskless, no-return, asset to be held as part of a portfolio; despite the fact that it does not promise any return. Whether or not it will be, what the optimum holding of it will be, what form its demand equation will assume, will all depend, as usual, on the investor's preference ordering and his estimates of the expectations of yield, and risks on the various assets. Likewise, his optimum choice of mean–variance will be achieved by the maximization of his expected utility subject to the equation for the frontier *OZB*;[19] but the optimum choice of assets implies the optimum mean–variance combination and vice-versa.

The mechanics of deriving the optimum holding of assets and their demand equation is exactly the same as in the case of one risky and one riskless asset, even though we now have more than one risky asset. The equations assume a similar format to those presented in equations (1.69) and (1.70) and are, in fact, as follows:

$$x_0 = -Me_1(\sigma_{12} - \sigma_2^2) + Me_2(\sigma_1^2 - \sigma_{12}) + W \qquad (1.85)$$

$$x_1 = Me_2\sigma_{12} - Me_1\sigma_2^2 \qquad (1.86)$$

where

$$M = (\partial U/\partial \mu_R)/(\partial U/\partial V).$$

CONCLUDING REMARKS

We have proceeded now as far as we need, with an exposition of the major analytical framework that has been utilized to explain the choice of portfolio by an individual. The basic ingredients of that framework have been set out, and I have demonstrated the central propositions that can be deduced from it in regard to the portfolio behaviour of the individual. The analysis has deliberately been kept on an individual basis, and the discussion has not strayed into an aggregate model for the reasons given in the Introduction. Furthermore, as mentioned there, the decision to invest in real capital has not been discussed. Since this is also sufficient for our purposes, discussion has been limited to the main manifestation of the application of the probability calculus to the portfolio selection problem, namely that founded on the Von Neumann–Morgenstern expected utility theorem. I have restricted myself to some comments, *en passant*, and footnotes on, for example, the Hicksian approach and (together with material presented in Appendix B) the Safety-First models of the kind developed by A. D. Roy.[20] Finally as mentioned in the Introduction, the chapter has not incorporated any ideas developed in the literature to handle situations where there is complete ignorance of states of nature,[21] or any philosophical discussion on objective and subjective probability.[22]

APPENDIX A: THE DERIVATION OF THE MEAN–VARIANCE EFFICIENT INVESTMENT FRONTIER FOR MANY ASSETS

My objective in this Appendix is to offer a proof that equation (1.55) contained in the main text of chapter 1 is the mean–variance frontier for the case of n assets. To repeat that equation for convenience, we have:

$$\sigma_R^2 [(e'\Omega^{-1}e)(i'\Omega^{-1}i) - (e'\Omega^{-1}i)(i'\Omega^{-1}e)] - \mu_R^2(i'\Omega^{-1}i) + 2\mu_R W(i'\Omega^{-1}e) - W^2(e'\Omega^{-1}e) = 0 \qquad A(1.1)$$

To prove equation A(1.1) we recall that we must:

$$\textit{choose } x \textit{ to min}: \quad \sigma_R^2 = x'\Omega x \qquad A(1.2)$$

$$\text{s.t.} \quad \mu_R = x'e \qquad A(1.3)$$

$$W = i'x = x'i \qquad A(1.4)$$

We form the Lagrangean Z:

$$Z = x'\Omega x + 2\lambda_1(\mu_R - x'e) + 2\lambda_2(W - x'i) \qquad A(1.5)$$

where λ_1 and λ_2 are Lagrange multipliers; and we have multiplied them by 2 since this simplifies the differentiation of Z with $x'\Omega x$ being a quadratic form.

The first-order conditions for a minimum value of Z are:

$$\frac{\partial Z}{\partial x} = 2\Omega x - 2\lambda_1 e - 2\lambda_2 i = 0 \qquad A(1.6)$$

$$\frac{\partial Z}{\partial \lambda_1} = 2\mu_R - 2x'e = 0 \qquad A(1.7)$$

$$\frac{\partial Z}{\partial \lambda_2} = 2W - 2x'i = 0 \qquad A(1.8)$$

It follows from equation A(1.6) that:

$$x = \Omega^{-1}(\lambda_1 e + \lambda_2 i) \qquad A(1.9)$$

This expression for the x vector cannot be substituted easily into σ_R^2, so deducing the equation for the frontier. Therefore, we first of all eliminate λ_1 and λ_2. This is done in the following way (which is a procedure that develops the ingenious and elegant proof given by A. D. Roy in a much-neglected paper on asset choice under uncertainty, namely 'Safety-first and the holding of assets', *Econometrica*, 1952, pp. 431–49).

Into the three basic equations, A(1.2)–A(1.4), we substitute equation A(1.9), so that:

$$\sigma_R^2 - (\Omega^{-1}(\lambda_1 e + \lambda_2 i))'\Omega x = 0 \quad \text{A(1.10)}$$

$$\mu_R - (\Omega^{-1}(\lambda_1 e + \lambda_2 i))'e = 0 \quad \text{A(1.11)}$$

$$W - (\Omega^{-1}(\lambda_1 e + \lambda_2 i))'i = 0 \quad \text{A(1.12)}$$

From A(1.9) itself:

$$\Omega x = \lambda_1 e + \lambda_2 i \quad \text{A(1.13)}$$

Now substitute this expression into equation A(1.10); this permits us to write:

$$\sigma_R^2 - [(\lambda_1 e + \lambda_2 i)'\Omega^{-1}(\lambda_1 e + \lambda_2 i)] = 0 \quad \text{A(1.14)}$$

(since $(\Omega^{-1})' = \Omega^{-1}$ as Ω^{-1} is symmetric).

Carrying out the premultiplication implied in the square brackets in A(1.14), remembering that λ_1 and λ_2 are scalars, we can re-write A(1.14) as:

$$\sigma_R^2 - [(\lambda_1 e + \lambda_2 i)'\Omega^{-1} e]\lambda_1 - [(\lambda_1 e + \lambda_2 i)'\Omega^{-1} i]\lambda_2 = 0 \quad \text{A(1.15)}$$

We can also re-write A(1.11) and A(1.12) as:

$$\mu_R = (\lambda_1 e + \lambda_2 i)'\Omega^{-1} e \quad \text{A(1.16)}$$

$$W = (\lambda_1 e + \lambda_2 i)'\Omega^{-1} i \quad \text{A(1.17)}$$

If we glance back at equation A(1.15) we can now see that it contains μ_R and W and can be written as:

$$\sigma_R^2 - (\mu_R)\lambda_1 - (W)\lambda_2 = 0 \quad \text{A(1.18)}$$

Additionally we can transform equations A(1.16) and A(1.17) into this form:

$$\mu_R - (e'\Omega^{-1} e)\lambda_1 - (i'\Omega^{-1} e)\lambda_2 = 0 \quad \text{A(1.19)}$$

$$W - (e'\Omega^{-1} i)\lambda_1 - (i'\Omega^{-1} i)\lambda_2 = 0 \quad \text{A(1.20)}$$

Thus, given the optimum x vector along the mean–variance frontier specified in equation A(1.9), we have reduced the three fundamental equations in σ_R^2, μ_R and W to three equations, A(1.18)–

A(1.20) in the two unknown Lagrange multipliers and writing:

$$\begin{bmatrix} \sigma_R^2 & \mu_R & W \\ \mu_R & (e'\Omega^{-1}e) & (i'\Omega^{-1}e) \\ W & (e'\Omega^{-1}i) & (i'\Omega^{-1}i) \end{bmatrix} \begin{bmatrix} 1 \\ -\lambda_1 \\ -\lambda_2 \end{bmatrix} = \begin{bmatrix} 0 \\ 0 \\ 0 \end{bmatrix} \qquad \text{A(1.21)}$$

This system of homogeneous equations will have a non-trivial solution (that is a non-zero solution vector) if and only if the determinant of the system is zero:

$$\begin{vmatrix} \sigma_R^2 & \mu_R & W \\ \mu_R & (e'\Omega^{-1}e) & (i'\Omega^{-1}e) \\ W & (e'\Omega^{-1}i) & (i'\Omega^{-1}i) \end{vmatrix} = 0 \qquad \text{A(1.22)}$$

Equation A(1.22) is the equation of the frontier since the Lagrange multipliers have effectively been eliminated by the use of the optimum x vector as a function of the multipliers given in A(1.9). Thus after some rearranging of terms, evaluation of the determinant in A(1.22) produces equation A(1.1).

From equations A(1.19) and A(1.20) we can derive the expression for λ_1 and λ_2 given in equation (1.57) of the text.

APPENDIX B: A MODEL OF RISKY ASSETS AND A RISKLESS ASSET: THE MARKET OPPORTUNITY LINE AND A. D. ROY'S ASSET CHOICE THEORY

We are now in a position where we can develop the material presented in Appendix A to consider the issue noted in chapter 1 concerning the efficient investment opportunity frontier when a riskless asset does exist alongside many risky assets. In effect, we can answer the question as to how the point Z on figure 1.7 is located. We can also offer some comments on one of the major alternatives to the expected utility or mean–variance approaches that has been offered as an explanation of portfolio behaviour in a probabilistic framework. That alternative has been developed by A. D. Roy (*Econometrica*, paper cited in Appendix A); and he has hypothesized that the investor will be safety-first, seeking to minimize the probability that the return on his portfolio falls below a predetermined disaster level, perhaps the level of his current wealth. It was in the course of propounding that theory that A. D. Roy produced the following method for locating the best risky asset bundle to trade with the riskless asset; the point Z on figure 1.7.

To discover that point in a way that enables us to convey the essence of Roy's own theory, we shall make the analysis more general by assuming that the riskless asset has a positive return. The situation where that return is zero, as it was assumed to be in the text of chapter 1 and hence in figure 1.7, is just a special case, as we shall see.

Let the riskless rate of return be denoted by $\bar{r}$. The risky asset frontier is depicted by AB on figure 1.8. The objective is to find how C can be discovered. It is usually assumed that the line drawn for $\bar{R}$ (where this equals $\bar{r}$ times W) is the 'market opportunity line' in discussions of the separation theorem and of capital asset pricing; it is alleged that the investor can lend (invest) as much of his wealth as he wishes at the given $\bar{r}$. Alternatively, he can borrow unlimited amounts of the asset at the given market rate. In the latter case his optimum portfolio would lie on the $\bar{R}C$ line extended. We shall assume that the investor does not borrow; but such an assumption has no implications for our ensuing analysis.

We have seen already, from Appendix A, that the risky asset frontier can be written as:

$$\begin{vmatrix} \sigma^2 & \mu & W \\ \mu & (e'\Omega^{-1}e) & (i'\Omega^{-1}e) \\ W & (e'\Omega^{-1}i) & (i'\Omega^{-1}i) \end{vmatrix} = 0 \qquad \text{B(1.1)}$$

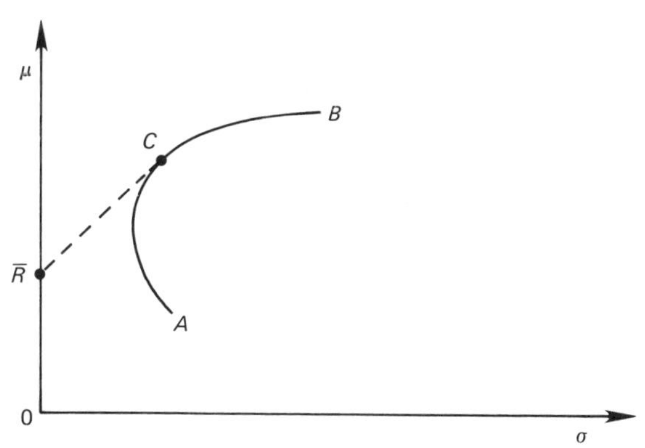

Figure 1.8 The efficient investment frontier for one riskless and many risky assets

The market opportunity line $\bar{R}C$ can be represented, in general, by:

$$\mu = \bar{R} + h\sigma \qquad \text{B(1.2)}$$

where h is the slope of the line. The market opportunity line will "cut" the frontier, the envelope $f(\mu, \sigma^2) = 0$, at a corresponding value of σ, for the value of μ given by B(1.2). If the market opportunity line cuts the envelope only once then the line *is* a tangent to the envelope. To unscramble the σ at which B(1.2) is a tangent to the frontier simply set μ in equation B(1.1) equal to μ from B(1.2). We need to determine the conditions under which the resulting quadratic equation in σ has only *one root*, for in that case there is only one σ which simultaneously satisfies B(1.1) and B(1.2) and the latter must be tangential to the former. Otherwise, for the case of two roots, σ_1 and σ_2, we have the kind of situation depicted in figure 1.9, where both equations are still satisfied at D and E.

From B(1.1) with μ replaced by B(1.2):

$$\sigma^2[(e'\Omega^{-1}e)(i'\Omega^{-1}i) - (e'\Omega^{-1}i)^2] - (h\sigma + \bar{R})[(h\sigma + \bar{R})(i'\Omega^{-1}i) - W(e'\Omega^{-1}i)][(h\sigma + \bar{R})(e'\Omega^{-1}i) - W(e'\Omega^{-1}e)] = 0 \qquad \text{B(1.3)}$$

or, in general notation:

$$\alpha\sigma^2 + \beta\sigma + \gamma = 0 \qquad \text{B(1.4)}$$

The condition that this quadratic in σ should, in effect, possess only one root follows directly from the standard formula for

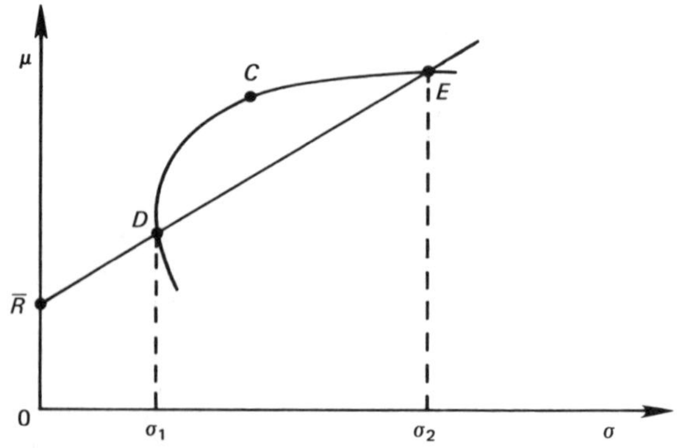

Figure 1.9 The method of derivation of the efficient investment frontier for one riskless and many risky assets

solving a quadratic equation:

$$\sigma = \frac{-\beta \pm \sqrt{\beta^2 - 4\alpha\gamma}}{2\alpha} \qquad \text{B}(1.5)$$

So the required condition is:

$$\beta^2 = 4\alpha\gamma \qquad \text{B}(1.6)$$

Here:

$$\alpha = [(e'\Omega^{-1}e)(i'\Omega^{-1}i) - (e'\Omega^{-1}i)^2 - h^2(i'\Omega^{-1}i)] \qquad \text{B}(1.7)$$

$$\beta = -[2h\bar{R}(i'\Omega^{-1}i) - 2hW(e'\Omega^{-1}i)] \qquad \text{B}(1.8)$$

$$\gamma = -\bar{R}^2(i'\Omega^{-1}i) + 2\bar{R}W(e'\Omega^{-1}i) - W^2(e'\Omega^{-1}e) \qquad \text{B}(1.9)$$

For B(1.6) to be satisfied it is necessary that:

$$h^2 = \left(\frac{\bar{R}}{W}\right)^2 (i'\Omega^{-1}i) - 2\frac{\bar{R}}{W}(e'\Omega^{-1}i) + e'\Omega^{-1}e \qquad \text{B}(1.10)$$

or:

$$h^2 = \left[e - \frac{\bar{R}}{W}i\right]'\Omega^{-1}\left[e - \frac{\bar{R}}{W}i\right] \qquad \text{B}(1.11)$$

So the slope of the market opportunity line is the square root of B(1.11). Given B(1.6), there is one and only one σ that satisfies equation B(1.4), namely:

$$\sigma = \left(\frac{-\beta}{2\alpha}\right) \qquad \text{B}(1.12)$$

From B(1.7)–B(1.9) we can re-write B(1.12) as:

$$\sigma = \frac{Wh}{[(e'\Omega^{-1}i) - (\bar{R}/W)(i'\Omega^{-1}i)]} \qquad \text{B}(1.13)$$

or, alternatively:

$$\sigma = \frac{Wh}{[e - (\bar{R}/W)i]'\Omega^{-1}i} \qquad \text{B}(1.14)$$

Having discovered *the* appropriate value of σ we can calculate the accompanying value of μ from B(1.2):

$$\mu = \frac{W(e'\Omega^{-1}e) - (\bar{R}/W)(e'\Omega^{-1}i)}{[(e'\Omega^{-1}i) - (\bar{R}/W)(i'\Omega^{-1}i)]} \qquad \text{B}(1.15)$$

or:

$$\mu = \frac{W[e - (\bar{R}/W)i]'\Omega^{-1}e}{[e - (\bar{R}/W)i]'\Omega^{-1}i} \qquad \text{B(1.16)}$$

To encompass the situation we have assumed in chapter 1, we simply have to let $\bar{R} = 0$ in B(1.14) and B(1.16).

Let us now define $\bar{D}(= \bar{R}) > 0$, as the disaster return the investor sets on his portfolio. To minimize the upper bound of the probability of the return on his wealth falling below $\bar{D}$ the investor should minimize:

$$\frac{\sigma^2}{(\mu - \bar{D})^2} \qquad \text{B(1.17)}$$

This follows from invoking Chebyshev's inequality that:

$$\text{Prob}\{|R - \mu| \geqslant \delta\sigma\} \leqslant \frac{1}{\delta^2} \qquad \text{B(1.18)}$$

or:

$$\text{Prob}\{|R - \mu| \geqslant \epsilon\} \leqslant \frac{\sigma^2}{\epsilon^2} \qquad \text{B(1.19)}$$

Thus let $\epsilon = (\mu - \bar{D})$. Then from B(1.19):

$$\text{Prob}(\mu - R \geqslant \mu - \bar{D}) = \text{Prob}(R \leqslant \bar{D}) \leqslant \frac{\sigma^2}{(\mu - \bar{D})^2} \qquad \text{B(1.20)}$$

To minimize the upper bound of the probability that $\bar{D}$ or worse will be the outcome the investor should maximize:

$$\left(\frac{\mu - \bar{D}}{\sigma}\right) \qquad \text{B(1.21)}$$

Call B(1.21) h, and the investor should then maximize h in:

$$\mu = \bar{D} + h\sigma \qquad \text{B(1.22)}$$

with $\bar{D} = \bar{R}$ this is the equivalent of the market opportunity line. The investor selects the highest h he can obtain given the risky asset investment opportunity frontier, AB, in figure 1.8. He therefore selects point C on that diagram (with $\bar{D} = \bar{R}$), as representing his best available portfolio. Thus, with $\bar{R}$ replaced by $\bar{D}$ in equations B(1.14) and B(1.16) we have the optimum value of μ and σ for the Royian Safety-First investor. From equations (1.56)–(1.58) the optimum holdings of the risky assets can be calculated.

It is apparent even from these necessarily cursory observations on Roy's approach that it is likely to lead to a different portfolio being selected by the investor from that which he would choose under expected utility maximization, for a given investment opportunity frontier. For a comparison of the two approaches and for a summary of the alternative safety-first criteria spawned by Roy's work see: D. H. Pyle and S. J. Turnovsky, 'Safety-first and expected utility maximisation in mean–standard deviation portfolio analysis', *Review of Economics and Statistics*, vol. 52 (1970), pp. 75–81.

2

An Outline of Professor Shackle's Theory

Professor Shackle's theory of choice of action, thus choice of portfolio or whatever, under uncertainty is predicated on his view that the probability approach cannot provide a reliable, *rational* foundation for action because the application of objective probabilities, relative frequencies, to decision-making is inadmissible, indeed irrelevant, because almost invariably decisions are *unique* phenomena. An individual, in essence, does not have the opportunity to, or the luxury to, indulge in infinitely repeatable 'experiments'. What might happen on the average, or for a large group of individuals taken collectively, is of no import for the individual. Consider then an individual investor endeavouring to select the best possible portfolio (and the example applies *in extenso* to all investment decisions). He will have a limited value of wealth. He stands to lose that wealth if he makes a totally wrong choice of portfolio. He might soon find himself 'out of the game against nature' that is portrayed in the probabilistic conception of decision-making. The chance of an infinitely repeatable investment of his wealth is, or could be, denied to him; he cannot rely on being able to trade on the relative frequencies of occurrence of particular yields on specified assets. For the individual, in short, a portfolio choice could be a one-and-for-all choice. What is true for society as a whole is not true for the individual.

Those logical difficulties had not gone unnoticed in the statistical and philosophical literature. They figured prominently in two well-known treatises – Venn's *The Logic of Chance* (1880) and more especially in various editions of Jeffrey's (1939) classic *Theory of Probability*. They had also been prominent in Keynes's *Treatise on Probability* (1921). It is from picking up the thrust of their arguments that Professor Shackle re-emphasized the (seemingly) fundamental weakness (we hesitate to use the word 'flaw') in the probability calculus. Also the concept that he proposed as an alternative to probability as the linch-pin of his own theory, namely *potential surprise*, possibly has as its antecedent the notion of surprise utilized by Venn.

The main gist of the argument against the use of the probability calculus is that decisions taken by human beings *per* individuals (or companies) are intrinsically, or overwhelmingly, *non-divisible non-seriable* experiments:

I want now to define the term *non-divisible non-seriable experiment*. When the question is: If I throw these dice 36,000 times, how often will they show a double six?, experience or thought may entitle us to answer: about one thousand times. The experiment is divisible into a large enough number of items, each consisting in a performance undertaken in some stable set of circumstances, to allow actuarial principles to give us an answer with the status of knowledge. When the question is: I am about to throw these dice once, what will they show?, no such division is possible, the experiment and its answer are a unitary whole and actuarial principles are not able to give that answer. We shall call such an experiment *non-divisible*. Sometimes, however, an experiment which can only be performed once by a single individual person can be pooled with similar experiments made by others so as to compose an experiment which, if all these people can be treated as a single entity, becomes divisible. The people *can* be treated as a single entity provided they agree to share out the result of the divisible experiment amongst themselves on some principle which to each one of them seems equitable. Thus although no-one can tell whether any particular person will live to be sixty, an insurance company can write him an endowment policy whose terms are based on knowledge. Then we can say that his experiment is *seriable*.[1]

We notice in this argument that reference is made to the fact that relative frequencies carry no information content if the experiment cannot be repeated in an unchanging set of conditions. For most decisions this will not be feasible; and for decisions made in an economic context this is most certainly likely to be the case. The very fact that an 'experiment' is being undertaken can destroy the circumstances in which it took place and make it impossible for it to be repeated. The situation where the investor has lost all of his wealth or had it altered by the 'experiment', the investment he undertook, mentioned previously, pertains to this. In addition, it is germane to point out that the general set of conditions present in the economy at any one investment point are not going to persist.

Shackle further castigates the use of objective probability in the analysis of investment decisions because probability is a *distributional* variable. Thus suppose that at one time n, mutually exclusive states of nature are possible. If the investor now revises his expectations about those states and arrives at the conclusion that $n + 1$, in effect, are possible, it is necessary for the probability of at least one of the n states of nature to be reduced to accommodate the extra eventuality. Why, Shackle asks, should an investor *have* to revise his estimate of any state of the world because another possible state emerges? Clearly there *is* a conundrum here. Should we think of probability as *subjective* probability then the essence of this difficulty remains.

Construction of a schema for investment decision-making on the basis of subjective probability reduces the force of the non-divisible non-serial experiment argument. However, it still cannot remove one of the underlying tenets of the probability approach which Shackle finds unacceptable and which forms the cornerstone of his own theory of expectations founded on potential surprise.

In chastising the proponents of the use of the probability calculus Professor Shackle used, as his examples, investment decisions which were based on the premise that the best decision was to choose that investment strategy which produced the highest *expected value of returns* or the highest discounted value of expected returns. An approach that is common in the choice of capital equipment/machinery to be purchased; and to which we shall make reference in chapter 6.

Since Professor Shackle says that objective probability is totally inapplicable to a non-seriable decision, such as the investment decision, he argues that:

> the decision maker . . . is reduced to using *subjective* probability, which has no claims to be knowledge, which cannot offer any objective support to such constructions as the mathematical expectations, cannot vividly or meaningfully be used to arrive at a *weighted average* outcome, save when this phrase has a purely formal meaning and indicates no more than that an arithmetical procedure of multiplications and additions of the resulting products has been performed. For now we are brought face to face with the core of the matter: when the experiment is a non-divisible one, the hypotheses regarding its outcome are cut-throat *rivals*, denying and excluding each other. What, then, is the sense of *averaging* them?[2]

Whilst, indeed, as we shall see, Shackle's own approach circumvents the 'averaging problem', it is perhaps a more subjective approach than that based on subjective probability.

In essence: if an investor is ranking various capital investment projects in terms of their (discounted) expected value of return; or is ranking unit-period investment portfolios on the basis (exclusively or partly) of their expected values of yield; can these exercises have any meaning? For each possible investment strategy, or portfolio, there will be a range of outcomes, which can be mapped out in a returns-matrix such as table 1.1; but the probabilities will now be regarded as subjective. For each strategy, however, only one outcome can occur; is there any ground in logic for combining those outcomes, by averaging them via their mathematical expectations, in such a situation? In a nutshell does such a procedure utilize all of the expectational data before the individual? Suppose that for states of nature 1 to k the outcomes for a given investment strategy are negative returns, whilst for k to n they are positive returns. Should the investor not take cognizance of such a characteristic of his expectations? Likewise, when comparing the various investment strategies open to him should he not pay special attention to the 'loss', 'gain', profile of outcomes for those strategies?

The common sense of answering those questions in the affirmative with respect to choice of capital investment projects based on the criterion referred to by Shackle is easy to appreciate. Thus, as a simple, illustrative, example let us consider the situation presented in table 2.1, where A and B refer to two possible pieces of equipment that could be purchased. These are assumed to be just four possible outcomes for each strategy; or four states of nature α if we think of these as states that last for the length of life of the capital equipment. The returns in those states can be thought of as the difference between discounted present values and asset prices. To avoid undue complexity we have assumed that each state has the same probability of being the true one.

Table 2.1
An investment pay-off matrix

α	1	2	3	4
A	–2	–2	4	4
B	0	0	2	2
Π_α	0.25	0.25	0.25	0.25

On the expected value of yield, or net return, criterion it is clear that the investor will be *indifferent* between purchasing *A* or *B*. They both promise the same expected yield. However, *A* offers the chance of negative yields, and, indeed, a 50 per cent possibility of such an eventuality. *B*, it is felt with 'certainty', can at worst only provide a zero yield; and it does so when there is a likelihood of negative yields, or losses, on investment *A*. For given states of nature and for the other 50 per cent of the time they both promise positive yields with investment *A* outstripping investment *B*.

A straightforward manipulation of the data to calculate expected yields masked that information on the pattern of the individual outcomes on *A* and *B*. That information tells us that no matter what might befall, as far as the investor sees the future, the yield on *B* must be non-negative; for *A* such a yield is only guaranteed for 50 per cent of the possible eventualities. If the investor bears that fact in mind he might well select strategy *B*. Ignoring that information he would be indifferent between *A* and *B*. In scanning the yield profile of the strategies he might then sift them into two categories: those that indicate a negative yield, or loss, and those that point to a positive yield or gain. Such, indeed, is the proposal that Professor Shackle makes in developing his alternative schema to that of the probability calculus.

If we reflect upon this issue in the context of portfolio selection we also see that it can be a relevant consideration, but it is not as obviously so as in the case of capital investment decisions. Should table 2.1 represent two possible portfolio return profiles from the investment of all the investor's wealth then if the investor is *risk-neutral*, so that his actual utility in actual returns (or actual wealth) is linear in that return, the outcome will be identical with that discussed previously when *A* and *B* denoted two capital investment projects. The investor's expected utility will be maximized by his selecting that portfolio which provides the higher expected value of return; therefore he is indifferent between the two portfolios. If the investor is a risk-averter he will select portfolio *B*; so he selects the same portfolio as we might expect him to do if he were to consider the whole gamut of potential returns on the portfolio rather than their 'conflated characteristics', such as their means and variances.

As an alternative imagine that the investor is confronted by the need to choose between portfolios I and II whose matrix of yields (where these are now to be thought of as the yields on assets I and II, respectively, scaled up by total wealth) are contained in table 2.2.

Table 2.2 An investment pay-off matrix

α	1	2	3	4
I	0	−1	−1	9
II	0	0	0	3
Π	0.25	0.25	0.25	0.25

If the investor is a *risk-averter* then his expected utility could be maximized by his choosing either portfolio; or he could find himself in the position where it did not matter which portfolio he chose. This is simply because the mean value of return on I exceeds that on II; but the variance on I also exceeds that on II. The mean–variance pairs are such, however, that an expected utility function could be posited from which we could deduce that those pairs lie along the same constant expected utility indifference curve. But that function could be such that I $\succ$ II or vice-versa. I $\succ$ II is perfectly possible because although II comes very close to dominating I stochastically (axion 5(a) chapter 1) it does not do so.

Because of his objections to probability and to the mechanical application of the probability calculus to expectational data Professor Shackle has proposed a radical alternative thought-scheme. As a replacement for probability he introduces the concept of *potential surprise*; and to overcome the objections that to telescope the expectational data on investment choices by some kind of averaging or 'concertina' process potentially ignores vital information and asks the human psyche to execute an inordinately complex operation (when it aims for simplicity since it is not capable of carrying forward a surfeit of information), he argues that the individual will partition his set of expectational data into a loss/negative yield subset and a gain/positive yield subset. Further, he will reduce the expectational information in each of those subsets to only one item by a simple sifting device in the form of the *ascendancy function*.

Now let us be specific. Consider the potential yields from investing a unit of wealth in a particular asset. The probabilistic methodological approach we recall is to specify the contingencies that can occur, the α's; for each contingency its probability is indicated;

and in each eventuality the investor forms a view as to the unit yield on the asset. Hence we have the matrix given in table 1.1 or tables 2.1 and 2.2. In Professor Shackle's schema the notion of state of nature does not appear in the explicit form it does in the traditional schema; and we shall dispense with it, but we shall find that it re-emerges later in a different guise. Rather we imagine that the investor maps out for himself (given his current information set, his past experiences, his view of future happenings that might influence his investment returns) the range of returns he believes could occur from investment in the asset. He then attaches a degree of potential surprise to each of those returns instead of a measure of their probability of occurrence.

Now the degree of potential surprise indicates the degree of surprise the investor would feel if a specified asset yield turned out to be true. The size of degree of potential surprise, which reflects the individual's *degree of belief* in an outcome, can range from zero to some (subjective, of course) maximum value, which would register complete *dis*-belief in the *possibility* that the outcome to which it was assigned could occur. The concept and measurement of potential surprise will be considered later. For now, in order to convey the essence of Shackle's theory we shall leave the matter here.

Once the degrees of potential surprise have been attached to the possible yields on the asset the investor then separates them into a gain and a loss set. If we denote potential surprise by y, and yield by r, then if for the sake of illustration at this stage we posit that the potential surprise function is continuous the investor has thus delineated:

$$y = y(r) \tag{2.1}$$

for the relevant asset. In general, we might anticipate that y increases in gain or with increases in the absolute value of loss; but this need not be the case, as we shall see. However, in most expositions of his theory Shackle assumes, for ease of *pictoral presentation* of his schema, that this is so.[3]

We separate out the potential surprise function into its two branches, that for gains (g) and that for losses (l):

$$y = y(g); \quad y = y(l) \tag{2.2}$$

We use the same symbol $y(.)$ for the two separate functions since we follow Shackle's notation.

The ascendancy function indicates the power of an expectational element, namely pair of (g,y) or (l,y) to arrest the attention of the individual. It is to be seen as a stimulus function and it is usually labelled the ϕ-function; so that:

$$\phi = \phi(g,y); \quad \phi = \phi(l,y) \tag{2.3}$$

again, following Shackle we use $\phi(.)$ to denote two functions, which could be quite different. In general, Shackle assumes that the properties of ϕ are as follows:

$$\frac{\partial \phi}{\partial g} > 0; \quad \frac{\partial \phi}{\partial y} < 0; \quad \text{and} \quad \frac{\partial \phi}{\partial l} > 0 \tag{2.4}$$

Note that the partial derivatives of the ϕ-function with respect to gains and losses are both positive. This is because Shackle defines losses as an absolute number. Thus, *ceteris paribus*, the higher is the gain on an asset the greater will be its power to attract the attention of the investor; and the larger is the loss on an asset the bigger will be its ascendancy in the mind of the investor. *Ceteris paribus*, as the potential surprise attached to a specified gain on an asset is increased, that gain will lose power to attract the investor's notice; this is the case similarly with an increase in the loss on an asset, since if the potential surprise on that loss falls there is less reason for the investor to pay attention to it, no matter what its magnitude happens to be.

Shackle makes the assumption that the ϕ-function is a continuous. one. Therefore, for each possible level of ϕ we can derive a ϕ-indifference curve which traces out for us the combinations of (g,y) or (g,l) consistent with the attainment of that level of ϕ. The resultant indifference curves will have positive slopes in (g,y) or (l,y) space given the conditions contained in (2.4). We shall also assume, along with Shackle, that the second-order conditions are satisfied that permit us to construct the ϕ-indifference curves as we have done in figure 2.1. On the latter we have also portrayed the potential surprise function; we have done so as if it were a continuous function. The function for the gain and loss branches can be identical or different. Only a selection of possible ϕ-indifference curves have been drawn, of course; and then solely for the case of gains. Those for losses might simply be a mirror-image of those for gains; but see later.

The ϕ-function, or ascendancy function, is now employed by the investor to sift out the expectational elements for gains/losses obtainable from a unit of investment in the asset. This is done in a way that states that the investor will use the ϕ-function as a

'ϕocusing' device; he will utilize it to telescope the information depicted in the profile of expectational elements to just *two* elements, one for the gain and one for the loss branch of the potential surprise function. He will therefore just focus his attention on two expectational elements. This focusing or sifting-out process is the analogue of the translation of the probability distribution of returns on the asset to the characteristics that epitomize that distribution *per se*, or to the characteristics that are required by the investor's expected utility function.

The sifting-out process is accomplished by the following route. At a point such as *E* on figure 2.1 the investor has maximized his ϕ-function. For at that point the highest value of ϕ has been attained *given* the constraint placed on it by the potential surprise function. The point *E* is an expectational element: it possesses a gain of *OF* and a degree of potential surprise equal to *OH*. That gain is labelled the *primary focus-gain* in Professor Shackle's theory. As we have indicated previously, it will have a concomitant primary focus-loss, namely, *ON*, with an associated degree of potential surprise, *OQ*.

Those primary focus-values are, as their name implies, the gain/loss values on which the investor focuses his attention initially. They have a first claim on his mind; they represent the 'best' that the investor can hope for and the 'worst' that he has to fear, *according to Shackle*. But they have attached to them a degree of potential surprise; or in general they will have, because, of course, there could be occasions when the gain and loss branches of the potential surprise function are coincidental at the origin of figure 2.1. The next step in the 'ϕocusing' process is one which removes the potential surprise element of the primary focus-elements. It is argued that the investor will need to have a common base upon which to compare the gains/losses from competing investment strategies. Therefore he will find an equivalent gain/loss for each asset/investment strategy where potential surprise has been discounted. Such equivalence is obtained by locating that gain/loss which is identical to the primary gain/loss in that it produces the same value of ϕ, but with zero potential surprise attached to it. Such a gain/loss is called the *standardized* focus-gain/loss, since the gain and the loss have been placed on the same, standard, footing. On figure 2.1 the standardised focus-gain is provided by *OG*; at *G* the investor is on the same level of ϕ as he is at *E*, but there is now zero degree of potential surprise attached to *OG*.

The expectational elements for the asset/investment strategy

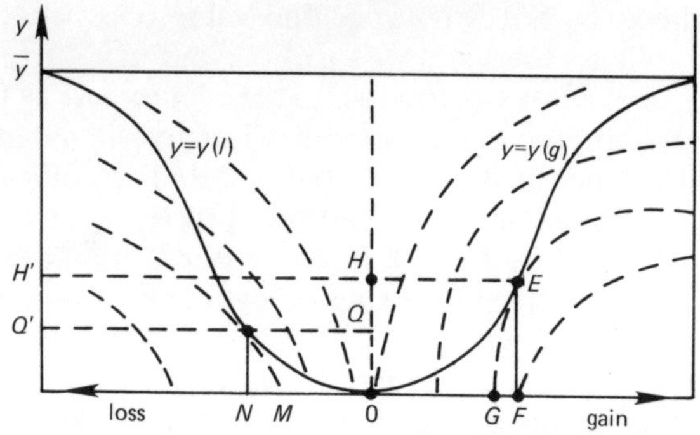

Figure 2.1 *The φ-indifference map and the potential surprise function*

have now been reduced to two monetary values – a gain and a loss. The analogue, but not, of course, the equivalent, counterpart in the probabilistic approach is the telescoping of the probability of returns on the asset/investment strategy, to characteristics of those distributions such as their means and variances.

The next stage in the choice of action entails the introduction of the *gambler-preference map*. Imagine that the standardized focus-values have been calculated for two assets and that the investor now has to decide how to allocate his wealth across those two assets. The Shackle schema sees this choice confronting the investor in this perspective. The standardized focus-values per £1 invested in each of the assets are scaled up by the total value of the investor's available wealth. This operation produces the *total* standardized focus-values on the two assets. The gambler-preference map epitomizes the investor's rankings of pairs of focus-values. Each indifference curves traces out those combinations that produce the same level of 'utility'. In the Shackle schema the latter is referred to only implicitly as an indicator of preferences; but we can regard that indicator as some 'U' or index; although it is conceptually advantageous to think of it as the former. We may write:

$$U = U(G, L) \tag{2.5}$$

where:

$$\frac{\partial U}{\partial G} > 0; \quad \frac{\partial U}{\partial L} < 0 \tag{2.6}$$

Here G and L denote, respectively, total standardized focus gains and loss. They are represented by capital letters to indicate that they do refer to total (wealth scaled up) values of focus values.

The hypothesis is that for a specified value of L, the higher is G the greater will be the investor's utility; and vice-versa, for a predetermined level of G, the lower is L the higher will be utility.

The gambler-preference indifference curves will assume the type of form and shape illustrated on figure 2.2. The curves are ranked (in ascending order) from the south-east to the north-west, by the hypotheses contained in (2.6). Points A and B might represent the (total) focus-values from investing the whole of wealth in either of the two assets individually.

The example given in figure 2.2 is one where the individual investor is indifferent between the two assets/strategies A and B. In chapter 3 we shall be investigating the possibility that the investor will find it optimal to invest in a *combination* of the two assets. As part of a wider enquiry into the application of Shackle's schema to portfolio selection, we shall be considering the kind of issues discussed in chapter 1 in the context of the probability calculus approach.

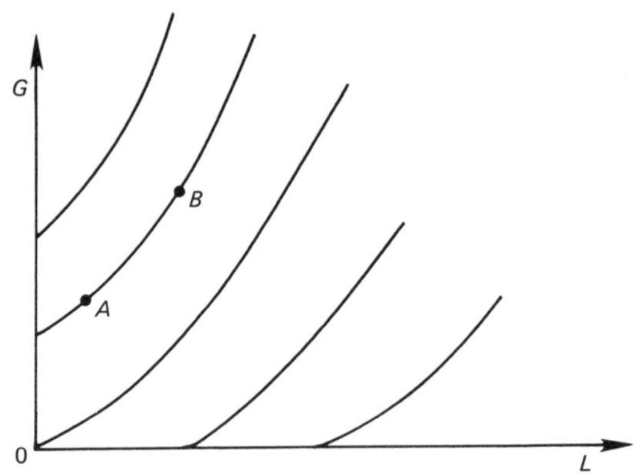

Figure 2.2 The gambler-preference map

The remainder of this chapter, however, will amplify several aspects of the main strands in Professor Shackle's model that have been covered only in a cursory fashion so far in an attempt to convey the essence and flavour of Shackle's conception of choice under uncertainty. It will be of assistance in the ensuing pages if a summary of the main stages embodied in the Shackle decision-making process were provided. These are as follows.

Stage 1. The investor specifies his potential surprise function for each asset, or investment strategy, as the case might be.

Stage 2. On the basis of his ascendancy, stimulus or ϕ function, the investor crystallizes the information contained in his potential surprise function into two outcomes that most catch his attention: a gain/positive return outcome and a loss/negative return outcome. These *primary* focus-values are to be looked upon as the best that the investor can hope for, and the worst he has to fear, according to Shackle.

Stage 3. The primary focus-values are transformed onto a common basis. This is accomplished by the calculation of *standardized* focus-values which have discounted the potential surprise attached to the primary focus-values.

Stage 4. The standardized focus-values on the assets, or investment projects, have to be ranked. This is achieved by means of the gambler-preference map. Choice of optimal action is then complete.

Thus in sum: the Shackle schema consists of three pieces of apparatus: the potential surprise function; the ascendancy or ϕ-function; and the gambler-preference map. Each one of these occupies a stage in the construction of the decision-making model, with the ϕ-function accounting for the two middle stages.

Before proceeding to consider each piece of apparatus in more depth it might be beneficial to pause and consider a simple example of the Shackle schema in operation. Let us suppose that the potential surprise functions for the gain (g) and loss (l) on two assets or investments A and B are as follows:

$$\begin{aligned} &\text{(i)}\quad y_A = a_1 g_A; &&\text{(ii)}\quad y_A = a_2 l_A \\ &\text{(iii)}\quad y_B = b_1 g_B; &&\text{(iv)}\quad y_B = b_2 l_B \end{aligned} \tag{2.7}$$

where all coefficients a_i, b_i are positive. We further assume that the ϕ-functions for gain and loss are given by:

$$(1)\ \phi_g = \alpha g + \beta y^2; \quad (2)\ \phi_l = \alpha_1 l + \beta_1 y^2; \quad \beta < 0, \beta_1 < 0 \tag{2.8}$$

These functions will assume a form similar to the ϕ-indifference curves illustrated on figure 2.1 and, of course, as in that figure, the potential surprise functions are continuous but are now linear.

Utilizing equations (2.7) and (2.8) we are in a position to evaluate the individual's perception of the primary focus-values on each of the investments. Thus, from the first-order conditions for the maximization of ϕ_g in (2.8) subject to equation (2.7)(i), we discover that:

$$g_A = \frac{-\alpha}{2a_1\beta} > 0 \tag{2.9}$$

This is the *primary* focus-gain on asset or investment A. With it there is a degree of potential surprise (obtained, of course, by merely substituting (2.9) into y_A) of:

$$y \mid g_A = \frac{-\alpha}{2\beta} > 0 \tag{2.10}$$

Maximization of ϕ_l in equation (2.8) subject to equation (2.7)(i) produces this result:

$$l_A = \frac{-\alpha_1}{2a_2\beta_1} > 0 \tag{2.11}$$

to which:

$$y \mid l_A = \frac{-\alpha_1}{2\beta_1} > 0 \tag{2.12}$$

Equations (2.9) and (2.10) enable calculations of the maximum value of ϕ attainable on the gain branch for asset A, namely:

$$\phi = \frac{-\alpha^2}{2a_1\beta} + \frac{\alpha^2}{4\beta} \tag{2.13}$$

The derivation of the *standardized* focus-gain for the asset or investment can now be accomplished. Such a focus-gain occurs, remember, when $y = 0$ and when ϕ assumes its maximum value attainable under the constraint of the potential surprise function, which is given by equation (2.13). Thus: set ϕ_g in equation (2.8)(1) equal to the value given in (2.13), and let $y = 0$; the outcome is the standardized focus-gain (sg), namely:

$$(sg)_A = \frac{-\alpha}{2a_1\beta} + \frac{\alpha}{4\beta} \tag{2.14}$$

Likewise from equations (2.8)(2), (2.11) and (2.12) we deduce that:

$$\phi \mid l_A = \frac{-\alpha_1^2}{2a_2\beta_1} + \frac{\alpha_1^2}{4\beta_1} \tag{2.15}$$

Therefore:

$$(sl)_A = \frac{-\alpha_1}{2a_2\beta_1} + \frac{\alpha_1}{4\beta_1} \tag{2.16}$$

In similar fashion we deduce that:

$$(sg)_B = \frac{-\alpha}{2b_1\beta} + \frac{\alpha}{4\beta} \tag{2.17}$$

$$(sl)_B = \frac{-\alpha_1}{2b_2\beta_1} + \frac{\alpha_1}{4\beta_1} \tag{2.18}$$

If A and B were investment projects the individual would be ranking the pair of focus-values epitomized in equations (2.14) and (2.16) against those given by equations (2.17) and (2.18). Should they be assets then those standardized focus values denote gains/losses per £1 invested in either of the assets. Should the investor be confronted by a choice of investing all of his wealth in one asset or the other then the focus-values need to be scaled up by his wealth (W). That is the choice considered explicitly in this chapter in order to concentrate on the essence of the Shackle schema *per se*. Chapter 3 will discuss the possibility that the investor can select (optimally) a mixture of the two assets.

Keeping to a choice between investing in one asset or the other (or either if his gambler-preference map indicates he is indifferent between them) we must specify the individual's gambler-preference function. Suppose it assumes this form:

$$U = \theta G + \lambda L^2; \quad \theta > 0; \quad \lambda < 0 \tag{2.19}$$

His gambler-preference map will then take on an appearance similar to that portrayed on figure 2.2. When the values defined by equations (2.14), (2.16), (2.17) and (2.18) are scaled up by W, we have the total standardized focus-values, G and L, for the two assets. Then:

$$U_A = \theta\left[\frac{W\alpha(a_1 - 2)}{4a_1\beta}\right] + \lambda\left[\frac{W^2\alpha_1^2(a_2 - 2)^2}{16a_2^2\beta_1^2}\right] \tag{2.20}$$

$$U_B = \theta\left[\frac{W\alpha(b_1 - 2)}{4b_1\beta}\right] + \lambda\left[\frac{W^2\alpha_1^2(b_2 - 2)^2}{16b_2^2\beta_1^2}\right] \tag{2.21}$$

If $U_A > U_B$ then asset A is selected (of course, as we should note in anticipation of discussion in chapter 3, if W can be held in the form of money, then U_A must also exceed that value of U that would obtain given the G, L characteristics of money).

Each of these pieces of apparatus will now be considered in more depth; They will be taken *seriatim*, but as will be observed, it is not clear whether the separate components of the model are always distinct.

Thus, in introducing his notion of *potential surprise*, Shackle comes close to arguing that the ϕ-function, rather than the gambler-preference map, is the arbiter of choice. For his underlying premise is:

> We decide on one particular course of action, out of a number of rival courses, because this one gives us, as an immediately present experience, the most enjoyment *by anticipation* of its outcome. Future situations and events cannot be experienced and therefore their degree of desirableness cannot be compared; but situations and events can be *imagined*, and the desirableness of these experiences which happen in the imagination can be compared. What gives imagined things a claim to be treated as the equivalents of future things? It is some degree of belief that the imagined things will take actual shape at the dates we assign to them. . . .
>
> Thus the entity which gives us enjoyment by anticipation (or distress by anticipation) or, as I shall say indifferently, by imagination, has two sets of characteristics. The first set specifies or describes the situation or sequence of situations, saying what it would be like if it were to happen . . . the picture can consist, for example, in a meeting with an actual and living friend, or the conferment on us of some honour, or success in some attempt. . . . The other set (of one member only) consists merely in our degree of belief that this picture will come true. But how is this degree of belief presented to our minds, and put on the same footing of concreteness, of capacity to influence our decisions, as the feelings aroused by the content of the picture?[4]

Shackle devoted little space in his original monograph to the concepts of degree of belief and potential surprise. His views can be summarized by the following:

> It is a man who feels very sure of a given outcome who can be greatly *surprised* by its non-occurrence. A degree of belief is not in itself a sensation or an emotion; but a high degree of belief is a condition of our being able to feel a high degree of surprise . . . we can use the degree of surprise which we judge would be caused to us by the non-occurrence of a given outcome, . . . , as an indicator of our degree of belief in this outcome. The range of possible intensities of surprise lies between zero and that intensity which would arise from the occurrence of an event believed impossible, or held to be *certain* not to occur. Within this range each one of us will find in his own past experience

particular occurrences . . . each of which has caused him some degree of surprise, the memory of which remains with him vividly enough to serve, in conjunction with the event which caused it, as one of a series of fixed levels, not necessarily even spaced, providing together a scale of potential surprise . . . and [we shall] treat surprise as a continuous variable defined in a certain range, and subject to manipulation by the methods of the differential calculus. . . . The measure so obtained is what we may call the *potential surprise* associated, by a particular person at a particular date, with the falsity of the answer or the non-occurrence of the outcome.[5]

Then Shackle comes across a conundrum and has to invert these notions so that we arrive at a concept of potential surprise related to the *occurrence* of an outcome:

This formula, however, is not quite satisfactory for our purpose. In answer to any questions about the future, there will typically be in the mind of any one person a number of rival hypotheses, and amongst these there will be a subset of which each member is superior, as regards his degree of belief in it, to any hypothesis outside the subset, but of which no one member is superior to any other member. In this case he cannot attach any degree of surprise greater than zero to the falsity or non-fulfilment of any one particular member of this subset; for to do so would *ipso facto* mark this member off as claiming a higher degree of belief than any of the others. The most he can do is to attach nil potential surprise to the *fulfilment* of any member of the subset. But he *can* attach some positive degree of potential surprise to every hypothesis *outside* the subset, and by doing so he will express its inferiority, in the matter of the degree of his belief in it, to every member of the subset. And further, he can attach different degrees of potential surprise to different hypotheses outside the subset. It will be convenient, therefore, to invert our formula, and say that by assigning different degrees of potential surprise to the occurrence, rather than the non-occurrence, of different hypothetical outcomes, he assigns to these outcomes positions on a scale of belief.[6]

Notice the reference to the 'inner subset', or for continuous outcomes, the 'inner range'. Any number of rival hypotheses about the outcome of an experiment, investment-decision, or whatever, can have zero potential surprise attached to them. Nevertheless, Shackle's own inclination is to suggest that there will be only a few outcomes for, say, a particular investment, that will carry zero potential surprise. Therefore the potential surprise function will take on the kind of structure conveyed on figure 2.1; but any form of that function is feasible. Thus there might be no gain branch or no loss branch; either branch might consist of one element of zero potential surprise, every other element carrying the maximum degree of potential surprise, if the investor is certain that only one gain/loss is possible. The project concerned might be one from which the investor would find small gains and extremely high gains perfectly possible, but which he feels will offer no chance of medium-sized gains; an all-or-nothing project would thus produce a ⎍ -shaped gain branch.

Out of an exhaustive set of rival hypotheses one at least must, naturally, carry zero potential surprise. However, in some decisions the list of outcomes might have to be made exhaustive by the inclusion of what Shackle calls the residual hypothesis. This stands as a shorthand for any outcome other than those particularized as possibilities, in short 'some other outcome', to which there will also be assigned a degree of potential surprise.

The existence of a residual hypothesis would make it difficult to consider potential surprise (or objective/subjective probability) as a distributional variable. But Shackle is insistent that potential surprise is non-additive and hence non-distributional:

> . . . there is no limit in logic to the number and diversity of suggested answers to a question, which can all simultaneously be accorded any given degree of potential surprise from zero to the absolute maximum. . . . Potential surprise is completely non-distributional.[7]

This conclusion remains, even if there is no residual hypothesis.

The replacement of dis-belief by belief has occasioned some difficulties for the interpretation of the concept of potential surprise. In writing of the two notions of degree of surprise and degree of belief, Robert Dorfman, for example, has observed:

> The problem is that while both of these concepts are intuitively appealing substitutes for mathematical probability, they are almost undefinable; reasoning based on the one contradicts reasoning based on the other, and no accepted basis for reconciling the two exists. The vagueness of the relationship between the two is illustrated by the fact that a man using a telephone has a low degree of belief in getting a wrong number but also a low degree of surprise if he does.[8]

Shackle's reply is based upon axiom 6 of the nine propositions by which he himself has axiomatized potential surprise as an analogue to the axiomization of probability.[9] That axiom states that:

> When *H* is any hypothesis, the degree of potential surprise attached to the

contradictory of *H* is equal to the *smallest* degree attached to any rival of *H* [italics in original].

This is obviously a logical proposition to make. It is used to counteract Dorfman's example in this fashion:

I can attach zero potential surprise to getting a wrong number, but also zero potential surprise to getting the right one. Thus both my degrees of belief in getting a wrong number, and my surprise if I do, will be zero.[10]

Shackle would now argue that zero potential surprise reflects *zero disbelief*. In *Decision, Order and Time* there is some ambivalence over the question of whether or not potential surprise should be related to belief or to disbelief. It seems that Shackle has a predilection for reverting to the emphasis on dis-belief that he had thought first of using in *Expectation in Economics*. This he does by emphasizing the general value of axiom 6:

When we consider together as one whole all the hypotheses which are rivals to a given hypothesis *H*, they constitute the *contradictory* of *H*. If, then, we wish to express the individual's *degree of belief* in a hypothesis, we shall think of this degree of belief as consisting in a degree of potential surprise associated with the hypothesis, and in another degree associated with its contradictory.[11]

The sentiment expressed in this paragraph is epitomized in axiom 1 of the nine axioms for potential surprise. That axiom, as we have stated previously, appeared in Shackle's first exposition of his new theory of expectations. However, as we have also seen from some of the quotes we have taken from the main text of that exposition, Shackle did not fully invoke that axiom in his definition of potential surprise as a measure of belief, when he endeavoured to switch from dis-belief in the occurrence of an hypothesis to belief in its occurrence. As a consequence, this made it possible for the key part of his apparatus to be challenged by others.[12]

It will be recalled that earlier on in this chapter it was shown that, initially, Shackle proposed that the measure of belief in an outcome reposes in the potential surprise the individual would feel if that outcome did not materialize. Thereafter, emphasis was placed on the occurrence of that outcome; to the effect that the scale of belief in that outcome depends upon the potential surprise attached to its occurrence. Our last quote from Shackle indicates that he is combining those two statements as he had really done already in his axiom 1 on potential surprise.

There is now no ambiguity over potential surprise and the potential surprise function for a project or strategy. That function, as portrayed here, indicates the degree of surprise the individual says he would experience if any specified outcome *occurred*. The degree of belief depends upon that degree of potential surprise, and that that would be felt if one of the alternatives to the project occurred. For projects for which the feasible outcomes constitute an exhaustive set and for which only one outcome – say, zero gain/zero loss – has zero potential surprise, it will follow that the rankings of the degrees of belief of the non-zero outcomes depend exclusively upon their potential surprise of occurrence; being correlated negatively with own-degree of potential surprise. The only exception here is that the degree of belief about the zero outcome with zero potential surprise could be identical with that of the first non-zero return. Potential surprise maps into degrees of belief, and for investment projects we are likely to encounter the kind of potential surprise function (such as that shown on figure 2.1) which would ensure this.

Therefore, to those critics who have argued that it is logically possible to assign zero degrees of potential surprise to two hypothetical outcomes whilst contending that the one is more likely to occur than the other, Shackle's reply is immediate and clear. To hold that the one outcome is more likely than the other must imply that there is an obstacle in the way of the other outcome's occurring. Therefore, it must be assigned a higher degree of potential surprise than the one outcome.[13]

The *ascendancy function* or the ϕ-function is involved in the second stage of the Shackle decision process. It is the vehicle that is supposed to sift out the expectational elements in the gain/loss branches of the potential surprise function for an investment project into two values upon which the investor focuses his attention and carries forward to the final stage of action-choice.

On the ϕ-function, Professor Shackle states:

> The account we shall offer of the selection of two elements out of a range of outcomes proceeds by describing a function connecting the characteristics of an expectation-element with what we shall variously call the *attention-arresting power, interestingness or ascendancy* of that element. These three expressions are to be taken as indifferent names for the same idea. We then look upon one element as having assigned to it a higher algebraic value of this function than another element. But this is not the end of the matter. The values of the function respectively assigned to this or that expectation-element merely

serve to *select* the element or elements upon which the decision-makers' whole attention will be concentrated. . . .

What will give on expectation-element ascendancy over another in the decision-maker's mind so that, if these two elements occupied the field alone, the former would capture and concentrate upon itself his whole attention to the neglect of the other? We say that such ascendancy will be the combined effect of the desiredness or distastefulness of the hypothetical outcome and of the potential surprise associated with it.[14]

So $\phi = \phi(r, y)$, where r represents either a gain or a loss and y denotes potential surprise. ϕ is only dependent upon those two magnitudes. It is assumed by Professor Shackle that $\phi_r > 0$, and $\phi_y < 0$. Since r refers to 'outcome' this means that if gain increases ascendancy will increase; similarly if loss increases then ϕ increases.

We have thought of ϕ increasing with positive G [gain] and also as increasing with numerical increase of L [loss] or negative G. This has always seemed and still seems to us natural. For let us remember that what ϕ means is not pleasure or pain, nor even encouragement or inhibition, but the power of expectation–elements to command attention. . . . I can be interested, engrossed, as well by the imagination of disaster as by that of triumph, and the part played by this response in our scheme of analysis does not seem to require or justify any distinction between the cases where it is a response to the one or to the other.[15]

The ϕ indifference curves or ϕ contour lines, as Professor Shackle sees them, are similar in form and shape to those depicted on figure 2.1 for gains/positive returns. The contour line for $\phi = 0$ is T-shaped: the top of the T being given by the upper bound on potential surprise, $\bar{y}$; the trunk of the T extending along the vertical line from zero-gain, zero-loss to $\bar{y}$. It is argued by Professor Shackle that:

Hypothetical outcomes which the decision-maker looks on as impossible will have no interest or relevance for him in his task of decision, and so we can say that ϕ will be zero everywhere on the line $y = \bar{y}$. Since we are in effect assuming that interest or relevance attaches to the *possibility of change* in the decision-maker's situation and if a given positive or negative gain which in the decision-maker's judgement cannot happen is, for that reason, of no interest, will not a zero-gain or loss which can happen be equally of no interest?[16]

This observation will apply whether we are dealing with gains/losses or with positive/negative returns. So the $\phi = 0$ indifference curve for gains is ┌-shaped and that for losses is ┐-shaped, with their axes coinciding with zero returns.

In our previous exposition of figure 2.1 it was stated that the ϕ-indifference curves for losses may be mirror-images of those drawn for gains. Frequently, in fact, Shackle follows such a line. However, it need not be the case that the ϕ-function is the same for gains and losses; indeed, in *Expectation in Economics* (by diagram, p. 20) and especially in *Decision, Order and Time* (by text and diagram, pp. 150–2) Shackle suggests that at times the ϕ-functions might differ.

Instead of representing the three-dimensional ϕ-surface, $\phi = \phi(y, r)$ in two dimensions by $y = \bar{\phi}(r)$ as in figure 2.1 in this book, we can construct the curve, $\phi = \phi(r, \bar{y})$: that is potential surprise is now constant (where $\bar{y}$ denotes the fact that y is at its maximum value). For a given potential surprise if the two branches of the ϕ-function are identical, they would also be mirror-images of each other on a $\phi = \phi(r, \bar{y})$ diagram. Professor Shackle suggests that they might not be such reflections of one another and that the situation might be similar to that portrayed in figure 2.3.

$\bar{\phi}$ represents an upper bound on ϕ, for as with y, it is assumed to have a limiting value. For fixed y, therefore, there are diminishing returns to gains and eventually $\partial\phi/\partial r = 0$; likewise for losses. The maximum value of ϕ is alleged to occur on the loss side where the loss is such as to represent the whole of the investor's wealth or investable resources. For small ratios of loss to wealth the investor's concern as loss increases will rise only slowly; but as the ratio rises the concern, ascendancy, in his mind of higher losses increases. Given the size of his wealth or investable resources, for an equivalent value of gain, the loss could induce a higher value of ϕ, as figure 2.3 suggests. The ϕ-function is meant to be used, as it was in figure

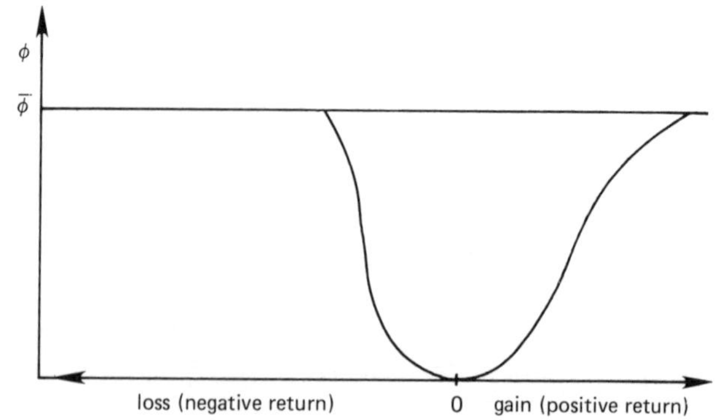

Figure 2.3 The ϕ-function

2.1, to telescope the information in the potential surprise function into an expectational element for each branch.

Reference to wealth and its effect on the ascendancy or ϕ-function provides a direct link with the third main element in Shackle's structure, namely the gambler-preference map. Shackle's own observations on that map and its constitution brings into focus the similarity between the sentiments expressed in the ϕ-function and those sentiments that are alleged to be encapsulated in the gambler-preference map.

That map is employed as the means by which the (standardized) focus-values obtained from application of the ϕ-function to the potential surprise function for various assets, investment strategies or whatever, are ranked and the choice of strategy finally made. The gambler-preference map is constructed on the supposition that the individual is a 'risk-averter'. However, at no time does Shackle argue that the gambler-preference indifference curves are derived from a gambler-preference function *per se*. Neither does Shackle begin his exposition of the choice-process under uncertainty with the premise that the individual will seek to maximize some kind of preference ordering. It merely transpires as the analysis unfolds that the individual is to be envisaged as maximizing his position on the gambler-preference map.

It seems from Shackle's presentation that he expects the typical gambler-preference indifference curves to have the shape depicted in figure 2.2. However, he wishes that each curve be not inextricably bound up with any other: each should be let free to express the individual's temperament. Nevertheless, for a choice of investment strategy the curves must be related, in some measure, if the individual possesses low risk-aversion, because Shackle propounds the view that the gambler-preference indifference curves are relevant only up to a barrier provided by the investable wealth of the individual:

> When the action-schemes being compared are investment schemes, the decision-maker will have in mind some definite available sum of money which is the most he can dispose of on behalf of himself or those who have placed their wealth at his discretion. This sum we shall call his fortune . . . it is the most that he can lose. . . . Thus at that point on the loss axis which corresponds to the decision-maker's fortune we erect, perpendicular to that axis, a barrier to the right of which the gambler-indifference curves would have no meaning. . . .[17]

He considers two broad categories of investor – namely 'the headlong gambler' and a person of more cautious temperament:

For the more cautious temperament, any point which threatens total ruin as one of its possibilities, that is any point on the 'barrier' . . . is more repellent than any point whose threat is less than total ruin. No point on the barrier, that is to say, can be contained in any of his gambler indifference curves, which therefore must approach the barrier asymptotically. . . . For the headlong gambler . . . there is no such restriction, his gambler indifference curves can meet the barrier at finite ordinates.[18]

Consequently, we have the preference maps assuming the form of those illustrated on figure 2.4; (a) for the 'headlong gambler'; and (b) for the (normal) risk-averter (see Shackle, *op. cit.*). The distance OW represents the investor's wealth or, alternatively, what he believes is the most he could afford to lose from his investment decisions.

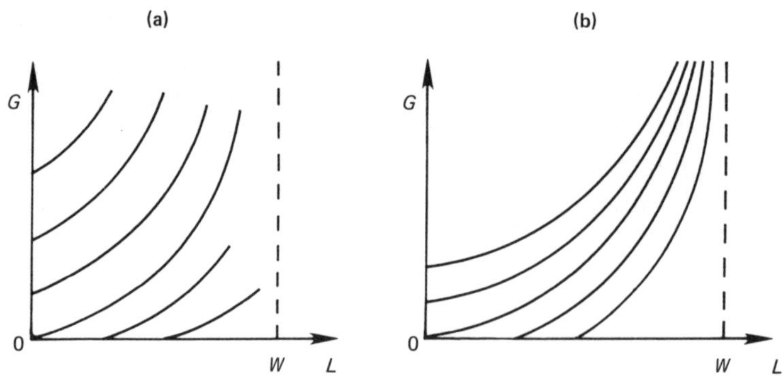

Figure 2.4 Wealth, the gambler-preference map and the attitude to risk

The gambler-preference indifference curve that passes through the origin is accorded special status: it is used as a method of measuring *risk-preference*:

The concept of the origin indifference curve leads us to a new and very simple definition of an individual's risk-preference, and enables us to measure the latter. A given individual in given circumstances will be able to name for any specific focus-loss a focus-gain such that if he is faced with this pair of focus-outcomes his situation seems to him neither more nor less desirable than if he had the assurance of experiencing neither gain nor loss. The ratio of the focus-loss to its compensating focus-gain will in general be different when the focus-loss is different. The set of all such ratios obtained by varying the focus-loss, other circumstances remaining unchanged, is what we shall mean by the *schedule of gambler-preference* of the given individual in these circumstances. It is evident that this is simply the set of ratios of abscissa to ordinate of all points on the origin indifference curve, when these ratios are placed in a one–one correspondence with the respective focus-losses concerned.[19]

The essential point to note here is that the précis of the nature of gambler-preference is not really the slip of the pen concerning *risk*, but the notion that wealth can influence gambler-preference orderings. Yet wealth is included as a possible factor in the weighting of expectational elements via the ϕ-function. The temperament of the individual embodied in the gambler-preference map is perhaps already subsumed in the ϕ-function. Maybe the gambler-preference map is dispensable; perhaps the ϕ-function should be used as a strategy-selection device rather than as a way by which expectations of asset returns or investment prospects are telescoped into manageable dimensions. Such a step might also restore uncertainty to playing a key role in the Shackle schema; for it disappears when primary focus-values are standardized and conjures up a view that perhaps at that stage the Shackle approach has lost its *point d'appui*.

All those (major) considerations will be within our purview in chapter 4. Prior to that, though, it is necessary to take a perspective on the Shackle schema *per se* and its applicability essentially to asset choice; chapter 6 will also provide more explicit observations on its value, along with that of the probabilistic approach to the real capital investment decision and to other decision-making processes.

Before proceeding to chapter 3 we should recapitulate on the essentials of Shackle's schema by noting these points.

(1) He disagrees with the probability approach because it uses a distributional variable to measure uncertainty and a variable that is not applicable to unique, i.e. non-seriable, non-divisible 'experiments'. If it were to be feasible to employ objective relative frequencies for assessing investment prospects of assets or strategies, then we would be in a world of risk and not of uncertainty. When objective probabilities can be used there is *ex definitione* no uncertainty; and if as is required the experiment *can be repeated an infinite number* of times in unchanging conditions, the outcome will equal its expected value. Thus, for a decision whether or

not to invest in this or that type of equipment or on this or that scale, where the decision is made on the basis of the expected (discounted) value of net returns, the outcome effectively is certain.

(2) The use of past data and past experience in the formation of expectations of yields on investments or assets is not dismissed. Such material could shape, or even dominate, the investor's view of future investment prospects.

(3) There are three main pillars to Shackle's new construct to replace the objective (also subjective) probability/orthodox approach to analysing choice of action under less than perfect knowledge. Potential surprise replaces objective probabilities (or states of nature) in that orthodox approach. The ascendancy or ϕ-function replaces the telescoping of the probability distribution of the investment or asset returns required in the conventional approach; those distributional characteristics that are relevant depend, of course, on the individual's utility function and/or the specific distribution those returns assume. Thus, if the individual's utility function is a quadratic in the actual portfolio return, only the means and variances of the asset return probability distribution are relevant. Likewise if the individual should possess a utility function that depends exponentially upon portfolio returns, if the returns on the individual's assets are normally distributed, their relevant characteristics again will be their means and variances.

The gambler-preference map is the analogue of the individual's utility function in total (portfolio) return. The latter permits the investor to choose the best combination of, say, mean and variance he can from investing all of his wealth, given the means and variances of the returns on the individual assets, which assets could constitute part of the optimum portfolio. To that optimal mean–variance pair there will be a unique composition of assets in the portfolio. The gambler-preference map, likewise, orders the relevant characteristics of the given assets or the given portfolios, namely their (total) standardized focus-values. Such an ordering procedure produces the best focus-value pair and hence the best asset portfolio.

3

A Detailed Study of Portfolio Selection and the Shackle Theory

In the preceding chapter the aim was to illustrate the essential points in the individual's decision-making process as portrayed in Professor Shackle's theory. This chapter will now examine the implications of his theory for portfolio choice. From chapter 1 it is recalled that there are three key questions to which we expect a theory of asset choice to offer us some kind of answer. These can be epitomized by the following:

(1) How does the investor decide the allocation of his wealth across alternative financial claims?
(2) Can the investor, acting rationally, allocate his wealth such that he holds a portfolio that is diversified over more than just two assets?
(3) (a) Can we deduce a set of equations to explain what does determine the purchase of a specific kind of financial claim by an investor?
(b) Can we sign the partial derivatives of these equations so that, for example, we can say what will happen to the holdings of 'bonds' if variable *a* changes?

Essentially I shall consider the three questions whilst accepting the whole of Shackle's apparatus *and* also all of the assumptions upon which I described it, which were also used in chapter 1. Here 1 refer especially to these assumptions: there is a one-period at a time decision process; financial assets are divisible; transaction costs do not exist; expectations are of zero inflation; there is no taxation.

A *fourth question* discussed in this chapter, which was also dealt with towards the end of chapter 1, concerns the *role of money* in the optimum portfolio. In the Shackle schema, as we shall see, the place of money is affected by the answer to question 2 related to the degree of asset-diversification feasible in the schema. We consider these questions *seriatim*.

In chapter 2, stage 4 of the Shackle schema provides us with the answer to question 1. It is implied that the investor has a 'utility' function over total standardized focus-values; and he maximises that utility subject to the best terms upon which he can 'trade' focus-loss for focus-gain. Those terms of trade are provided by the analogue of the budget line in consumer choice theory, namely the efficient investment frontier; as in the probabilistic approach described in chapter 1. If g_i and l_i, respectively, denote the standardised focus-gain (positive return) and focus-loss (negative return) on asset i, then for two assets A and B, the efficient investment frontier is derived by:

$$\max_{x_A, x_B} \quad G = g_A x_A + g_B x_B \tag{3.1}$$

$$\text{s.t.} \quad L = l_A x_A + l_B x_B \tag{3.2}$$

$$W = x_A + x_B \tag{3.3}$$

where, as hitherto and subsequently, for simplicity, G and L denote total standardized focus-gain (positive returns) and loss (negative returns) wherever it is necessary to set out equations in those values. Since we have only two linear constraints in two unknowns the optimum (*) values of x_A and x_B at all points along the efficient investment frontier can be derived directly from equations (3.2) and (3.3). Thus:

$$x_A^* = \frac{L - l_B W}{l_A - l_B} \tag{3.4}$$

$$x_B^* = \frac{l_A W - L}{l_A - l_B} \tag{3.5}$$

The efficient investment frontier being, therefore:

$$G = \left(\frac{g_A - g_B}{l_A - l_B}\right) L + \left(\frac{g_B l_A - g_A l_B}{l_A - l_B}\right) W \tag{3.6}$$

Now equations (3.1) and (3.2), and hence the efficient investment frontier, have been developed on the assumptions contained in, especially, *Expectation in Economics* and Shackle's other writings. Thus Shackle assumes that the total focus-values will be linear combinations of the focus-values of those for the two assets. In the only detailed critique of Shackle's theory of portfolio selection, developed by Dr R. A. D. Egerton,[1] it has been claimed that Shackle's assumption requires that the correlation between the expected gains/losses on the assets be unity: for in that case it is argued that if, say, the focus-gain on one asset occurs, so too will that on the other asset. This contention will be examined at length in chapter 4; we proceed on the supposition that if the correlation between identically named focus-values on the two assets is unity it will definitely be legitimate to evaluate total standardized focus-values in the way shown in equations (3.1) and (3.2).

The frontier is efficient in the sense that the x's have been chosen in such a way that it is not possible by any reallocation of wealth across the assets, for any given L, to increase G. Of course, it happens to be the case, in the two-asset model, that the efficient set of x's coincides with the efficient set. Also, in deriving the frontier we have used the implicit constraint that x_A and x_B are both non-negative. When the whole of the investor's wealth is allocated to asset A, G will equal $g_A W$ and L will equal $l_A W$; similarly for the case where all of the wealth is allocated to asset B. If $g_A < g_B$ and $l_A < l_B$, with all focus-values positive, equation (3.6) can be represented by the line AB on figure 3.1. Given his 'utility' function he would choose point E as providing the best asset portfolio on U_1. At E there are, of course, unique values for x_A^* and x_B^* which can be deduced from equations (3.4) and (3.5), given the characteristics of the two assets and the value of wealth. Alternatively, the optimum values of x_A and x_B can be obtained directly by choosing x_A^* and x_B^* to maximize 'utility' subject to the specification of G and L for given wealth. This latter method, naturally,

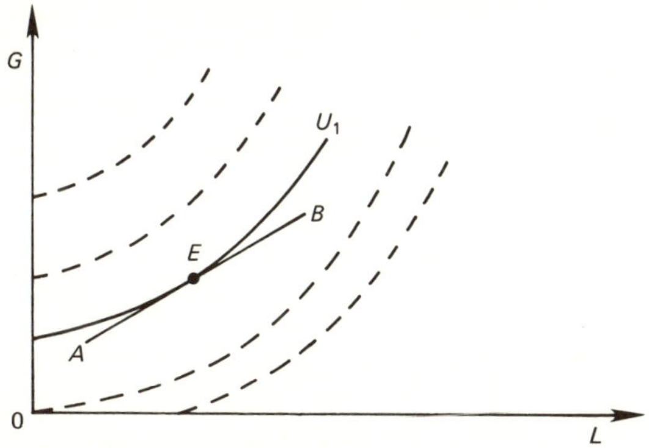

Figure 3.1 *The gambler-preference map and the investment opportunity line*

is potentially the more convenient one to adopt in a situation where the investor, potentially, has a choice of investing in several financial claims. Before proceeding that far attention must be given to consideration of question 2 posed above.

Discussion of that question will begin in the simplest possible way; that is: assume that the individual investor has a choice of investing in three assets; then investigate whether or not it is feasible for a rational investor to hold all three assets. Assets will be labelled *A*, *B* and *C*; and the ranking of their standardized focus-gains (positive returns) will be presumed to be in reverse alphabetical ordering, and that of their standardized focus-losses (negative returns) to be in alphabetical order. In such circumstances it will follow from equation (3.6) there will be a linear frontier connecting the gains/losses from alternative amounts of investment in assets *A* and *B* and such a frontier epitomizing the gains/losses from the possible investments in assets *B* and *C*. The situation can be depicted in general by figure 3.2.

If we consider figure 3.2, on the supposition of perfectly positive correlation between the focus-gain and focus-loss for any asset, we can appreciate immediately that there is also a linear frontier connecting *A* and *C*, with respect to feasible investment in those assets. We can now appreciate that should the focus-value characteristics of the three assets be such that the line *ABC* is not linear, as is the case on figure 3.2, it is *inefficient* for the investor to hold three assets. The reason this is so is that the efficient frontier must be *ABC*. *AC* cannot form part of the efficient frontier because it is dominated by *AB* and *BC*. That is, for every point along *AC* there is a point on *AB* or *BC* which promises a higher value of total

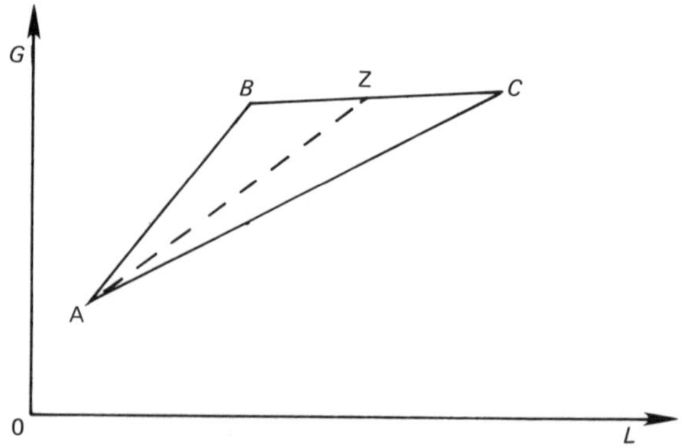

Figure 3.2 Investment opportunities with three financial assets

standardized focus-gain for any given value of total standardized focus-loss. Along *AB* or *BC* only two assets can be held. Therefore three assets can only be held within the triangle *ABC* on figure 3.2. Suppose that we select some arbitrary point along *BC*, such as *Z* on figure 3.2, then we can permit the investor to retain the holding of asset *C* consistent with the point *Z* while he trades his holdings of asset *B* for some of asset *A*. That can only be carried out *efficiently* along a *straight line* connecting the points *Z* and *A*. Anywhere between *A* and *Z* on the dotted line on figure 3.2 the investor will be holding three assets. But *AZ* itself cannot be on the efficient boundary because it is dominated by *AB* and *BC*. All holdings of three assets within the triangle *ABC* are dominated by the frontier *ABC*; so only two assets at most can be held by a rational investor.

It will be possible for three assets to be held if figure 3.2 is amended so that the stretch *BC* is merely the segment *AB* extended. Such a situation will occur if and only if:

$$\frac{g_A - g_B}{l_A - l_B} = \frac{g_B - g_C}{l_B - l_C} \tag{3.7}$$

provided all values of g and l are non-zero. If such a condition obtains, in effect, it means that the marginal rate of 'transformation' of loss into gain by the investor's switching from asset *A* to asset *B* is identical to that rate with respect to assets *B* and *C*. It might be thought from equation (3.6) that it is also necessary for:

$$(g_B l_A - g_A l_B)/(l_A - l_B) = (g_C l_B - g_B l_C)/(l_B - l_C) \tag{3.7a}$$

But this is not so because the lower point of the *BC* frontier, namely *B*, must always coincide, *ex definitione*, with the upper point of the *AB* frontier.

That the condition specified in equation (3.7) must be satisfied to permit three assets to be held as an optimum portfolio can be demonstrated formally. Thus, to derive the efficient frontier for three assets the procedure is:

$$\max_{x_A, x_B, x_C} \quad G = g_A x_A + g_B x_B + g_C x_C \tag{3.8}$$

$$\text{S.T.} \qquad L = l_A x_A + l_B x_B + l_C x_C \tag{3.9}$$

$$W = x_A + x_B + x_C \tag{3.10}$$

Letting λ_1 and λ_2 be the two Lagrange multipliers on the constraints (3.9) and (3.10) respectively, we discover from the first-order conditions arising from the exercise epitomized by equations

(3.8)–(3.10) that:

$$\begin{bmatrix} 0 & 0 & 0 & l_A & 1 \\ 0 & 0 & 0 & l_B & 1 \\ 0 & 0 & 0 & l_C & 1 \\ l_A & l_B & l_C & 0 & 0 \\ 1 & 1 & 1 & 0 & 0 \end{bmatrix} \begin{bmatrix} x_A \\ x_B \\ x_C \\ \lambda_1 \\ \lambda_2 \end{bmatrix} = \begin{bmatrix} -g_A \\ -g_B \\ -g_C \\ L \\ W \end{bmatrix} \tag{3.11}$$

A glance at equation (3.11) reveals that the matrix of coefficients on the dependent variables is singular. Hence it cannot be inverted to enable us to obtain *unique* solutions for the values of x_A, x_B and x_C. This, of course, does not mean that a solution might not exist. Since (3.11) is a system of non-homogeneous equations there will be a set of non-trivial solutions (x_A, x_B and $x_C \neq 0$) iff the rank of the coefficients matrix on the vector of dependent variables is the same as its augmented matrix.[2]

The maximum rank of the coefficients matrix on the endogenous variables in (3.11) is, naturally, four. In fact, provided the focus-losses of the three assets are different, and provided that their focus-gains are also such that it will be possible *prima facie* for all assets to lie on the same frontier (so that the assets' focus-values are ordered in a similar fashion, for example, to those on figure 3.2), if the rank of the coefficients matrix is, indeed, four. The rank of the augmented matrix (Z) will turn out to be less than five and hence must also be of rank four, if:

$$|Z| = (l_A - l_C)[l_A(g_B - g_C) - l_B(g_A - g_C) + l_C(g_A - g_B)] = 0 \tag{3.12}$$

where $|Z|$ has been evaluated by means of the second column of Z, its first column having been deleted.

Since, *ex hypothesi*, $l_B \neq l_C$, it follows that the only way that $|Z|$ can equal zero is if the term in square brackets in equation (3.12) is itself zero. Such an outcome can only materialize when the asset characteristics *do* bear the relationship to each other given in equation (3.7). In that case, and only in that case, can three assets be held in an optimum portfolio.

Although a solution to (3.11) does exist provided the conditions stipulated in (3.7) or (3.12) are met, that solution for the x vector, of course, is not unique. The solution, indeed, is one wherein we can assign an *arbitrary* value to the holding of one of the assets:

provided that that value is less than investable wealth, this will be consistent with the holding of some of both of the remaining assets. Thus, for example, a point on the segment *BC*, on figure 3.2, such as *Z*, is consistent with the placing of wealth into three assets or with the holding of just two assets, *B* and *C*.

Thus, if we preassign a value to x_A, say $\bar{x}_A$, this is a 'given' in equations (3.8)–(3.10) so the maximization of *G* under the *L* and the *W* constraints results in this set of equations from the first-order conditions:

$$\begin{bmatrix} x_B \\ x_C \end{bmatrix} = \begin{bmatrix} l_B & l_C \\ 1 & 1 \end{bmatrix}^{-1} \begin{bmatrix} L - \bar{x}_A \\ W - \bar{x}_A \end{bmatrix} \tag{3.13}$$

from which we deduce that along the *ABC* frontier drawn on figure 3.2, x_B and x_C exist, for a value of x_A less than *W*. So, if we refer back to the stretch *BC* as an example, we can see readily that, as stated hitherto, as well as being consistent with the holding of assets *B* and *C* it is compatible with the holding of all three assets. For, given that:

$$L = l_A \bar{x}_A + l_B x_B + l_C x_C \tag{3.14}$$

and

$$W = \bar{x}_A + x_B + x_C \tag{3.15}$$

it follows that we can write (3.14) as either:

$$L = (l_A - l_C)\bar{x}_A + (l_B - l_C)x_B + l_C W \tag{3.16}$$

or as:

$$L = (l_A - l_B)\bar{x}_A + (l_C - l_B)x_C + l_B W \tag{3.17}$$

Here $l_C W$ and $l_B W$ represent, respectively, the total standardized focus loss on assets *C* and *B* when all of wealth is held separately in those assets. Thus from (3.16) when $\bar{x}_A$ and x_B are positive, given the orderings of focus-losses pictured on figure 3.2, *L* will be less than $l_C W$; whilst from (3.17), if x_C is also positive, *L* can be greater than $l_B W$.

Naturally, where the individual investor will be on the efficient frontier depends upon his gambler-indifference map; but it will be *immaterial* to him whether he selects a portfolio of three assets in the case where the assets have characteristics which make it feasible to construct a three-asset frontier. In essence, his utility can be maximized by his selecting a portfolio consisting solely of only two assets and conceivably consisting of only one asset. There is *no* predilection to the investor's favouring a three-asset portfolio; a two-asset portfolio is capable of achieving for him everything that a three-asset portfolio can. Therefore, at the best we can only posit that a three-asset portfolio is feasible, it might never be selected; and in sum, there is no benefit to be derived by the investor from his choosing a three-asset portfolio.

That conclusion can be demonstrated to hold up in a situation where the investor can choose a portfolio from n assets. In that circumstance the equivalent of equation (3.11) becomes:

$$\left[\begin{array}{c:c} O_1 & H \\ \hdashline H' & O_2 \end{array}\right] \left[\begin{array}{c} x \\ \hdashline \lambda \end{array}\right] = \left[\begin{array}{c} -G \\ \hdashline Q \end{array}\right] \tag{3.18}$$

Here: O_1 is an $n \times n$ null-matrix; O_2 is a 2×2 null-matrix (for there are two constraints); H is an $n \times 2$ matrix. The first column of H is $l_1, l_2, \ldots, l_n$, where the assets are $1, 2, \ldots, n$; in the second column of H all of the elements are unity. X is an $n \times 1$ matrix of the n asset holdings (the x's); whilst λ is a 2×1 matrix. The elements of G are $g_1, g_2, \ldots, g_n$; and Q is a 2×1 matrix whose elements are L and W respectively. The determinant of the partitioned matrix in (3.18) is zero. Again we can show that its rank is $n - 1$. Having formed the augmented matrix we can establish for the n-asset case that the equivalent of equations (3.7) and (3.11) must be satisfied if an efficient frontier can exist for n assets.

It is not surprising that these conclusions emerge, since the analysis of the feasible number of assets that could be held along the gain/loss investment frontier is similar to that developed by Professor Kelvin Lancaster[3] in the characterizations approach to consumer theory, with the assets here being chosen with respect to their gain/loss characteristics. Also, we have been employing implicitly the concepts inherent in activity analysis upon which the Lancaster analysis is based, for in the Shackle framework assets, and hence their characteristics seen *in toto*, are divisible.

The manifestation of the previous analysis is that except in very special conditions it will be irrational for an investor to possess more than *two* assets in his portfolio; but even the existence of those 'very special conditions' cannot guarantee that an investor will purchase more than two assets.

There exists only one means by which we can guarantee the existence of asset diversification over more than two assets without our amending the premises of the Shackle model. This can be accomplished by the introduction of a constraint on the investment portfolio of the investor besides that imposed by his wealth. Constraints can assume a number of forms, but they will be essentially of two kinds:

(1) a stipulation that the investor has to hold at least a specified proportion of his investable wealth in one type of asset or another or in a range of assets;
(2) a limit on the value of the holding of one type of asset or another – in effect, the investor's asset holdings are subject to rationing.

As far as asset choice is concerned, as a matter of empirical observation, the appropriate form of constraint is provided by (1); but then, for the most part, such constraints are imposed on investors seen as firms, such as commercial banks, rather than on private, individual, investors.

Nevertheless, let us assume that for one reason or another – say, because the government or the monetary authority impose this restriction on the individual for precautionary or safety-first reasons – the investor has to hold at least a certain proportion, α, of his wealth in asset A. Assume also that the constraint is binding and effective in the Kuhn–Tucker sense: so $x_A = \alpha W$. Then the investor's choice of portfolio reduces to setting on one side αW as investment in asset A, and spending $(1 - \alpha)W$ on assets B and C. with x_A 'given' by the constraint the efficient frontier becomes a two-asset frontier again. Indeed, the equations for x_B and x_C are none other than those set out hitherto for the holdings of assets B and C when x_A has been preassigned a positive value, in the situation where the ABC frontier was as drawn on figure 3.2 and could support the holding of a three-asset portfolio.

Imagine that figure 3.2 does epitomize the investor's choice set without the constraint on the holding of asset A. Then, for the sake of illustration let the constraint be introduced with α taking the value of one-half. The choice set of the investor is scaled down to become $B'C'$ on figure 3.3. The value of x_A is 'chosen' according to the constraint; then the optimum allocation of the residual wealth $(1 - \alpha)W$ between B and C has to be decided upon along $B'C'$ by reference to the function $U = U(G, L)$. But the very fact that the choice over three assets has been transformed in this fashion means that three assets can exist in the optimum portfolio; because the frontier has been translated into the familiar two-asset frontier. For at all points along $B'C'$, naturally, x_A equals αW.

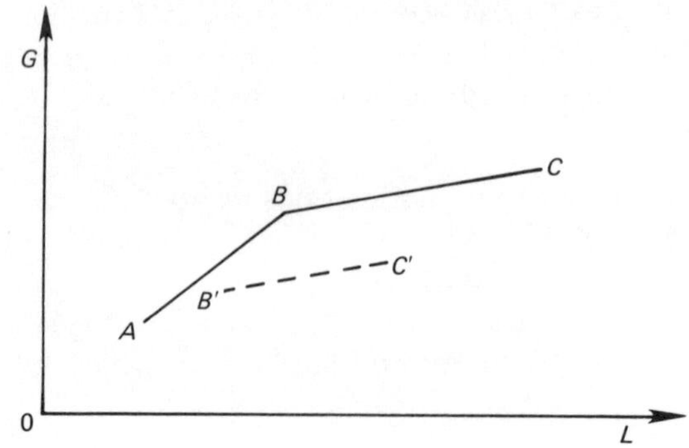

Figure 3.3 *The investment opportunity frontier and constraints on asset choice*

At this juncture we have said all that is germane to the degree of asset-diversification within the strict confines of the Shackle model. We move on, therefore, to offer some observations on question (3) posed in the preamble to this chapter, which – to recapitulate – relates to the possibility of deriving equations to explain the optimum purchases of specific kinds of financial claims by the investor, together with information on the signs of the partial derivatives of those equations, should any equations be deducible.

Remember that the objective of the Shackle investor, or at least his implied ultimate objective, is to:

$$\max U = U(G, L) \tag{3.19}$$

where G and L again represent total standardized focus-gain and focus-loss, respectively. In Shackle's model *per se* the only constraint on asset choice is the level of the investor's wealth, W. Let the Lagrangean expression for the maximization of (3.19) subject to W be:

$$Q = U(G, L) + \lambda(x_A + x_B - W) \tag{3.20}$$

where it has been assumed that the investor can choose over only two assets once more.

The first order conditions for a maximum of (3.20) are:

$$\frac{\partial Q}{\partial x_A} = \frac{\partial U}{\partial G}\frac{\partial G}{\partial x_A} + \frac{\partial U}{\partial L}\frac{\partial L}{\partial x_A} + \lambda = 0 \tag{3.21}$$

$$\frac{\partial Q}{\partial x_B} = \frac{\partial U}{\partial G}\frac{\partial G}{\partial x_B} + \frac{\partial U}{\partial L}\frac{\partial L}{\partial x_B} + \lambda = 0 \tag{3.22}$$

$$\frac{\partial Q}{\partial \lambda} = x_A + x_B - W = 0 \qquad (3.23)$$

These first-order conditions for a maximum of utility, U, are simply the wealth-constrained marginal utility equations for the value of the holdings of the two assets, x_A and x_B. For equilibrium to exist it follows that the marginal utility of the two asset holdings must be identical. It is the marginal utility equations that determine whether a mixed portfolio is held and how much of wealth is placed in either asset. Thus suppose that the marginal utility equations for each asset happen to be a linear, decreasing function of the value of the holding of that asset, and of that asset alone: then the situation might be as depicted on Diagram 3.4, which depicts the constraint via wealth that exists on the $\partial U/\partial x$. The optimum portfolio obtains at a common value of $\partial U/\partial x$ of OB. At that value OA of wealth of OW is placed in asset A, the remainder of wealth, AW is invested in asset B. Should it happen that the marginal utility of each asset at given x is independent of the level of the investor's wealth, then an increase in that level of wealth to OW_1 will change the optimum values of x_A and x_B, enabling the purchase of both assets to be pushed to the point at which their marginal utilities become zero. (An increase in wealth in excess of WW_1 will mean, under the assumptions made (especially the assumption that marginal utilities are independent of wealth) that some *money* has to be held in the optimum portfolio; because the marginal utility of money is zero: but more about the role of money later on in this chapter.)

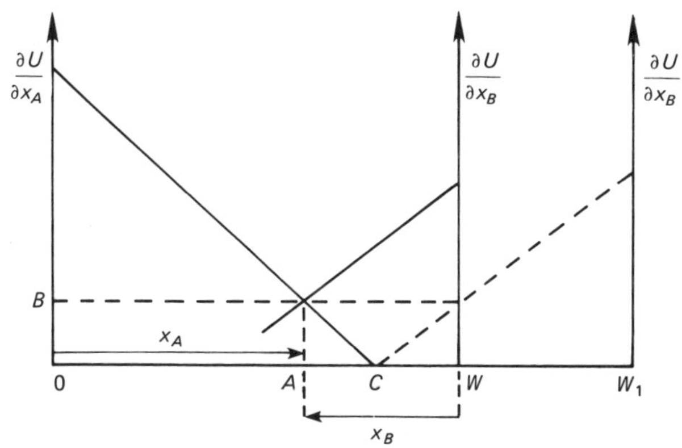

Figure 3.4 Marginal utilities and the selection of the optimum portfolio

We can, of course, discover how the marginal utility curves for the assets must have changed when the data (the focus-values on assets, the level of W) surrounding the investor's choice of portfolio have altered by analysis of the demand equation for the assets which are derivable from equations (3.21)–(3.23). However, we see from the latter that, unless we specify the form of the investor's 'utility' function, so that x's appear in $(\partial U/\partial G)$ and $(\partial U/\partial L)$, we can only deduce the responsiveness of asset holdings to changes in information by implicit total differentiation of those equations, in the manner familiar from traditional consumer choice theory under certainty. Even then, as we shall see, few clear-cut conclusions can be attained without specifying the U-function. We adopt this notation:

$$\frac{\partial U}{\partial i} = U_i \quad \text{and} \quad \frac{\partial}{\partial j}(U_i) = U_{ij};$$

recall also that:

$$\frac{\partial G}{\partial x_i} = g_i \quad \text{and} \quad \frac{\partial L}{\partial x_i} = l_i.$$

After totally differentiating equations (3.21)–(3.23) and simplifying by allowing just W to vary we have:

$$\begin{bmatrix} a_{11} & a_{12} & 1 \\ a_{21} & a_{22} & 1 \\ 1 & 1 & 0 \end{bmatrix} \begin{bmatrix} \dfrac{\partial x_A}{\partial W} \\ \dfrac{\partial x_B}{\partial W} \\ \dfrac{\partial \lambda}{\partial W} \end{bmatrix} = \begin{bmatrix} 0 \\ 0 \\ 1 \end{bmatrix} \qquad (3.24)$$

where:

$$\begin{aligned} a_{11} &= g_A^2 U_{GG} + g_A l_A U_{GL} + g_A l_A U_{LG} + l_A^2 U_{LL}; \\ a_{12} &= g_A g_B U_{GG} + g_B l_A U_{GL} + g_A l_B U_{LG} + l_A l_B U_{LL}; \\ a_{21} &= g_A g_B U_{GG} + g_A l_B U_{GL} + g_B l_A U_{LG} + l_A l_B U_{LL}; \\ a_{22} &= g_B^2 U_{GG} + g_B l_B U_{GL} + g_B l_B U_{LG} + l_B^2 U_{LL}; \end{aligned} \qquad (3.25)$$

and where $U_{GL} \equiv U_{LG}$

The matrix on the left-hand side of equation (3.24) is the bordered Hessian of the system and by the second-order conditions for the maximization of U its determinant (say, Det) should be positive. From equation (3.24) we deduce that:

$$\frac{\partial x_A}{\partial W} = \frac{a_{12} - a_{22}}{\text{Det}} \tag{3.26}$$

$$\frac{\partial x_B}{\partial W} = \frac{a_{21} - a_{11}}{\text{Det}} \tag{3.27}$$

Since Det $= a_{12} + a_{21} - a_{11} - a_{22}$, the Engel Aggregation condition holds on the asset demand equations. It is also clear from equations (3.25)–(3.27) that equations (3.26) and (3.27) cannot be signed without placing restrictions on the form of U since, for example:

$$\frac{\partial x_A}{\partial W} = \frac{g_B(g_A - g_B)U_{GG} + g_B(l_A - l_B)U_{GL} + l_B(g_A - g_B)U_{LG} + l_B(l_A - l_B)U_{LL}}{\text{Det}} \tag{3.28}$$

$g_A < g_B$ and $l_A < l_B$ is not sufficient information upon which to sign $\partial x_A / \partial W$. As with the orthodox approach to asset choice, and as indeed with most models of decision-making under uncertainty, no definitive answers can be obtained without more details of the individual's 'utility' function.

The same conclusion emerges if we differentiate equations (3.21)–(3.23) with respect to any of the focus-value characteristics. The only conclusion that emerges therefrom is that the Cournot Aggregation condition holds. Symmetry might or might not hold, depending upon the form of the utility function. Given these obvious results it is not worthwhile to devote space to the supporting mathematics. Rather we can content ourselves with a diagrammatic exposition of the effects of changes in data on the investor's optimal holding of assets; an exposition which is sufficient to highlight the difficulties involved, and is sensible given that we only have a two-asset world.

Thus, suppose that the investor experiences a *ceteris paribus* increase in wealth in this Shackle model. The effect is simply to shift out the investment frontier parallel to itself in figure 3.5, so that if wealth doubles, focus-gain and focus-loss at A', for example, are twice their respective values at A. Suppose that the original optimal position was at E on U_1. If when wealth does increase the investor's utility function is such that L is a non-inferior character-

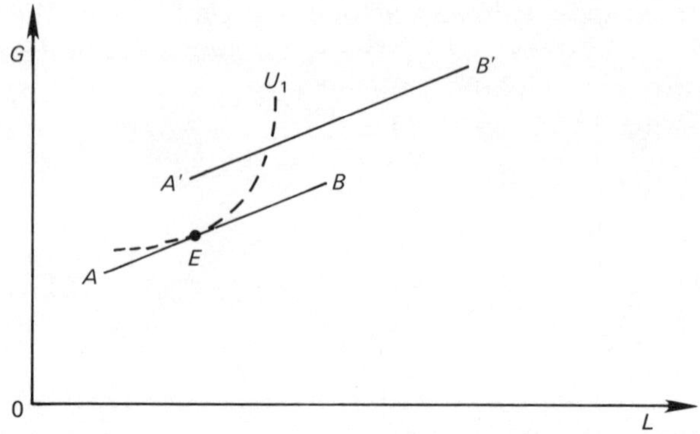

Figure 3.5 An increase in wealth and the Shackle investment frontier

istic then it must follow, obviously, that the holding of the asset with the higher loss/higher gain (asset *B*) must have increased. This is simply because if *L* remains constant or increases, *G* must increase.

Suppose now that there is a *ceteris paribus* increase in g_B. The effect on x_A and x_B depends as usual upon the relative strengths of the substitution and wealth effects in the investor's utility function. If the former effect dominates the latter the investor will take on more *L* and hence, without question, he will switch some of his wealth from asset *A* into asset *B*. An increase in g_B will increase the gain per unit of loss that the investor can now obtain from his given level of wealth. So at the *margin* there is an inducement to accept more loss (risk) than previously, if the investor is a loss (risk) averter, *ex definitione*. With only two assets in the model, with fixed wealth, the substitution effect then will mean that more x_B, the riskier asset, is purchased. However, there is a counterweight to this inducement to increase the loss taken on, because the marginal gain per unit of loss has increased; that counterweight is provided by the wealth effect. For any given total loss the investor can now obtain more total gain than hitherto; so he experiences the equivalent of some increase in wealth. The *average* relationship between total gain and total loss has now also improved: to put the situation in a more appropriate manner, to obtain the same total gain that he previously enjoyed he now needs to take on less loss (risk). Accordingly, the wealth effect might work in any way; it might lead to less, to the same, or to more, total loss being assumed. It all depends again on whether total loss is a normal or an inferior characteristic.

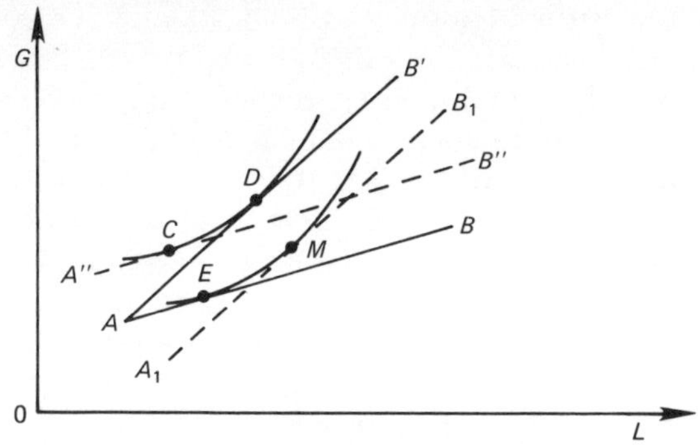

Figure 3.6 *The investor's response to asset yields*

Thus, let us consider figure 3.6. The line AB is the initial two-asset efficient investment frontier; the line AB' is the new frontier that confronts the investor when the standardized focus-gain on asset B increases, all other expected gains/losses and wealth remaining constant. Given the gambler indifference curves the original optimum point is E on AB. The new equilibrium, likewise, is denoted by the point D on AB'. The move from the one position to the other can be envisaged as involving a wealth effect from M to D and a *pure* substitution effect from E to M along the indifference curve upon which both those points actually lie: $A'B'$ is parallel to AB'.

Figure 3.6 assumes, in fact, that the wealth effect on total loss (L) is negative and that it is so negative as to dominate the positive substitution effect for a loss (risk) averter which inclines him to move along a given indifference curve and assume more total loss (E to M on figure 3.6).

Thus in a two-asset Shackle model, as we would expect, x_A and x_B can be shown to depend upon their focus-value characteristics and upon wealth. For given properties of the U-function we can sign all of the partial derivatives of asset demands with respect to those characteristics and wealth. Those derivatives must obey (*ex definitione*) the Cournot and Engel Aggregation conditions.

One question only remains to be examined in this chapter, and that is concerned with the place of *money* in the Shackle model. Given the assumption specified in the latter, money will possess neither a focus-gain (positive return) nor a focus-loss (negative return). Therefore, on the total standardized focus-values diagram the opportunities available to the investor from holding all of his wealth in the form of money will be fixed at the origin. Consequently, if we should suppose that an investor has several other assets in which he could invest, labelled, say, *A*, *B* and *C*, then if they promise non-zero focus values it is highly likely that money will be dominated out of the portfolio. Thus, in this case, the *ABC* frontier on figure 3.2 has to be extended, as a linear frontier still, of course, from the point *A* to the origin. Any point along the new extension, between *O* and *A*, will represent a combination of money and asset *A* in the optimum portfolio should the investor's gambler-preference function have the properties that result in his selecting a point along *OA* as his best strategy.

Money cannot be held with more than one asset unless the ratio of focus-gain to focus-loss for all assets is the same. In that case the 'risky asset' frontier can be extended naturally to the origin of the gambler-preference diagram as in figure 3.7. As shown in the preceding analyses in this chapter, even if such a configuration of asset characteristics should occur, it will not guarantee that money and many other assets are held. In the optimal portfolio the investor *need* hold only two assets at most.

Unlike the situation that emerges from the expected utility approach, the Shackle construct is unable to demonstrate that money and a many-'risky' asset portfolio should be held optimally. It is highly likely that pure money will be dominated and will not appear in an optimal portfolio. As in the expected utility approach, if there exists a 'money substitute' with a positive focus-gain (positive return) and no loss, such as a building society deposit or share, then money must be inferior to it, and so money cannot be held in the optimum speculative portfolio.[4]

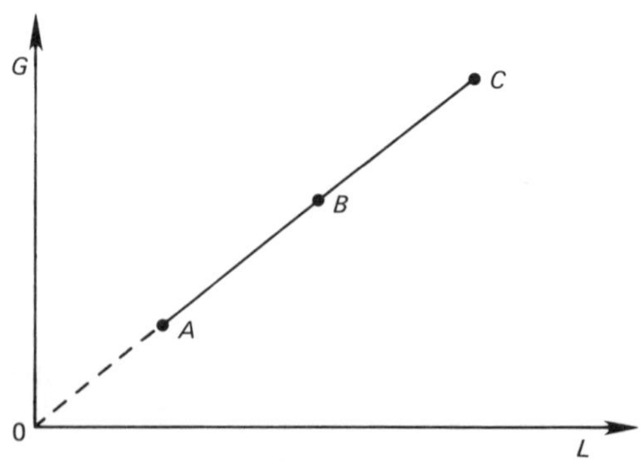

Figure 3.7 Money and the investment frontier

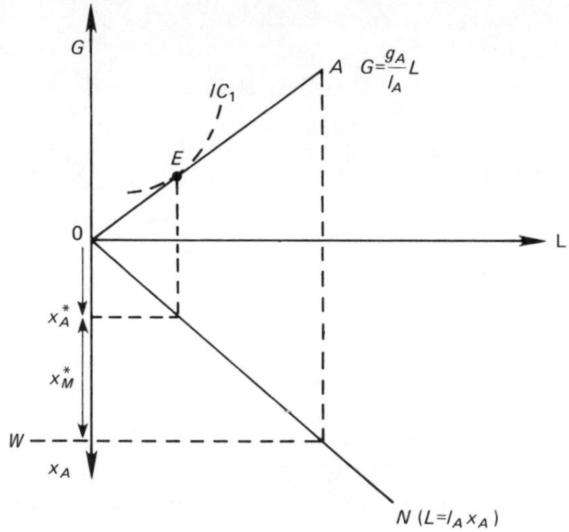

Figure 3.8 The optimum mix of money and bonds

Additionally, as with the expected utility model, if the investor can only purchase money and one other 'risky' asset his choice set and the optimum portfolio selected can be portrayed on one simple picture of the kind introduced by Professor Tobin and used here in chapter 1. Thus, if we assume that asset *A* promises focus-values of g_A and l_A and money (*M*) offers zero valued focus-outcomes, we have $G = g_A x_A$, $L = l_A x_A$, with $W = x_M + x_A$. Then the situation confronting the investor can be depicted by lines *OA* and *ON* in figure 3.8.

Assuming that the investor's utility ordering is such that his best position is at *E* on IC_1 and *OA*, he will elect to hold x_A^* of his wealth in asset *A* and the remainder x_M^* in the form of money.

4

The Shackle Schema: A Critical Exegesis

I have drawn attention to several difficulties with the Shackle schema and to its apparently limited value in accounting for asset portfolio behaviour. Some of these have merely been noted or considered to a limited extent. In this chapter I intend to rectify that omission; and, *passim*, will also provide more detail on the Shackle schema *per se*. An essential element in my analyses will be to consider the most prominent of the critical evaluations of either the constituent parts of, or of the whole of, the Shackle framework that have figured in the literature and have been latent in my previous analyses. The examples used to clarify the issues under discussion will be based on portfolio choice, but they can be replaced easily by examples from the capital investment decision, and, indeed, by illustrations drawn from other models of action-choice under uncertainty, as shown in chapter 6. However, the reference to investment decisions permits consideration of action-choice where, in principle, gain and loss branches of the potential surprise function can coexist. Some decision-making frameworks require only a gain branch, or its analogue, to exist. So a free evaluation of the Shackle schema is not possible in those cases.

Within the context of portfolio selection it will be feasible then to consider these fundamental issues: the appropriateness of using focus-values to epitomize expectations of the prospect of returns on assets; the need for both the ϕ-function and the gambler-preference map; and the vital question of the derivation of the gambler-opportunity line, with its attendant implications for the feasible range of optimum asset diversification. Apart from this last consideration all these matters are key issues in general in the Shackle schema, but the last issue has its own special importance, we recall from the Introduction, because it was, in part, the apparent failure of the Shackle approach to predict the rational holding by investors of multi-asset portfolios that led to the approach being abandoned in the literature.

It will simplify matters if the issues for consideration are set out by means of a series of questions which I shall seek to answer, even though the questions are not mutually exclusive. Thus:

(1) Is the concept of standardized focus-value a valid one?
(2) Is it possible to amend the Shackle theory, if it appears that the concentration on standardised focus-values to the neglect of primary focus-values is invalid, so that the choice-process is seen explicitly to take cognizance of uncertainty or potential surprise? In other words, can the gambler-preference function be changed so that it no longer merely has two arguments in it, namely total standardized focus-gain and total standardized focus-loss?
(3) As a corollary of this, is the *form* of the potential surprise function, rather than just its mere existence in the mind of the investor, of any influence, in the Shackle theory *per se*, on his choice of focus-values?
(4) Is there a separate role, indeed can there be a separate role, for the ϕ-function and the gambler-preference map in the selection of the optimum investment strategy?
(5) Is it correct that Shackle's gambler-opportunity line, for portfolio investment, is only linear because it is implicitly being assumed that the expected prices (or returns) on the available assets are perfectly correlated? Furthermore, how can the notion of correlations between asset prices (or returns) be accommodated within an approach such as Shackle's; and can taking explicit cognizance of those correlations enable *multi*-asset portfolios to be held?

Finally, a matter which so far has only been noted in chapter 2, but which has been mentioned a number of times in the literature, needs to be considered. This concerns the very foundations of Shackle's model of uncertainty and expectations, namely the claim that probability is not appropriate and must be replaced by a concept like potential surprise. It has been argued that the latter is nothing other than a translation of subjective/objective probability onto another scale of measurement. Therefore it is incumbent upon us to give full consideration at the end of our deliberations to this question, even if, logically, it should be discussed before

(1)–(5) above:

(6) Can an index of potential surprise be re-cast in terms of a conventional probability index? If so, would such a re-casting have any meaning and behavioural content? In any event, would the use of a transformed index affect the analysis of portfolio choice, and hence the actual optimum portfolio that is selected, assuming the rest of Shackle's apparatus? Would that apparatus have any *raison d'être*?

Questions (1)–(4), especially (1), (2) and (3) do, in fact, overlap considerably and although discussion will start with question (1), it will not be sensible (indeed, feasible) to consider the questions *seriatim*, until observations on questions (1)–(4) are complete.

Question (1) accepts the notion of the potential surprise function; it also accepts the concept of the ϕ-function. That question is concerned with the propriety of using standardized focus-values; and *a fortiori* it is concerned with the method by which the ϕ-function is employed to process the potential surprise function for an investment into just two (focus)-values.

To appreciate the difficulties that can arise if standardized focus-values are used rather than primary focus-values we shall consider a simple portfolio problem. Suppose that the investor is contemplating investment in two assets A and B in a situation where it is assumed that neither asset will yield a loss: that is, the loss branch of the potential surprise function for either asset does not exist. Let the gain branches of that function be as illustrated on figure 4.1. The primary focus-gain and the standardized focus-gain of asset B exceed those gains for asset A. Translating this information onto the gambler-preference diagram would lead to the investor having to choose between points on the (total) standardized focus-gain axis of that figure: he must choose only one asset, since the gain on B exceeds that on A. The investor does *not*, and should *not*, diversify.

However, if we take a closer look at figure 4.1 we see that though asset A is inferior in terms of its primary focus-gain characteristics it is not inferior if we take account of the potential surprise, or uncertainty, that is attached to its primary focus-gain. According to the investor's expectations and view of the world, the primary focus-gains attainable at points Z and E on figure 4.1 can only be attained if the investor is prepared to accept the degree of disbelief that surrounds them; there is a price to pay for the primary focus-gains.

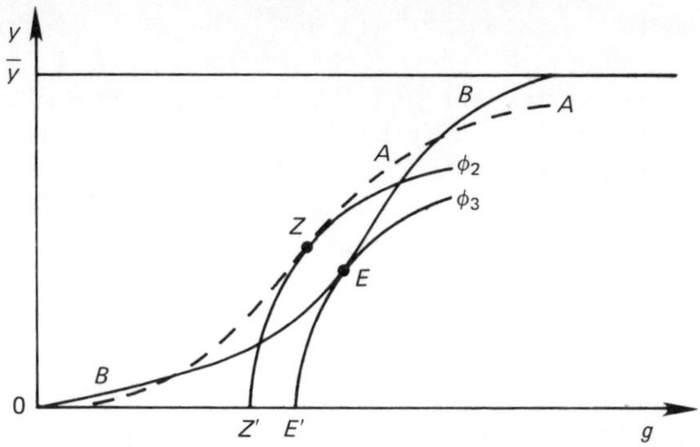

Figure 4.1 *Primary and standardized focus gains*

To put the matter the other way round, the investor himself believes that there is some price to pay for focus-gains represented by Z and E: he sees that there is no certainty about those focus-gains being realized at the end of his investment period. However, by the very nature of the ϕ-function he is prepared to accept the concomitant doubt (lack of perfect possibility) associated with Z and E when selecting the best point along each potential surprise function via his ϕ or stimulation function.

Thus the ϕ-function will, as a general rule, select best (and where relevant worst) outcomes by means of their characteristics; their promise of monetary gain and the degree of doubt surrounding that promise. What Shackle does is then to simplify the end-product of the maximization of ϕ-function subject to the potential surprise function by removing or discounting the degree of potential surprise attaching to the primary focus-gain. For, as shown in chapter 2, he suggests that the primary focus-gain should be replaced by its standardized value; with respect to points Z and E on figure 4.1, the standardized focus values are represented by points Z' and E'. The latter have no disbelief attached to their occurrence and they lie on the same ϕ indifference curve as their counterparts, the primary focus-gains. It is in this way that Shackle seeks to place focus-gains from all possible investments on *the same (standard) footing*.

Shackle, in fact, says this about that procedure (using the capital-investment choice decision as his reference point):

Suppose the enterpriser should wish to compare ventures in regard to their desirable aspects only, . . . their respective primary focus-gain. . . . These . . .

cannot be immediately compared with each other by a direct comparison of their respective values of x (their focus-gains); each must be replaced by an expression *equivalent* to it and such that both equivalents carry *equal potential surprise*. What must we mean here by an equivalent combination of gain and potential surprise? Plainly it is one having equal power to afford the enterpriser enjoyment by anticipation. . . . That is, two points in the xy plane will be equivalent if they lie on the same projected (ϕ) contour-line. In order to compare two primary focus-gains we must choose for them equivalents whose respective values of y are equal to each other; . . . it will be natural and convenient to reduce all primary focus-outcomes invariably to *zero* potential surprise. . . . We shall call such equivalents standardised focus-outcomes. . . . These . . . are in effect simply values of x, and as such they are all legitimately comparable amongst themselves.[1]

Intuitively the simplicity and aesthetic quality of this proposal can be grasped, and it is easy to appreciate the value of being able to compare gains on investments by means of a common yardstick; indeed by means of just *one* yardstick. Yet this leaves the uncomfortable feeling *prima facie* that somehow the adoption of such a measuring rod could deprive the Shackle model of its very essence: for what the standardization of focus-gains does it to obliterate outcomes other than the 'perfectly possible' outcomes.

The basis of the difficulty here is that the potential surprise function, even if it is a self-imposed, hence subjective, psychological, as opposed to an objective, externally-given, constraint *is* a constraint. Even if Z and Z' are equally stimulating and hence Z' is the 'certainty-equivalent' of Z, the investor's expectations are such that a gain of Z' will not occasion zero potential surprise: in the investor's mind, in other words, it is not possible to have the combination (Z', zero potential surprise). To say that it is, is to distort the information contained in the potential surprise function.

As an illustrative example consider the situation portrayed in figure 4.2. In the latter there is a potential surprise (y_A) function for the gain on asset A; but it is the investor's view that the potential surprise function for asset B consists of $\bar{y}$ for all gains except OB. In effect, that gain is one that, if it occurred, would present *no surprise* to the individual. Further, and of more importance, is the fact that that zero degree of potential surprise, the perfect possible value OB, is held with *certainty*. Not only is it a perfect possibility in the opinion of the investor, but it is the only gain outcome that is possible, so it must be regarded as a perfectly certain outcome.

As portrayed in figure 4.2 the highest ϕ value that can be attained

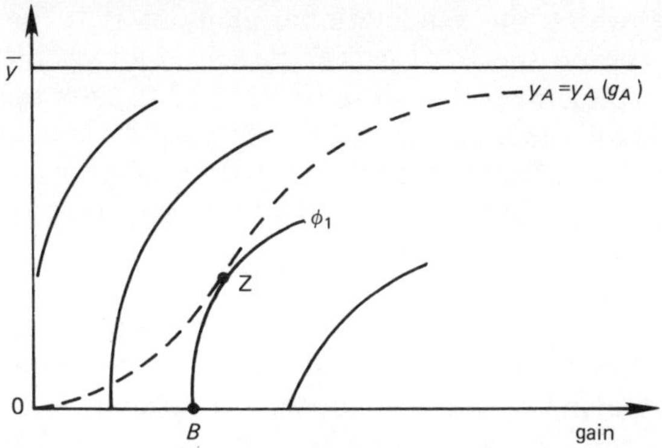

Figure 4.2 *Potential surprise functions and focus gains*

with the potential surprise function for A, $y_A = y_A(g_A)$, is ϕ_1. At the latter level the standardized focus-gain on asset A is identical with that on B. Should both assets have no loss branch to their potential surprise functions then a choice between a portfolio wholly of asset A or wholly of asset B (or a choice between projects A and B) assessed by reference to the gambler-preference map would reveal that the investor was indifferent between them. They offer the same pair of focus-values.

The point that has been highlighted and amplified with the preceding comments on figures 4.1 and 4.2 has an affinity, of course, with the ideas advanced in the literature that the Shackle 'ϕocusing' procedure is inadequate and misrepresentative of the uncertainty of returns confronting the investor because it discards the information embodied in the whole of the potential surprise function; an issue to which I shall return shortly. The main gist of the point I have been developing, however, is that even if the 'ϕocusing' device is permitted to operate it will in general produce only *hypothetical* returns on the assets; these will not be returns, in general, that the investor thinks are feasible. Thus in figure 4.2 a gain of OB with zero potential surprise on asset A is not even considered to be a possibility by the investor.

This matter will be considered further when we proceed to examine question (4) on the importance or unimportance of the whole of the potential surprise function. At this stage we move on to consider briefly question (2) which takes as its premise the view that it is not an appropriate, or valid, procedure to discount away potential surprise and that as a consequence if the ϕ-function is a vehicle by which an expectational element is to be selected to epitomize the prospects of gain (return) on an asset (project) that expectational element *in toto* must be used to rank the investment prospects. Can the gambler-preference map be amended then to incorporate 'potential surprise'? Unfortunately, in regard to portfolio choice, the answer is no!; and why this is the case can be seen quite readily.

When evaluating a portfolio strategy, as we have seen, it is necessary to *scale-up* the gains(returns)/losses(negative returns) on the relevant assets by the value of the holding of those assets – the scale factor being wealth, of course, if a comparison is being made solely between investment in asset A or in asset B. Suppose that it is just such a comparison that is being contemplated. If primary focus elements are now to be used in that comparison, what is required is an estimate of the degree of potential surprise attached to the *total* gain/loss from investment in the one asset or the other. The only logical step open to us is to utilize the degrees of potential surprise that accompany the (per unit) primary focus-values on the assets (Professor Shackle confirmed in correspondence dated 20 April 1976 that this was the correct procedure.) As shown in chapter 2, potential surprise is *ex definitione* a *non-additive* concept. Essentially, this means that we cannot write, as an example:

$$Y_T = y_A \cdot x_A + y_B \cdot x_B \tag{4.1}$$

where Y_T is 'total' potential surprise; y_A and y_B are, respectively, the degrees of potential surprise accompanying, say, the focus losses on the two assets, A and B; and x_A and x_B are, as usual, the values of the holdings of those two assets. *Ipso facto*, we cannot state that:

$$U = U(G, L, Y_T^L, Y_T^G) \tag{4.2}$$

where Y_T^L, for example, is the total degree of potential surprise for a given level of loss taken on by the investor; G and L denote total (now primary) focus gain and loss. It is not obvious how we could arrive at values for Y_T^L and Y_T^G.

If it had been possible to combine degrees of potential surprise, and in a linear way, as portrayed in equation (4.1), then because equation (4.2) is a utility function over four arguments which arguments are linear combinations of the individual focus-values/potential surprises of the investment project, by the arguments advanced in chapter 3, this would have allowed a situation in which the investor could hold, optimally, four assets in a portfolio. In such a way the potential degree of asset diversifications in the Shackle model would have increased. The very essence of the concept of potential surprise renders it a concept that cannot be employed in an exercise designed to discover the optimum *combination* of assets. However, for a ranking of assets on an individual basis then the gambler-preference map could be amended so that it is four-dimensional and the assets *per assets* are evaluated according to their returns/potential surprise characteristics. *In effect*, on an asset-by-asset basis such a comparison is none other than one which ranks the assets by their primary expectational elements. Again the interdependency between the questions for consideration in this chapter become obvious, for at this point we are faced with the possible conflicts and overlaps between two of the three key elements in the Shackle schema, the ϕ-function and the gambler-preference map. That issue, has however, been reached too early again; simply because of the interlocking nature of the vital issues being tackled.

It is necessary to digress at this point, in order to discuss the important matter of the incorporation of potential surprise into the decision-making process. If the individual is comparing capital investment projects (such as whether to buy this piece of equipment or that; whether to set up a plant in this industry or that) then potential surprise can figure legitimately in his decision. This is because he will simply be ranking the feasible projects *per projects*.

Let us pass on to the wider issue regarding the role of potential surprise and reflect on question (3) in the preamble to this chapter. That question suggests that consideration might be given to all elements on the potential surprise function for an asset, and implicitly to a comparison of the potential surprise functions for competing assets or investment projects. It has indeed been argued fairly forcibly in the literature that the rational investor will bear those considerations in mind.[2] To illustrate the central issues here it is possible to utilize another simple diagrammatical example.[3]

Consider the situation, depicted on figure 4.3, where again for expositional ease it is assumed that there exist only two assets, or projects, in which the individual can invest. The continuous line represents the potential surprise function for A; the dotted line that for B. It is assumed that both assets could produce losses as well as gains; although the analysis would be unaffected if, as hitherto, we had posited that both loss branches did not exist. What this picture informs us is that the assets have identical

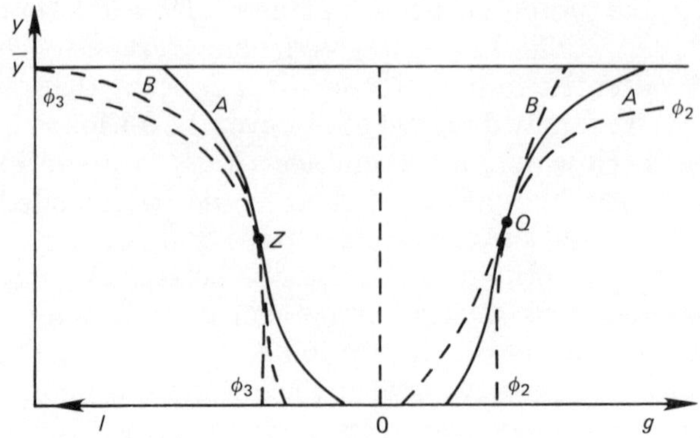

Figure 4.3 Primary and standardized focus gains and losses

primary focus-values. These two ventures have provided the same stimulus or level of ascendancy for the individual, but project *A* offers higher potential gains for a given level of potential surprise than *B* does, except at one point *Q* where they both give the same promise of gain with the same degree of potential surprise. Similarly, a comparison of the loss branches of the two potential surprise functions indicates that except at *Z* where the two assets offer the same expectations-element, asset *A* promises to bring with it less loss per unit of investment at any degree of potential surprise.

On a 'Pareto criterion' or by 'stochastic dominance' *A* is the superior asset. In effect, this epitomizes the notion that asset *A* is superior on grounds analogous to the axiom of absolute preference (axiom 5(a)) given in chapter 1. Naturally, pursuing this argument to this extent means that the assets are being ranked by their potential surprise functions. This implies two things: the first is that the gambler-preference map can be dispensed with; the second is that the ϕ-function as it stands serves no meaningful purpose within the decision-making process, for it only selects *an* expectational element from the potential surprise function and as it is construed, formalized, in the Shackle schema it cannot consider the potential surprise function in its entirety.

As the Shackle schema is structured the ϕ, ascendancy, function's purpose is only to condense information; to select an element from each of the branches of the potential surprise function that the investor can carry forward in his mind as best representations of the expectational characteristics of a specific asset. The ascendancy function is a simplifying function. Professor Shackle's retort to the critics of focus-values is unequivocal on that point:

The notion of focus elements has been criticised along several lines. Their selective aspect is objected to by those who, while perhaps accepting the idea of potential surprise, say that to base decision, in effect, on only two points of the potential surprise curve . . . is to 'waste information'. . . . This criticism betrays, indeed, a radical misconception of our whole approach and of the purpose which we conceive the act of decision to serve. . . . In brief, we say that the hypotheses whose assigned degrees of possibility are expressed by the potential surprise curve are mutually contradictory and that therefore it is as senseless to try to follow all of them as it would be to book tickets for trains travelling simultaneously in divergent directions; that because of this uselessness of aggregation, because of the need for selection which the very nature of things imposes, the decision-maker is free, and is bound, to select rather than add together the unaddable. . . .

It is, in our view, not only legitimate but essentially necessary, in basing decisions on that form of uncertainty judgement which the potential surprise curve expressed, to use the curve as a means of selection and not as a means of averaging. By contrast a probability distribution, legitimately used to discover the (undoubted) outcome of a divisible experiment, must of course be used in its entirety, since every one of the contingencies represented in it will, if the distribution is correct, help to compose the total outcome of the divisible experiment. . . . To lop off part of a probability distribution and neglect it . . . would plainly be not merely to waste information, but grossly to distort and invalidate the information contained in the distribution as a whole. Of the potential surprise curve nothing of the sort would be true if the lopping off were performed *after* the curve had been applied to its selective task. . . . Once the selection of the focus elements has been performed, the legitimacy of discarding the rest of the curve, . . . springs from the non-distributional nature of potential surprise.[4]

This obscures one further, fundamental, matter, however; that is that the ϕ or ascendancy function is not seen as a means by which assets or investment strategies can be ranked. The ascendancy function is the means to an end; the end is accomplished via the gambler-preference map. This raises the issue that has been near the surface of all the discussions so far in this chapter; an issue that is summarized in question (4) in the preamble. Is there a separate role for the ascendancy function and for the gambler-preference map? Is the latter subsumed in the former? Can the latter not be in conflict at times with the former?

The kind of paradoxes elaborated on up to this point have prompted the view in the literature that as far as rational behaviour is concerned they are not just paradoxes but produce unacceptable results; as a consequence the gambler-preference map should be discarded, leaving the ascendancy function to rank investment opportunities.[5] Since ϕ is measured cardinally it has been argued that the ranking can be achieved on the basis of a ranking of the *net ϕ values*, that is by the algebraic sum of the ϕ values for the loss and the gain branches of the potential surprise function for the particular investments, ϕ^l and ϕ^g, respectively. Note, at this stage, however, that this does *not* mean that the *whole* of the potential surprise function is being assessed. That is a very important point because nowhere in the literature has the 'absolute preference' issue been dealt with adequately in the critical literature on the Shackle theory. When the onus for choice of action has been placed on the ascendancy function it has been done on the supposition that that function is achieving the same ends as is the gambler-preference map; they are seen as inseparable. The introduction of the ascendancy function as the ranking device would mean, however, that the problem highlighted in figures 4.1 and 4.2 when potential surprise is artificially discounted in the construction of standardized focus-values, disappears *ex hypothesi*, since the value of ϕ is identical for an asset, or investment strategy, at the primary and standardized focus-values.

What does Professor Shackle have to say on this vital issue? It appears that over the years he has shifted his ground, discernibly even if slightly, and that there is some ambivalence in his mind about the role played in his schema by the ascendancy function. Even in his first pronouncements on the nature of that second pillar in his 'three pillars' theory of expectations an enigmatic view is perceptible. Thus, in *Expectation in Economics* he wrote as follows:

> This . . . brings us to our central problem: how will an individual choose between different courses of action when the outcome of each cannot be known in advance, but is only represented in his mind by a whole set of differing hypotheses?
>
> In order to assess the merits of any given course of action, a man must find some way of reducing the great array of hypotheses about the relevant consequences of this course, which will usually be present in his mind, to some compact and vivid statement. The real incentive for embarking on some given venture, whose objective results will not develop and their character become known until some date in the future, is the immediate mental experience which the decision to embark on this course will give us, namely the *enjoyment by anticipation* of a high level of success. . . . I do not believe that the impossibility of feeling certain that a particular unique result will be

attained . . . implies that the individual will not desire a unique focus for his imagination, that is to say, that he will not centre his hopes on *one particular* level of success. He will, it seems to me, desire a single clear-cut mental image concerning the outcome to provide the *content* of his hope, and this will need to be given, as it were, an extra dimension by association with a sufficiently low degree of potential surprise, to render it a motive for entering into his decision. . . . In most cases there will be some positively hurtful outcomes which will be not less insistently present to our minds than the favourable ones. Here again the individual will tend, I think, . . . [to select] *one particular* degree of misfortune to represent what he 'stands to lose'.[6]

The question is then posed: how can the particular level of success and of misfortune be determined? The answer provided is that the ascendancy function will perform that task. We perceive here that although the ascendancy function is being employed to select an expectational element from each branch of the relevant potential surprise function, it is in part envisaged as a conventional utility function, for we observe the emphasis on enjoyment by anticipation. It is as if the *attractiveness* of the asset, or project, was being assessed on the gain/loss side by the ascendancy function. A different sentiment is being expressed from one which says that the individual cannot carry forward in his mind all or many of the conceivable outcomes on an asset, with their associated degree of potential surprise; so that on the gain, or success, side, and on the loss side he has to reduce that information to manageable proportions and, say, to one element on each side, 'a best' and 'a worst' outcome. To say that this is accomplished by a procedure such as the ascendancy function – because which element will capture the investor's thoughts is the one that has the greatest power to make him stop and think, as it were – is a different matter from describing the ascendancy function as a vehicle which encapsulates the *attractiveness* of, the enjoyment provided by, an asset or an investment project and it pushes the ascendancy function closer to the realm of action choice and to move it out of the expectations-telescoping arena. There is a genuine difficulty in describing the properties of the ascendancy function without slipping into the use of language that carries emotive connotations; but the issue is not just one of semantics.

However, in answer to those critics of his who had suggested that the ϕ-function was more than a selection device and could replace the gambler-preference map, Professor Shackle reaffirms his own position and does so by use of language which is tighter and more formal, so that he leaves the reader in no doubt as to his intentions in devising the ϕ or ascendancy function:

> If both of the primary focus elements are to be thought of as present in the decision-maker's thought throughout his act of decision, this presence could take either of two forms. Interpreting ϕ as the measure of an element's power not simply to command the decision-maker's attention, but even directly to influence him for or against the particular action-course, and treating ϕ as negative when it arises from a hypothesis of loss . . . we could . . . suppose the decision-maker to form the algebraic sum of the ϕ values of the two primary focus elements. That sum when obtained for each of the available action-courses . . . would show which of them most strongly attracted him. . . . This method has a formal simplicity which must be weighed against what we may call the psychic simplicity of our own alternative. But the scheme of thought to which ϕ belongs when interpreted as a direct pull or push on the decision is an essentially different one from our own. ϕ for us is not the attractiveness or repulsiveness itself of an expectation-element, but the relevance or *attention-arresting power* which belongs to a highly attractive or highly repellant hypothesis not too much enfeebled by an air of unreality.[7]

Seen as a 'ϕocusing' apparatus or an ascendancy, attention-arresting phenomenon, the expectational element selector is so defined. Seen by its alternative name, the stimulation function, the situation is not so clear-cut.

Professor Shackle's more recent opinions on the ϕ-function indicate that although his *intention* is clear in regard to the role to be played by the ϕ-function, the attempt to wrestle with the kind of paradoxes which that function can engender reintroduces the element of ambivalence and uncertainty concerning its role and interpretation. Thus (in correspondence) the notion was proposed to him that, in the light of the type of conditions depicted in figure 4.1 above:

(1) the standardization of focus-values was potentially misleading; and
(2) that as a consequence the two investment strategies A and B should be compared by reference to their (primary focus gains, degrees of potential surprise), so that the gambler-preference map should embrace some measure of 'uncertainty'.

In answering these queries (correspondence dated 26 April 1976) Professor Shackle made explicit reference to the role of the ϕ-function. He wrote as follows:

> The ϕ surface (or rather, the notion of ascendancy itself) is here being used

for two different purposes: first, to identify the primary focus-outcomes; secondly, to identify a pair of *hypothetical* outcomes (gain and loss) which would give the investor the same degree of stimulus to invest in the asset in question.

Thus the nub of the matter is: are these two purposes *both* served by the same ϕ-function? That they are is the essence of my meaning for the ϕ-function, and for ϕ itself. (italics in original).

Further to our *suggestion* concerning the portrayal of the situation in figure 4.1 by a generalized gambler-preference map, namely that:

The excess of the focus-gain for *B* over *A* may not be enough to compensate for the excess of its potential surprise over that of *A*'s.

Professor Shackle *answered*:

The fact that *B*'s primary focus-outcome is on a higher equal ϕ-curve than *A*'s shows that it is enough.

In extenso, these verdicts inform us that in the situation portrayed in figure 4.2 the investor would be indifferent between the two assets or projects. The problem is not confined: the reference to the ϕ-function by its alternative name, the *stimulation* function, transfers the emphasis embedded in the ϕ-function or the ascendancy function into one of attractiveness or stimulus rather than one of attention-arresting power.

These observations lead us to speculate that Shackle's attitude has shifted considerably over the years. In the past, whilst wishing to emphasize that the dominant characteristic of the ϕ-function is that it acts as a filter of expectations, he has been prepared to give some credence to the view that aspects of the factors that determine an individual's choice of action do creep into the function. Until recently it was never conceded explicitly that more, if not all, of those aspects were encapsulated in the ϕ-function. Thus, when writing immediately following the first appearance of the suggestion that the gambler-preference map could be discarded[8] and net ϕ values used to rank action schemes, Professor Shackle expressed this opinion:

[This] is not acceptable, for it means that when a scale for ϕ is given, and a particular form is specified for the ϕ surface with respect to that scale, the shape of every gambler indifference curve is thereby also specified, and in consequence, the slopes of the gambler indifference curves are not independent of each other, they have no freedom to express that aspect of the individual's temperament which it is the purpose of the gambler indifference-map to express. . . . The gambler indifference-map is free to reflect a different aspect of the individual's attitude to uncertainty from that reflected by the ϕ surface.[9]

The point being propounded here is that if ϕ is measured cardinally and *net* ϕ values are used to order investment strategies this predetermines the relationship between total (now again *standardized*) focus-values on the gambler-preference map. That map has no independent existence. There should be and can be no separate role for the map. Shackle is arguing that there should be, and that to use net ϕ values deprives the gambler-preference map from serving its true purpose. To use net ϕ values (with ϕ positive for gains and negative for losses) does not mean that the assets or investment projects are not being ranked by the gambler-preference map. The contention is that indeed they are; but that the latter map is otiose.

This can be demonstrated formally in the following way *where it is assumed that the ϕ-functions for gain and loss are identical.* ϕ^g and ϕ^l represent, respectively, the level of ϕ for gain and for loss. So:

$$\phi^g = \phi^g(g, y); \quad \phi^l = \phi^l(l, y) \tag{4.3}$$

Given that ϕ^g and ϕ^l possess a cardinal scale we may define their difference, which we label a net Φ-value, as:

$$\Phi_{i-j} = \phi_i^g - \phi_j^l; \quad i, j = 0, 1, \ldots, n \tag{4.4}$$

Thus, a gain ϕ-value ϕ_1^g together with a loss ϕ-value of ϕ_0^l for a given investment project would yield a net Φ-value of 1. Remember that for any project, for example ϕ^g, will be the same value at the standardized focus-gain as it is at the primary focus-gain: so that to a given ϕ^g, via equation (4.3), as shown in chapter 2, we can discover g by letting $y = 0$. Thus, importantly, to each ϕ_i^g there is a value of standardized focus-gain.

Consider then the derivation of the net Φ indifference curves, their relationship to each other and the implications they carry for the gambler-preference map. Let us take the ϕ_0 indifference curve first of all. From equation (4.4) this entails taking all ϕ_i^g and ϕ_j^l where $i = j$. When $i = j = 0$, by the nature of the Shackle ϕ-indifference map as reported in chapter 2, $\phi^g \equiv \phi^l \equiv 0$. Thus the ϕ_0 indifference curve must pass through the origin of the standardized focus-values diagram. At $i = j = 0$, standardized focus-gain and focus-loss on the project or asset are both zero. So, if those focus-values apply to an asset, they are still zero on the total standardized focus-values diagram. When $i = j \neq 0$, since we have assumed that in equation (4.3), $\phi^g(.) = \phi^l(.)$, it follows that $g_i \equiv l_j$, for $\phi_i^g = \phi_i^l$. Therefore, under our assumptions, we can deduce additionally that the ϕ indifference curve must be linear. As we increase $i = j$ from zero, each ϕ_i^g, ϕ_i^l, naturally produce unique, and increasing, values of standardized focus-gain and loss. So Φ_0 *is* drawn over standardized focus-gain and standardized focus-loss space.

Suppose now that we wish to trace out another Φ indifference curve, say Φ_1. We proceed by noting that:

$$\Phi_1 = \phi_i^g - \phi_{i-1}^l \tag{4.5}$$

Then, remembering that we have $y = 0$ always:

$$\Phi_1 = f(g_1) - f(l_0) = f(g_1) \tag{4.6}$$

$$\Phi_1 = f(g_2) - f(l_1) \tag{4.7}$$

$$\vdots$$

$$\Phi_1 = f(g_n) - f(l_{n-1}) \tag{4.8}$$

so that $f(g_1) = \phi_1^g$, namely a value of ϕ^g of unity. Note that $f(l_i) \equiv f(g_i)$, therefore (4.6)–(4.8) can be simplified to:

$$\begin{aligned} f(g_1) &= \Phi_1 = 1; \quad \Phi_1 \equiv 1 \\ f(g_2) &= 2\Phi_1 = 2 \\ &\vdots \\ f(g_n) &= n\Phi_1 = n \end{aligned} \tag{4.9}$$

Equation (4.9) shows that the slope of the $\Phi = 1 = \Phi_1$ indifference curve is constant. From (4.6) it can be seen that the intercept of Φ_1 on the focus-gain axis exceeds that (of zero) for Φ_0. So, Φ_1 lies above and parallel to Φ_0. *In extenso*, it follows that all the net ϕ indifference curves are linear and parallel to each other in the total standardized focus-values plane.

Therefore all of the gambler-preference curves are inextricably interrelated; not only are their slopes related but they are identical.

If one asset or investment project has the same standardized focus-values as another they would be equivalent investments on the gambler-preference map *per se*, and they are also identical projects by the net ϕ scale.

On occasions Shackle permits the gain and loss ϕ-functions to differ from each other. In that case the net ϕ indifference curves will indeed be curves but they will still be interdependent and they will imply a particular form of the gambler-preference map.[10]

The latter, however, is not really a gambler-preference map in the Shackle sense. Once net ϕ values are the yardstick by which investment strategies are ranked, then a choice over total standardized focus-values of the strategies is implied, but it does not require stating explicitly. So, in one sense, the argument that the form of that choice is prescribed by placing reliance on net ϕ values is an empty box, for that choice is not now an open choice via the specification of a preference over total standardized focus-values.

It is an ineluctable fact, however, that a model designed so that choice over actions is governed by net ϕ values obliterates the Shacklesque gambler-preference map. The two approaches are rivals. Professor Shackle is adamant, as we have seen, that his approach is a valid one, and although the ϕ-function and the gambler-preference map are related they are not conveying exactly the same information about the investor's psyche. They reinforce one another:

> . . . in so far as the shape of the gambler indifference curves, and the form of the ϕ-surface, of a given indidivual are influenced by, or express, the same traits of his character, these two formal statements of certain aspects of that character, are, of course, not independent of each other; if, by inspection of his ϕ-surface, we should learn something about his audacity or caution, or about his taste for or dislike of uncertainty, then we shall learn the same thing, or a broadly similar thing, from inspection of his gambler indifference map. The schedule of gambler-preference may not, as it were, give true readings in an absolute sense, but it will still serve very well for comparisons of the frame of mind of the same individual at different times, and of different individuals.[11]

How dissimilar indeed are the ϕ-function and the gambler-preference map? The smaller the divergence between the concepts the nearer we find ourselves to a position in which choice of action can be described by the ϕ-function, and it ceases solely to be a percolator for the expectational elements in the potential surprise function.

We must now exercise our minds on question (5), namely that concerned with the issue of asset return correlations on available assets and the mathematical form of the gambler opportunity line or investment frontier. Inevitably this will draw us into discussion of the scale of asset-diversification that is feasible within Shackle's schema.

As noted in chapter 3, Professor Shackle was fully aware of the limit imposed upon the extent of asset diversification by his theory as we have described that theory in chapters 2 and 3. Thus in chapter IV of *Expectation in Economics*, he wrote:

But this outer boundary . . . will be simply the gambler opportunity-chain line . . . and we know that any point lying below and to the right of this chain will be inferior to some point of the chain itself, that is some point on one of the straight-line segments composing the chain. Thus (except in the case where the points for these goods [assets] all lie on the same straight 'link' of the chain) any combination of more than two goods will be inferior to some combination of not more than two goods.

If, then, combinations of more than two goods are ever chosen, one or other of two things must in such cases be true; either some qualities of the combination besides its focus-gain and loss are being taken into account; or else the assumption that the focus-gain and loss of such a combination can be obtained from the potential surprise functions for the ratios of price-change of the individual goods in the direct way we have described does not always hold.[12]

In his *Investment Decisions under Uncertainty* (1960) it was precisely the method by which Shackle had combined focus-values to arrive at total focus-values that was challenged by R. A. D. Egerton, as noted in chapter 3. Recall that those total focus-values are found by weighting the separate focus outcomes of the assets by the holdings of those assets: total focus-gain is thus a linear combination of the focus-gains of the assets that the investor could invest in, the weights being equal to the holdings of each of the assets. On this issue Egerton argues as follows:

The Shackle theory cannot explain risk spreading because of the way in which it assumes an investor to look at the total focus-outcome of a composite holding of assets. An investor is assumed to think that either all the focus-gains or all the focus-losses will occur, and, if he does think in this way, there is no advantage to him in holding more than two assets. But it is doubtful if an investor would think in this way unless he believed there to be a high degree of positive correlation between price movements of the assets. If an investor beleived that there was no, or only slight, correlation between the price movements of certain assets it would be curious for him to consider the outcome of holding a composite portfolio of them as being simply the sum of their separate focus-outcomes, because it would presumably cause him considerable surprise if they all did yield either their focus-gain, or if they all yielded their focus-loss. Where any two assets have a high degree of positive correlation in their price movements, Professor Shackle's method of aggregation is appropriate; but when two assets have a high degree of negative correlation in their price movements, the total focus-outcome of a composite holding will be found – not by adding the focus-gains and the focus-losses – but by adding each focus-gain to the focus-*loss* of the other. But either method of addition is strictly proper only when the correlation coefficient (either positive or negative) is unity.[13]

This question of the role of the correlation between asset prices raises a number of issues which are mentioned, in part, by Dr Egerton in the preceding passage. The first, more general, issue that springs to mind is one concerning the basis upon which the potential surprise functions themselves are formulated. Dr C. F. Carter (now Sir Charles Carter) suggested in his paper entitled, 'A revised theory of expectations', (1953)[14] (wherein he advanced a new theory of expectations based on a simplification of Shackle's theory) that there should be, *effectively*, a potential surprise curve for each asset for every 'general state of the economy', an idea taken up later by Dr Egerton.

Carter begins by challenging Shackle's notion of a *continuous* potential surprise curve for any asset *per se*:

Now the human mind does not, I think, carry very easily a picture of a continuous variable.

Attention will at once be concentrated on *typical outcomes* in imagined future situations; the first rule of simplification being that all variables must be reduced to a few discrete values. The number of typical outcomes depends in part on the liveliness of the imagination in conjuring up alternative future situations, and in part on the distance of the image-date (i.e. on the time available for disturbing elements to enter in). . . .

Now the various typical outcomes, associated with imagined future situations, command various degrees of belief. . . .

It seems to me likely that, just as the mind simplifies a continuous distribution of outcome by concentrating on a few typical outcomes, so also it will simplify the degrees of belief. It will not be sensitive to small differences of belief, or (rather) it will never give that minute attention to differences of circumstance which would enable small differences of belief to appear. Instead, it will rank outcomes in broad groups, the 'perfectly possible', the 'just possible', and so on. It seems to me that Professor Shackle's 'potential surprise' properly appears as a result of this simplification. . . .

> We now have a picture of degree of belief like a short staircase, perhaps of one, two, six or ten steps. On each step stands a number of typical outcomes of varying height (i.e. attractiveness). . . . Let us call the set of outcomes thus selected for consideration, *primary typical gains and losses.* Each has associated with it two rankings, one in the scale of utility and one in the scale of belief. Now let us compare the course of action typified by these expected outcomes with another course of action. . . .
>
> Now I think that it is realistic to suppose that the courses of action (call them A and B) will in the first place be compared *in each of the imagined future circumstances*; that is to say, separately for each of the steps of belief. This seems to me to be the natural way of thinking. 'Course A will be better than Course B if there is inflation; but B is wiser if there is to be a change of Government . . . ' and so on (if two of these imagined circumstances carry the same degree of belief, one will, of course, compare the bigger, or primary, outcome). This step is a departure from Professor Shackle's theory, in which A and B are *first* summarised into focus gains and losses and *then* compared.[15]

This commentary epitomizing Carter's views on the need to introduce circumstance/situation potential surprise functions has been drawn together from several pages of his text, as reported. Hopefully, the conflation of what he has said does not do an injustice to the clarity and accruity of his observations.

As Carter points out, his suggestions conform to Shackle's theory in one instance: that is when there is only one step on the staircase of belief. In essence, however, what Carter proposed is in direct conflict with Shackle's thought-schemes. Carter's method of relating the 'typical' outcomes on an asset to the degree of belief of the circumstances that would be responsible for their occurrence is identical with one of the main pillars of the probability approach to asset choice. What Carter posits, essentially, is that there exist in the mind of the investor several 'states of nature', 'eventualities' or 'circumstances', one of which he feels certain will materialize by the end of the investment period. For each and every asset, gains/losses per £1 invested in them can be formulated: each of those typical outcomes has a degree of belief assigned to it via the 'states of nature'. Therefore the continuous potential surprise curve for an asset in Shackle's theory is replaced by a discontinuous curve, but a curve which has the outcomes (gains or losses) mapped into degrees of belief (rather than degrees of potential surprise).

The unique standard upon which the 'distribution' of gains/losses can be compared is the degree of belief. It seems that comparison is being made in Carter's framework by a preference function ('utility index') which has two arguments, on the gain side and on the loss side separately, namely gain/loss and degree of belief: $U_g = U(g, b)$; $U_L = U_L(L, b)$; where g is gains, L is loss and b is degree of belief. Since for any given 'state of nature' there is only one b, the U function can be written as: $U = U[(g, L), b]$.

A U function such as this gives the degree of belief a central role in the choice process: in Shackle's theory the degree of belief (let us say, equals the degree of potential surprise) and so *uncertainty* is filtered out of the final choice process. In emphasizing that belief Dr Carter's methodology also entails the investor using the *whole of the degree of belief functions* to order and to compare alternative investment strategies. One of the consequences of this is that if for all b two assets yield per £1 invested the same loss, but the one promises a higher yield than, or the same yield as the other asset, a rational investor should choose the one asset in preference to the other. Such a procedure satisfies the absolute preference criterion implied in the axioms of von Neumann-Morgenstern that is one of the linch-pins of the expected utility theory: that criterion we have made reference to earlier on in our analysis of question 3. A more extreme situation when the absolute preference criterion would be met is clearly one wherein the one asset also promises for some, or for all, 'states of nature' less loss than the other asset.

However, there will be situations, Carter indicates, where it may not be possible to state that, say, outcome A is uniformly better than B. Where an unequivocal answer is not possible he suggests that there are four strategies that are feasible:

> One is to look for a third course of action which can beat the other two. . . . Another is to delay action; if that is possible. . . . A third possibility is to do *both* the actions . . . : this is surely the origin of hedging. A fourth is to trust to chance, to toss a coin. . . . [16]

If we hypothesize that the investor has considered all of the alternative asset strategies so that there is available no other asset whose gain/loss characteristics will allow the deadlock to be broken, then it will follow that if the investor is to act rationally, if he does decide to delay his choice of action, *money* must be seen to be preferable to holding assets on the $U = U[(g, L), b]$ criterion; also the possibility of hedging cannot be turned *a priori* into a certainty that that is what the investor will do because, in the axioms that implicitly lie behind the construction and use of the U criterion, it would be assumed ordinarily that the investor *can order* the various degree of belief functions. This would mean that we would have an axiom of this form:

$$U[(g, L), b]_i \gtreqless U[(g, L)', b]_j; \quad \text{for all } i, j \quad i \neq j \tag{4.10}$$

Here i and j refer to assets/investment strategies: > means 'preferred to' and = means 'indifferent to'. In short, all 'distributions' can be compared; the investor can choose over them; if he cannot, he is indifferent between them. Therefore, he can choose any *one* of them: he could, or might, choose more than one of them, but he has no need to do so. To conclude that he must is to imply that U depends upon other factors besides (g, L) and b.

Additionally, b is an ordinal measure, *ex definitione*; hence it, like potential surprise, is not an additive concept. Hence a U-function over gain, loss and degree of belief can only hold for individual assets. Transformation of the U-function into an ordering over combinations of assets is not possible. Carter's theory seems, therefore, to take us no further forward than Shackle's theory.

However, Egerton has suggested that we should adopt Carter's idea that we should consider expectations based upon several 'general' economic situations, but he has applied that idea to asset choice in a way that differs from the path followed by Carter:

> It is probable that the trouble with the concept of potential surprise is that it is really useful in connection with only one of the two sorts of uncertainty with which an investor is usually faced. One sort of uncertainty is expressed in the form of such questions as, in these circumstances, how profitable is this venture likely to be? Or, in these circumstances, which looks to be the most attractive investment? The other sort of uncertainty is expressed in such questions as, is a slump likely within twelve months? The uncertainty which faces an investor is uncertainty both about general economic conditions and about the outcome of a particular project, given the general conditions.
>
> If an investor makes his investment decisions on the assumption of certain general conditions . . . , there are no difficulties involved in using the potential surprise concept, and the investor may reasonably hold only two assets. . . . The difficulties arise when an investor can visualise the occurrence of one out of more than two mutually exclusive sets of future general conditions.
>
> Suppose that an investor would not be surprised if within the relevant near future there was either peace-time full employment, or a slump, or war-time full employment. Suppose that he finds that a combined holding of two assets L and M places him at the preferred point on his gambler indifference map. Would he be sensible to hold only L and M if both will achieve their focus-loss if there is war (which could not surprise him)? Surely, he would be more sensible to hold also some other asset N which will yield its focus-gain if there

is a war, even if its focus-outcome, taken in isolation, is unattractive relative to the focus-outcomes of L and M.[17]

The approach by Egerton leads to a different attack on the question of asset diversification because what distinguishes his approach from that of Carter is that Egerton seems to envisage there being a potential surprise function for each asset for each general situation. From each potential surprise function there is a pair of focus-outcomes just as in Shackle's analysis; but now each pair of focus-values for an asset depends upon a particular 'state of nature'; each state of nature, it appears, is assigned a potential surprise of zero. So we have returned completely to the Shackle framework: the only difference now is that for each asset, if, as Egerton does, we assume that there exist three perfectly possible states of nature, we have three pairs of focus-values.

Since for any asset the three states of nature have attached to them the same, zero degree of potential surprise the investor, following the Shackle model, would choose just one pair of focus-values to epitomize his expectations of gains/losses from investing in the asset. There might be one pair which has simultaneously the largest focus-loss and the largest focus-gain, but if this is not so, because the pairs of focus-values all carry zero potential surprise by Professor Shackle's ascendancy, or ϕ-function, the highest focus loss and the highest focus gains on the asset, *independent of the state of nature*, will be carried forward as the investor's estimate of the worst to fear, and of the best to hope for, from investment in the relevant asset.

The logic of this argument, which is merely an extension of that of Professor Shackle, seems unimpeachable. It means, therefore, that the notion that extra assets will be introduced into the investor's portfolio if we characterize potential surprise curves/functions by reference to the occurrence of a state of nature, cannot be upheld. Dr Egerton's assets *L*, *M* and *N* will be ranked on a common basis, of zero potential surprise; either one asset will be superior to the other, or one combination of any two assets will be superior to the other asset combinations and to any one asset. Asset diversification cannot be over more than two assets, save fortuitously, as already discussed in chapter 3.

However, Dr Egerton's amendments to the concept of potential surprise come nearer than do Dr Carter's to finding a means whereby asset diversification can be magnified. Essentially what Dr Egerton is seeking to do in the lengthy quote presented above, is to introduce the idea of *correlation* between the focus-values on the assets by which he set so much store, as seen at the outset of the discussions on question (5).

In the immediately preceding quote Dr Egerton is implying that in one state of nature (war) asset N will yield a gain (and, he implies, it will yield no loss) whilst in that state (of war) assets L and M will yield losses (but no gains). He also seems to be implying that in the two other states (peace-time full employment, or a slump) asset N will yield losses and no gains, while, analogously, assets L and M will yield gains but no losses.

The situation can be summarized in Table 4.1, where we return to our customary notation, so that l and g represent loss and gain per £1 invested, respectively. On Professor Shackle's decision criteria the investor would choose any one asset to invest in, or any combination of two assets: on Dr Carter's criteria he is 'likely' to choose L or M. However, Dr Egerton's proposal is that the investor should choose a combination of all *three* assets.

Table 4.1 The potential surprise pay-off matrix for three assets and three states of nature

	Asset		
State of nature	*L*	*M*	*N*
War	$l_L > 0$ $g_L = 0$	$l_M > 0$ $g_M = 0$	$l_N = 0$ $g_N > 0$
Peace	$l_L = 0$ $g_L > 0$	$l_M = 0$ $g_M > 0$	$l_N > 0$ $g_N = 0$
Slump	$l_L = 0$ $g_L > 0$	$l_M = 0$ $g_M > 0$	$l_N > 0$ $g_N = 0$

I have said 'proposal' because Dr Egerton advances no criteria by reference to which choice can be made. The main factor behind his proposal, of course, is the idea of hedging. This is based on the fact that the gains (positive returns) on some assets might be accompanied by losses (negative returns) on others and vice-versa; in other words prices for particular assets might be negatively correlated to some degree.

Table 4.1 arises, of course, as a consequence of a set of assumptions in which negative price correlation is prevalent. A quick glance at that table would lead one to the view that it is eminently sensible to diversify across assets, in a situation where the states of nature are mutually exclusive and are judged to be equally likely to occur. However, more concentrated study of Table 4.1 will reveal that only two assets L and N or M and N might be held after all. A simple alteration to Table 4.1 could make it seem more likely *a priori* that the investor would hold three assets; basically, all that is needed is an adjustment to the table so that the Peace and Slump elements for L and M read as shown in Table 4.2. This shows strongly, but less than perfectly, negative correlation between the returns on all three assets.

Table 4.2 The potential surprise pay-off matrix for two assets and two states of nature

	L	M
Peace	$l_L = 0$ $g_M > 0$	$l_M > 0$ $g_M = 0$
Slump	$l_L > 0$ $g_M = 0$	$l_L = 0$ $g_M > 0$

The major difficulty with the introduction of correlation into the Shackle model is the obvious one that the model is one which eschews any reference to probability distributions upon which the formal definition of correlation is based; also, as a corollary of this, though the investor is choosing (still) over focus-values, there is no formal way in which correlation can be introduced into the calculation of those focus-values for combinations of assets because asset focus-values have not been derived from the potential surprise distributions as if those distributions were probability distributions *and* by a procedure such that say, risk (= 'potential loss') was measured by the dispersion of the potential surprise distribution around its 'expected value'. If a measure of dispersion is employed then clearly at the aggregate level when we are considering all possible combinations of wealth allocation the total dispersions (of returns) in any portfolio will depend upon the dispersions of the returns on individual assets and on the correlation between the various asset returns; all of this, naturally, as in conventional portfolio theory discussed in chapter 1 of this book.

Again, however, it is an easy matter to appreciate that some progress can be made if the degree of correlation between asset prices/returns does happen to be *exactly* plus one or minus one (where we interpret correlation in a rather looser way from that derived from statistical theory). Thus suppose that we consider the choice of investment in only two assets and we do so in the Shackle construct: it then follows that if we hypothesize that the potential surprise functions of the assets are for *a* particular state of nature (being the only one expected), if the focus-gain on the other asset does materialize then so will that on the other asset; an analogous statement can be made for the focus-losses. It follows, therefore, as Egerton has maintained strongly in his writings (see chapter 3 of this book) that it is legitimate, say, to add the focus-gains weighted by the holding of the relevant asset to the weighted focus-gain of the other asset in order to arrive at a value for total focus-gain from the given allocation of total wealth.

We could argue that Shackle set up his model of the potential surprise function for each asset under *an* assumed economic climate; for him each of the possible values of gain and loss within that climate were the variables which were mutually exclusive, and so, in his theory, non-additive. Therefore, perfect correlation between asset prices is, or could easily be, an integral part of Shackle's theory. If so, the investment frontier for two assets is linear, and all that has been said in previous chapters about asset diversification in the Shackle model holds good.

What happens when considering the other polar case of perfect negative correlation between asset prices? Again asset diversification is possible only over two assets, because all two-asset investment frontiers are linear; and except in the special conditions, of a kind similar to those detailed in chapter 3 for the case of perfect positive correlation, a frontier for three or more assets cannot be derived.

Precisely how do we construct the frontier when there is perfect negative correlation? If the returns on the assets are negatively correlated we may interpret this as meaning that the focus-gain on, say, asset A would be accompanied by the focus-loss on asset B, and vice-versa. Consequently, we would add the focus-gain on asset A to the focus-loss on asset B (both weighted by the value of the holdings of the respective asset) to find one focus-value for a portfolio consisting of both assets, and to discover the other focus-value we would add the (weighted) values of the focus-loss on A and the focus-gain on B. In some instances this could produce aggregate focus-values which are either *both* gains or both losses.

Generally, for perfectly negative correlation in our current example:

$$G = g_A x_A - l_B x_B \tag{4.11}$$

$$L = g_B x_B - l_A x_A \tag{4.12}$$

and $$W = x_A + x_B \tag{4.13}$$

Here the notation is the same as that used previously: so that g_A, for example, is the standardized focus-gain or focus positive return on asset A, and G is the total value of such gain or positive return for the given set of placings, x_A, x_B out of the fixed wealth.

The (G, L) frontier implied by equations (4.11)–(4.13) is:

$$G = \left(\frac{g_A g_B - l_B l_A}{g_B + l_A}\right) W - \left(\frac{g_A + g_B}{g_B + l_A}\right) L \tag{4.14}$$

Assume that $g_A / l_A > l_B / g_B$: then the frontier will be in the positive quadrant and have a negative slope as depicted on figure 4.4. At C the optimum portfolio will be:

$$x_A^* = \frac{g_B W}{g_B + l_A}\ ; \quad x_B^* = \frac{l_A W}{g_B + l_A} \tag{4.15}$$

If the investor is a risk-averter that is the portfolio he will choose. Should $g_A / l_A < l_B / g_B$ the frontier will extend in a north-westerly direction so that L *will be negative* along it; hence *gain* will be available on both axes of the frontier. A combination of x's will be chosen in the north-west quadrant; that combination promises only gain.

So far the discussion of the importance of asset price correlations for asset diversification has been concerned with two special

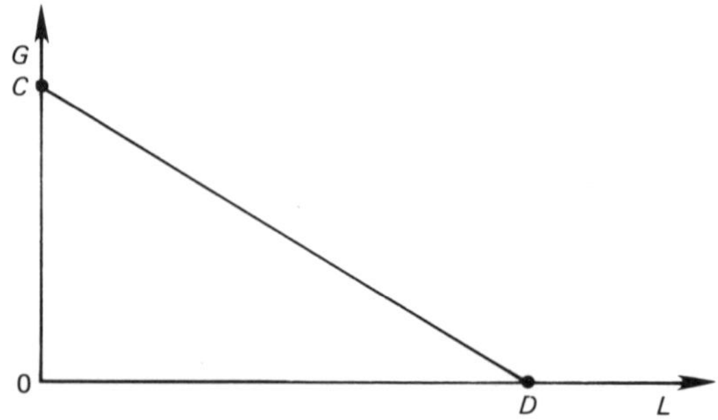

Figure 4.4 *The Shackle investment frontier with perfectly negative correlation between asset yields*

cases. In the second case of perfect negative correlation it has been possible to show that diversification will take place over two assets; this is something likely to occur, but which need not occur, in the case of perfect positive correlation. Nevertheless, the discussion of perfect negative correlation has been undertaken in the context solely of two assets. However, an extension of the analysis to three assets is not possible except in special circumstances, by analogy with the discussion in chapter 3 on the problems of extending the case of positive correlation to more than two assets. When there is negative correlation the equations for G and L are still linear in the value of the asset holdings.

This leads us on naturally to two important issues, namely: how can we handle situations where the degree of correlation between asset prices lies *between* plus one and minus one? Would such alternative degrees of correlation increase asset diversification? Clearly, the former question is the prior one and without a satisfactory answer to it the second question becomes otiose.

Let us now turn our attention to that first question. Unfortunately there is no satisfactory answer to it. The reason for this can be stated immediately: it is that the definitions of total focus-gain and total focus-loss are not in any way connected with the statistical moments of a probability distribution. Only if potential surprise is equated with probability, and loss equated with risk as measured by standard deviation, can the degree of correlation between asset prices or asset returns be introduced systematically. However, there is one classic attempt in the literature on portfolio selection to introduce risk and correlation into portfolio choice *without* reference to a measure of risk such as the standard deviation or variance of return on the whole portfolio. Here I refer to the paper by E. D. Domar and R. A. Musgrave.[18] That paper is concerned initially with an analysis of the optimum level of risk from the investment of a given level of wealth, and thereafter with the effects of different forms of income tax on risk-taking by investors.

In setting up their basic behavioural framework for the investor Professors Domar and Musgrave make essentially the same assumptions made in this book about the circumstances surrounding the investor's one-period-at-a-time decision model (e.g. he has a given level of wealth, investments are divisible . . .). They then state that:

To handle our problem, quantitative values for the yield and the degree of risk of an investment are needed; and in the absence of a better approach, they are obtained by means of a probability distribution which the investor will construct for each available investment opportunity. Each possible yield, positive or negative, will include the recurrent income from the investment . . . as well as the change in capital value which the investor expects to realise. . . .

From the probability distribution thus constructed, the investor will compute the mathematical expectation of the percentage yields (y). . . . It will prove helpful in the following discussion to separate y into its negative component r and its positive component g. Thus, if $q_1, q_2, \ldots, q_k, q_{k+1}, \ldots, q_n$, are the expected rates of return, such that $q_i < q_{i+1}$ and $q_k = 0$, and if the probability of the occurrence of q_i is p_i, so that

$$\sum_{i=1}^{n} p_i = 1$$

we arrive at the following definitions:

$$(1)\quad r = -\sum_{i}^{k} q_i p_i$$

$$(2)\quad g = \sum_{i=k+1}^{n} q_i p_i$$

$$(3)\quad y = \sum_{i=1}^{n} q_i p_i = g - r$$

The magnitude of the actual value is not the only factor determining the investor's choice. Other characteristics must also be considered, though for purposes of this analysis their number must be limited.

Investment decisions are made in spite of uncertainty with respect to the relevant data and their implications. . . . Yet it is extremely difficult to express the degree of uncertainty involved in workable terms. For our purpose it is sufficient to say that the prevalence of uncertainty may induce the investor to require a somewhat higher return than would be required otherwise.[19]

In attempting to make allowance for uncertainty they continue:

Of all possible questions which the investor may ask, the most important one, it appears to us, is concerned with the probability of the actual yield being less than zero, that is, with the probability of a loss. This is the essence of *risk* . . . the coefficient of risk should be defined more precisely as a function of losses and their probabilities. This can be done most simply by defining risk as . . . r.

By considering r, the most relevant aspect of the dispersion of the probability distribution is accounted for in our analysis. . . . That is not to say that the dispersion of the distribution will not be a factor in investment decisions. A more elaborate analysis would allow for additional variables defining the shape of the probability distributions; for example, in terms of the standard deviation. . . .[20]

Accordingly, in their analysis, (total) y and r determine the choice of investment strategy. On that basis Domar and Musgrave proceed to consider the case where the investor can invest in two assets, A and B. They then argue that the (y, r) frontier, given wealth, for the holding of the assets will assume the form of the line AB in figure 4.5, if the values of y and r for assets A and B are completely interdependent, whilst if:

. . . they are more or less independent, the r of each combination will be more or less below the weighted average of the r of the components (assets A and B). This reflects the principle that diversification reduces the dispersion of a probability distribution. Therefore, the r's and y's will fall on a curve such as ACB [on figure 4.5].[21]

In these observations, epitomized in figure 4.5 (where it is assumed that $y_B < y_A$, $r_B < r_A$), Domar and Musgrave are arguing by analogy with the mean–variance portfolio selection model. However, although y is equivalent to μ, the mean value of the return on an asset or on a total *portfolio* as appropriate, r is not equivalent to the standard deviation or variance of the returns on individual assets or as relevant, on the whole portfolio; this is true *ex definitione*, and it is conceded, as we have seen, by Domar and Musgrave.

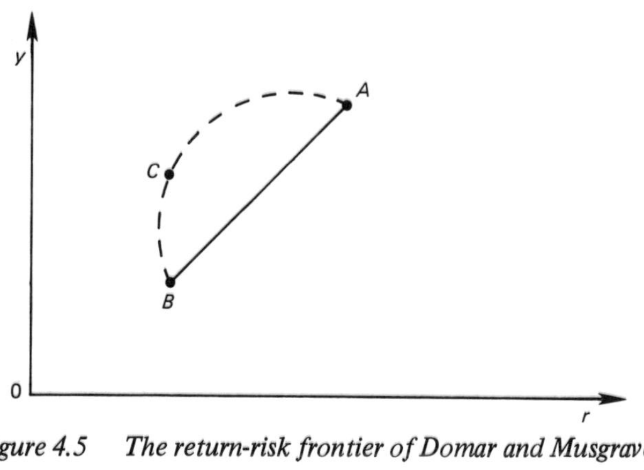

Figure 4.5 The return-risk frontier of Domar and Musgrave

Should r be defined as that standard deviation or variance we can then deduce that a curvilinear frontier (such as *BCA* on figure 4.5) can exist if the correlation between the returns (positive and negative) on the two assets are negatively correlated. That, and more, has been demonstrated and discussed already in chapter 1. But without risk being assessed in that way, it is not possible to envisage asset diversification over more than two assets as an optimum hedging strategy for the investor.

If we could interpret Domar and Musgrave's r as the dispersion of asset returns then we could justify their observations on the (y, r) frontier; but no indication of the dispersion of the probability distribution of returns on any assets, and hence on a combination of assets, can be provided by r: it is not even a measure of semi-variance, even though the base value for the calculation of r is (a return of) zero. In short, r, like y, is a linear function of each asset return that is negative; unlike any measure of dispersion, it does not involve squared values of asset returns, q_i. *Ergo*, the aggregate, across-the-whole-portfolio, value of r, cannot involve squared values of each of the asset holdings, as it would if r were a measure of dispersion. Despite the fact that it cannot incorporate asset price/return correlation, the Domar–Musgrave analysis has been applied to investigations of risk-taking and investment.[22]

As far as we can see, therefore, the Domar–Musgrave approach becomes essentially the same approach as Professor Shackle's: the real differences are only ones of semantics. This is despite the view of Domar and Musgrave that Shackle's potential surprise approach, to investment decision and so the effect of taxation on the willingness to invest and to assume risk, was inadequate and had to be replaced by the probability framework.[23] In essence, Domar and Musgrave were arguing in support of one of the main premises in the Shackle model that losses (negative returns) should be treated separately from gains (positive returns); risk to them enters the investor's scheme of things via potential losses on assets or portfolios. This is why r is used as a variable that affects the investor's choice. The only difference between the Domar–Musgrave framework and that of Shackle is that they see gains/losses as being epitomized by their mathematical expectations. That, of course, is anathema to Shackle; in his opinion the mutually exclusive losses (gains) cannot be combined. To combine them, to average them, is a logical contradiction.

Given all of these observations, it would follow that if they have any foundation when we revert to the potential surprise model we cannot readily incorporate situations of other than perfectly negative/positive asset price correlations into our analysis. Even if we assume the special intermediate case of zero correlation we cannot determine how that would affect the shape and position of the (G, L) frontier even for two assets. If it could have been demonstrated that, unlike the frontier for perfectly positive correlation, it was curvilinear, we would have been able to extend the degree of asset diversification so that a multi-asset portfolio was possible. Logically that is not feasible in the Domar–Musgrave model; in the Shackle model there is the added drawback that we are not dealing with the probability calculus and hence there is not even the possibility of introducing correlation through dispersion of returns.

It was shown early on in this chapter, and in chapter 3, that Shackle was well aware of the limited asset diversification that his theory would produce. He suggested that the way that asset gains/losses were amalgamated – to provide the total gain/total loss frontier – could be inappropriate, (this is the question we have just analysed). He also raised the possibility that focus-values of returns on assets might themselves be inadequate means of representing the characteristics of assets. He did not amplify that point but in the second edition of *Expectation in Economics* he offers a suggestion as to why that might be so.

The substance of what he said was that his model of asset choice was developed on the basis of money gains/losses, whereas it should have been couched in terms of *real* returns. In his model he argued that there was one kind of asset, money, which because of the assumption of zero inflation, was safe, so that the proportion of his wealth that was placed in money was secure. He then argued that:

> In contrast to this, we might assume the individual to feel that no single kind of asset could be relied on not to suffer a large and rapid fall of its rates of exchange for most other kinds of asset. If in that case he thinks of loss in terms of general command over goods of all sorts, that is as loss of some amount of general purchasing power, and if there is some degree of such loss which would entail 'catastrophe' for him, and if we assume that he will select his relative quantities of different kinds of assets with the whole purpose of reducing his fear that such catastrophe may occur, he must resort to 'spreading of risks'. The principles on which this ought to be done have been discussed by Mr A. D. Roy . . . in an extremely distinguished article called "Safety first and the holding of assets" (not yet published).[24]

The article to which Professor Shackle referred was subsequently published in *Econometrica*, 1952; and was referred to previously in chapter 1 and in appendix B. That paper was indeed a veritable *tour de force*, as noted; but it was a paper predicated on the probability approach to portfolio decision-making under 'uncertainty' even though it paid tribute to Professor Shackle's approach. It did so, in effect, by supporting his claim that an investor's concern about a portfolio or investment strategy was focused on the potential *losses* or negative returns; and that we could contemplate the degree of his concern, hence his 'risk-aversion', being influenced by the ratio of possible loss to wealth. Those two points are enveloped in the Roy model by his assuming that, as his objective, the investor seeks to minimize the probability that the return on his portfolio (wealth) will fall below a specified level, which he labels the disaster level. That level could be taken to be one at which his wealth is at least maintained over the investment period; invariably it will be a higher level than that. For example, for an institutional investor, such as an insurance company or a discount house, we might think the Roy model is an appropriate one. We might argue *a priori* that we could proxy the portfolio behaviour of such institutions by stating that they seek to minimize the probability that their portfolio returns fall below the cost of capital, which for discount houses is measured by the cost of the call loans they take on for the commercial banks, without which they could not conduct their business.

So, despite the fact that Dr Roy also uses subjective probability instead of objective probability, his framework does not make any *effective* concessions to the Shackle schema. It does explain multi-asset portfolios but that is irrelevant in this context. So it is not an avenue by which to explore multi-asset diversification in the Shackle model. Additionally, it should be noted that the use of *real* returns, rather than money returns, does not affect the structure and hence conclusions of that model. This is so whether we assume the existence of only one state of nature in the construction of the potential surprise function or of many; because for any such function for any asset, and hence for any strategy, the investor will now simply be setting out the positive/negative real returns rather than money returns with their associated degrees of potential surprise.[25]

We *can* allow for the disaster level/rate of return in the Shackle model if we so wish; but this will not improve the chances of being able to say that an investor will hold a true multi-asset portfolio.

Allowance can be made for a disaster level d by either setting up the investor's utility function in terms of $U = U(G, L/W)$ with, say, the disaster being that $L \geqslant W$; or by deflating just the asset focus-gain by the disaster level per unit of wealth.[26] Even so, because we are not moving outside the basic tenets of the Shackle construct we cannot possibly produce other than linear, two-asset, investment frontiers.

The only means now available, to increase the general degree of asset diversification in the Shackle model, is to introduce the idea of rationing or constraints mentioned in chapter 3. The essential point is that if we place constraints or rationing quotas on the holding of various types of assets this can, if the investor's wealth is large enough, lead to a very diversified portfolio. For example, we could say that the value of the holding of a number of assets (x_j) should be equal to $\alpha_j W$. If $\Sigma\alpha_j < 1$, then at least $j + 1$ assets will be held. Additionally, we might find that the monetary authorities impose rationing restrictions on the x_{j+1} assets that can be held; such that $x_{j+1} \leqslant V$. Then, if given the investor's utility function he would have desired to have, given his residual wealth $(W - \alpha_j W)$, a greater x_{j+1} than V, asset diversification will be increased even further as the investor endeavours to allocate all of his wealth across available assets; since by the Kuhn–Tucker theorem the constraints would be binding and effective.[27] But such constraints only have importance for institutional, and not for private, investors.

A position is now reached where there is only one more question about the Shackle schema remaining unanswered: that is question 6 which concerns the possibility of translating Professor Shackle's index of potential surprise into a subjective probability index; with the validity of such a translation; and, furthermore, with whether or not such a probability index would affect the optimum portfolio selected by the investor.

It is, in fact, perfectly possible to transform the index of potential surprise into one of subjective probability. Various mappings between the two have been proposed.[28] That this is so is not remarkable; for since at least one of a set of exhaustive hypotheses must carry zero potential surprise, there will be a one-to-one mapping of the set of potential surprises, for an investment, to a set of numbers π_i, where $\Sigma_{i=1}^{n} \pi_i = 1$; so that the π_i become subjective probabilities. One very simple mapping is provided by W. Krelle,[29] who believes that the plausibility of any outcome i can be measured by the difference between $\bar{y}$ (the maximum degree of potential surprise) and y_i. He then suggests this mapping:

$$\pi_i = \frac{\bar{y} - y_i}{\sum_{i=1}^{n} (\bar{y} - y_i)} \tag{4.16}$$

and:

$$y_i = \frac{-\pi_i}{\pi_{j\max}} \bar{y}(1 - n\pi_{j\max}) + \bar{y}(1 - n\pi_i) \tag{4.17}$$

for given 'arbitrary' value of $\bar{y}$.

Since the mapping of y into π is isomorphic the rankings of the potential surprises are maintained. The high values of y_i are associated with low values of π_i; but are such mappings of any meaning? Though they preserve all of the orderings and essential properties of the potential surprise index, and though they are simply transformations of one unit of 'measurement' into another, it could be argued quite forcibly that they have no *subjective* meaning in the Shackle model. That is to say, they cannot represent the thought processes and expectational complex of the investor. If we ask the investor to set out his scale of potential surprise about a set of hypotheses concerning the yields on an investment, we are asking him to think in a different way from a situation where we ask him to specify the likelihood or probability that a particular yield will materialize. An investor might not be surprised if the yield on the investment was, say, zero; though he might consider it most unlikely that such a yield would materialize. A zero potential surprise does not mean that the outcome concerned is expected to occur with certainty, unless the individual attaches the maximum degree of potential surprise to all other, rival, outcomes.

Again, to touch on another issue raised in chapter 2, if we look at a mapping such as equation (4.16) we see that if suddenly we believe that some other return, which we had not thought of before, could materialize so that the set of 'exhaustive' hypotheses increases, the probability, π_i, attached to any return has to fall. Thus though the potential surprise for return *i* might not have changed as a consequence of the extra information the investor feels he has, since the denominator of (4.16) must increase, *ceteris paribus*, so that for any *i*, the numerator is the same, so π_i falls. This is attributable to the fact that probability is a distributional variable; and, of course, summation of π_i in (4.16) produces a value of unity.

That is the main thrust of Shackle's rebuttal of the use of a mapping of potential surprise into subjective probability:

The very word *possibility* in the subjective sense I wish to give it is essentially an acknowledgement of a state of mind quite the opposite of that of a man who constructs a probability distribution. When a man speaks of probability he pushes ignorance so far as he can into concealment and an inconspicuous role; when he speaks of possibility he recognises his knowledge as merely setting bounds to a wide spectrum of mutually exclusive ideas. To sum the degrees of *potential* possibility assigned to various rival hypotheses is to fall back on the idea that it is the *number of its rivals* which gives a hypothesis its status, rather than its own particular character. . . . To do what Professor Krelle suggests would give to a *perfectly possible* hypothesis a share, which might be a very small one, of the total

$$\sum_{i=1}^{n} (\bar{y} - y_i)$$

It is precisely this idea, that a *small share of a total*, and a share that *varies with the size of that total*, can suitably indicate the status of *perfect possibility*, that I cannot agree with.[30]

How would the choice of optimum portfolio be affected, if at all, in the Shackle model, if we were to use subjective probabilities instead of degrees of potential surprise? The short answer is, not at all! All that will have happened is that we will have transformed the potential surprise function by transforming potential surprise; once we transform the ϕ-function appropriately, the focus-values on assets will be as they were before the transformation.[31]

Thus let us assume that π is a *strictly* decreasing function of y, $\pi = \pi(y)$, which it will be, given the function specified in equation (4.16). We also assume on figure 4.6 that ϕ attains a maximum at x^*, where we consider only the gain branch of the potential surprise function for simplicity. The value of ϕ at x^* is given by $\bar{\phi}$; so the equation of that ϕ-indifference curve is $y = \bar{\phi}(x)$. The potential surprise function is $y = y(x) = P(x)$; it and $\phi(x)$ are tangential at $y = y^*$.

Therefore x^* is a *unique*, *global* maximum of x.

Now, let us define:

$\pi = y^{\pi}(x)$ is defined by $\pi = \pi(y(x))$

$\pi = \bar{\phi}^{\pi}(x)$ is defined by $\pi = \pi(\bar{\phi}(x))$

with $\bar{\phi}$ equal to the curve $y = \bar{\phi}(x)$.

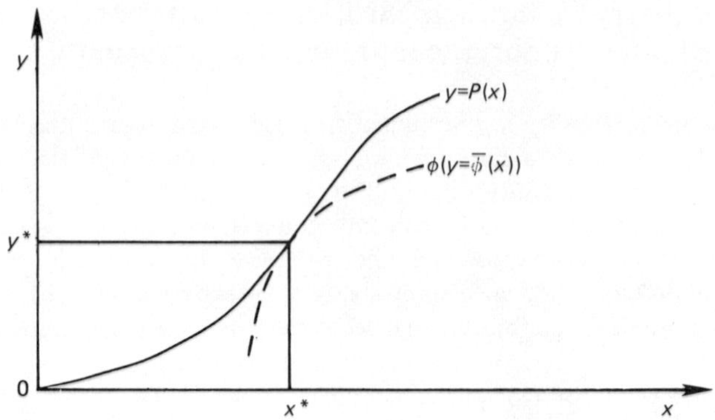

Figure 4.6 *The selection of focus values and potential surprise*

From figure 4.6 we have:

$$y(x^*) = \bar{\phi}(x^*)$$

But:

$$y^{\pi}(x^*) = \pi(y(x^*)) \quad \text{(by definition)}$$

$$\bar{\phi}^{\pi}(x^*) = \pi(\bar{\phi}(x^*)) \quad \text{(by definition)}$$

$$\therefore \quad y^{\pi}(x^*) = \bar{\phi}^{\pi}(x^*) \qquad (4.18)$$

Equation (4.18) proves that x^* will also be the maximum value of x, and hence the primary focus-gain on the relevant asset.

Thus figure 4.6 can be translated into figure 4.7. The standardized focus-gain (focus positive return) will be identical with that obtained when potential surprise is used explicitly. *Mutatis mutandis* the same is true of the standardized focus-loss (focus negative return).

The conditions under which the mapping of potential surprise into 'subjective probability' has been developed must be borne in mind. In essence, it has been assumed that we have been presented with the individual's potential surprise function: the mapping process merely transforms that function into one of 'subject probability'. No individual has been asked to supply his potential surprise function for the returns on a specified asset or a particular investment project, and his own representation of a subjective probability density function for the returns on the asset or project, so that a comparison can be made between that density function and the result of the mapping procedure. One consequence of this

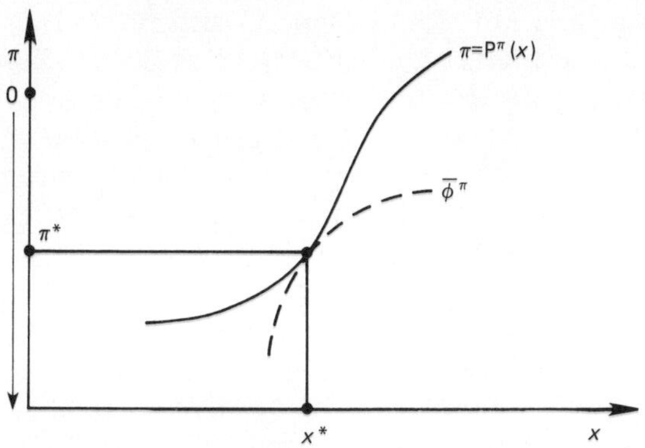

Figure 4.7 The selection of focus values and subjective probability

is that we cannot run into situations of the kind where the individual stipulates that he assigns the same degree of potential surprise to two outcomes, but states that he would attach a higher degree of probability of occurrence to the one outcome than he would to the other.

Such a situation would mean, naturally, that the mapping process could not produce a subjective probability density function that matched the one provided by the individual himself. Furthermore, although we might think *prima facie* that from introspection we might, say, assign zero potential surprise to two (rival) outcomes, such as a Labour or Tory victory at the next election, but attach a higher probability to the one rather than to the other, this has been ruled out as being illogical, irrational, within his scheme of things by Shackle himself. Recall from the commentary in chapter 2 that Shackle argued that in such conditions the individual would assign different degrees of potential surprise to the two outcomes, in view of the fact that he has different degrees of belief in their occurrence.

As far as empirical matters are concerned it is not obvious how we could establish an experiment to determine which is the primitive concept, potential surprise or subjective probability. Naturally, by means of questionnaires and interviews it would be possible to ascertain from individuals what their potential surprise function looked like for given investment projects. Thereafter, they would be asked to repeat the exercise of evaluating investment prospects by means of a subjective probability distribution. Comparisons could then be made between that distribution and one derived by the mapping function from potential surprise. *Ceteris paribus*, an assessment could then be made of the value of the mapping process in capturing for a project the expectational complex of the individual. From that assessment it would not be possible automatically to decide upon which was the primitive, basic, concept. It may be the case that individuals do think in terms of potential surprise first and foremost; and that a subjective probability equivalent can then be derived from potential surprise. It is possible (many would no doubt say, likely) that the reverse mechanism is true in reality. Only a direct question to that effect could elicit any worthwhile answer, because a comparison of subjective probability distribution based on mappings with the declared subjective probability distribution of the individual can alone inform us about the accuracy of the mappings.

There seems to be every likelihood indeed, as noted previously, that potential surprise and subjective probability are based on two distinct thought processes; accordingly we would not expect the mappings to prove to be empirically sound. Shackle would argue that they are intrinsically different, apart from the fact that the one is a distributed variable whilst the other is not.

However, as will be argued in chapter 5, once we have a model in which the individual, when confronted by the need to choose a course of action in an uncertain world, has set out his expected outcomes from the choices open to him, by means of potential surprise, we can then convert that concept into one akin to, or what we might call, subjective probability. Such a methodological procedure makes no presumption about the existence of a subjective probability density function in the mind of the investor, nor about its equivalence to a potential surprise function.

5

The Critical Exegesis in Sum and An Axiomatic Treatment of the Shackle Model

The presentation and analysis in chapter 4 has demonstrated unequivocably the ambivalence that exists at times in the literature about the exact meaning of, and role played by, some of the central parts of Shackle's theory, and that that ambivalence on occasions creeps into Shackle's own exposition and defence of his schema. This book has also advanced critical analytical points in respect of the Shackle schema *per se*, and of the exegital literature on it.

So, it seems a worthwhile step to attempt to summarize what emerge as the essential messages of chapter 4 on the central elements of the Shackle construct. It can be demonstrated how, in effect, the criticisms of the construct can be circumvented by alternative specifications of the Shackle schema *per se* which produce what we might call Shacklesque models.

A synthesis of the views contained in chapter 4 is best presented by reference to the three major elements of the Shackle construct taken in their logical sequence.

POTENTIAL SURPRISE

The discussion in chapter 4 offered no substantial counter-weight to the concept of potential surprise, except by consideration of the view that potential surprise could be explained readily by subjective probability. Despite the fact that mappings of potential surprise into subjective probability can be devised, our position was, in essence, that such devices were only of a mechanical nature. In any event the impact on the Shackle model of such translations is minimal. They can only replicate the inferences of that model for portfolio choice and on the wider canvas are unable to embrace anything other than two-asset portfolios because when subjective (or objective) probability is the sole emendation to the Shackle model there remains no place for the moments of the resultant probability distribution. Thus, in fact, the ascendancy function and the gambler preference-map of the Shackle framework are preserved. *Ex hypothesi*, the asset diversification, and other concomitant properties of the orthodox probabilistic approach, cannot emerge from the Shackle model when it is changed, essentially, in nomenclature alone. The replacement of potential surprise by a distributional variable is nothing more than a cosmetic change (within the Shackle model *per se*).

Some, but only some, discussion there has been of the notion, of the very concept, of potential surprise. This has largely focused on two points. The one is that it is hard to envisage an individual investor being able, perhaps even taking the time, to fine-tune, as it were, his potential surprise function for any one asset or for any potential investment strategy. Therefore, he is not likely to, or able to, map out all the possible returns with an attached degree of potential surprise. The gradations necessary are not likely to be feasible, or the investor is seen – from a psychological viewpoint – to divide the range of returns by reference to various major groups of 'perfectly possible', 'very possible', 'not so possible', and 'impossible', simply because, adopting Shackle's own standpoint, the investor will seek a simplification of the expectations-forming process. Within his purview he will not find it within his faculties to specify in precise detail and fine detail the expectational complex for any investment strategy.

Such considerations may be seen to be important if we reflect introspectively on our own decision-making processes. The psyche might only be able to cope with such a complex and complicated procedure by extreme simplification; but such an issue does not affect the Shacklesque schema in any fundamental sense. It is perfectly consistent with the Shackle impression that individuals will seek to, will indeed find it necessary to, simplify the expectations-formation process. It merely goes further than Shackle does along those lines. Additionally the further simplification, envisaged in the replacement of finely graded degrees of potential surprise – by broader categories of 'possible', of the kind suggested by Carter – makes no difference to the findings of the Shackle model. Then, for each broad category of 'possible', the investor selects the best positive outcome (highest loss) as epitomizing the prospects of return on the said asset or investment strategy, under the specified 'level' (staircase) of possibility. That level is effectively a degree of potential surprise in the Shackle sense; it is not a surrogate for it. In sum, all that this telescoping of the concept of potential surprise achieves is a truncation of the Shackle potential surprise function for any asset or investment strategy.

THE ASCENDANCY FUNCTION

It is probably fair to say that it is the ascendancy function that has caused most of the doubts in the literature and in this presentation of the Shackle schema. Some of the confusion over the very concept itself has permeated Shackle's own writings. There are two major difficulties over the ascendancy function; the one relates to the very existence of the function, to its *raison d'être*; the other is concerned with the utilization of the function, leaving aside the prior question of its role, to construct focus-values; but these two issues are not entirely unconnected.

The fact that the ascendancy function is frequently referred to as the stimulus function highlights the ambivalence that seems to exist over the rationale for, and the role of, the function. It is apparent that underlying all the pronouncements concerning the function that have been made by Shackle himself is the theme that the ascendancy function is meant to be a vehicle through which an investor can sift out the range of possible returns on any investment strategy into a manageable data set; a set, in effect, which consists of only one expectational element for either gain or loss. The investor will have an inherent desire to simplify the expectational complex by which he is confronted. On the gain side of an investment project he concentrates on what Shackle calls 'the best he can hope for'; such an expectational element has claimed his attention, has gained ascendancy in his mind.

When the alternative form of wording is used to describe the function, the impression is gained (indeed, it is often given) that 'the' expectational elements that are selected from the gain and loss branches of the potential surprise function have stimulated the investor to action, to think of investing in the specified project or to follow the given investment strategy. He is stimulated by the imagination of the prospects on the project or strategy.

Such a portrayal of the situation, and in such language, throws into sharp relief the question as to whether the ascendancy or ϕ

function should be viewed as a telescoping, 'ϕocusing', device for selecting expectational elements, or as a route for the selection of investment strategies. Viewed in that light the issue is more than one of semantics. Shackle's position (despite the semantic and language problems that arise in his endeavours to support this position) is that the two selection procedures are entirely separate, and that the purpose of the ascendancy, ϕ, stimulus function is to serve as a conflator of expectational elements into focus-values.

At the semantic level, naturally, it could be contended that some of the uncertainties surrounding the ascendancy function's role could have been obviated by a more suitable form of nomenclature. Clearly, if some other name had been chosen to describe the ascendancy function, even if less elegant, but more poignant, such as expectations telescoping function, there would have been no doubt as to what role that function was to perform in the scheme of things. This would have been doubly so if an alternative nomenclature had been reinforced by the avoidance of 'ophelemity-based' phraseology centred round words such as ascendancy and, more obviously, stimulus. Such steps might well have prevented the critical debate over the redundancy of the gambler-preference map, from arising. Otherwise the connotations of the ascendancy/stimulus function and gambler-preference map are identical. Furthermore, if the stimulus function is judged by its literal meaning, as Shackle at times wishes it to be, then it can be appreciated why critics have indeed argued that the gambler-preference map is otiose; and net Φ values should be employed to rank investment choices. On occasions, as can be recalled from chapter 4 especially, Shackle maintained that the risk-preference, as he himself labelled it, of the investor can be given a different expression in the gambler-preference map from that implied in the ascendancy function. On the occasions when that is not so the gambler-preference map can be discarded; yet where it is so, it is doubtful whether the use of more direct, less ambivalent description of the function introduced to conflate the potential surprise function ultimately would have removed the doubts about a conflator function *per se* and hence about the seeming incongruity of the gambler-preference map.

In terms of the behaviour of our psyche – and perhaps to make it feasible for us to make the choices involved in everyday decision-making, of whatever kind and complexion – we do, and do need to, simplify the range of choices with which we are confronted. However, we can only speculate on that from introspection; we cannot make definitive statements. Indeed, it is likely that the depths of the human psyche will remain an arcanum. In any case, some of the simplification we engage in can be the result of economic and social constraints which have imposed costs on the patterns of information to check out the rightness of the choice before us. All of the simplification we would expect, *a priori*, cannot be ascribed to the need to simplify *per se* because of the limited capacity of the brain to store and process data. Be that as it may, we must remember that in the Shackle model the investor is assumed to have little difficulty in tracing out the pattern of returns, with concomitant degrees of potential surprise, for assets on investment strategies. Once he has done so, to use a conflator function (such as the ascendancy function) followed by use of a function (the gambler-preference function) that ranks the information provided by the conflator function, is to *discard information that the investor does have at his disposal.* To sift that information by means of an ascendancy function requires no less demanding a mental exercise than one which involves the investor's employing the whole of the potential surprise function.

The previous chapter showed how the Shackle ascendancy function cannot rule out instances where the *absolute preference axiom* is contravened. Likewise it was shown that even if the investment prospects facing the investor always rule out any conflict with that axiom, it is not sensible to argue that, when the ascendancy function is employed to select a focus-gain or focus-loss, those values can be *standardized.* In general such a procedure will entail the investor's expecting a return to materialize with zero potential surprise that he believes cannot be the case; indeed, he would be surprised if it did materialize. It is necessary, therefore, to employ the primary focus-values with their associated degrees of potential surprise to evaluate the investment strategy that should be adopted. In that event, the gambler-preference map as constituted in Professor Shackle's theory is deficient. I have demonstrated, however, that the required emendation of that map is not sufficient to improve the extent of asset-diversification that is feasible in the Shacklesque model.

As I have stressed, it is in a sense paradoxical that a theoretical apparatus which is designed to capture expectations and uncertainty in a more imaginative way (in both meanings of the word) and to do so explicitly, becomes one which to all intents and purposes is devoid of those vital and all-powerful ingredients. It is odd, too, that while it is maintained that the human psyche feels a compelling need to simplify choices, it is alleged to be able to formulate and utilize such a concept as the ascendancy function; and that when it does so it is only on a half-hearted basis; discarding and distorting the information which it has formulated itself.

THE GAMBLER-PREFERENCE MAP

It is apparent from the deliberations of the previous chapter that the concept and the role of the gambler-preference map has come under heavy and quite persistent attack as a direct consequence of the evaluation of the logically prior concept of the ascendancy function. I have already reiterated that point in the preceding summary of the position in regard to the ascendancy function.

Shackle's position again is unequivocal on the need to retain the gambler-preference map, but at times he is prepared to make concessions, as we have made clear, when the ascendancy function and the gambler-preference map are made conformable in their representation of the risk-aversion of the investor. In instances where they are not so conformable, Professor Shackle has insisted that the two pieces of his apparatus are both required, each playing its own role. On that basis he is not prepared to accept the notion, often advanced by his critics, that we can dispense with the gambler-preference map and use net Φ values to order investment strategies.

Despite the fact that I have not drawn attention to this point, it will not have passed unnoticed that the gambler-preference map almost hangs by its own bootstraps in the Shackle schema. What do I mean by such a bald statement? Simply this: in the traditional approach to the analysis of individual choice in economic theory, whether that choice concerns the selection of best consumption bundle under certainty, or of the best asset portfolio in an uncertain world, we start with the *a priori* hypothesis that the individual has a stated objective in view, such as the maximization of 'utility' or of expected 'utility'. In the Shackle theory the maximand is never stated explicitly and it is definitely not invoked at the outset of the unfolding of the new theoretical apparatus, as the *raison d'être* of that apparatus. This is reason enough for the role of uncertainty to be diminished, for expectational data to be ignored and for confusion to arise over the roles of the ascendancy function and the gambler preference map.

An explicit specification of an objective function for the individual investor who is endeavouring to discover the best asset portfolio or investment strategy, in an environment where uncertainty is characterized by potential surprise, would have preserved a key role for uncertainty besides leading to the conclusion that a conflator function is not required. Indeed, it might not even have been entertained as an idea.

This point is made simply because if it had been posited that the individual investor's objective was to maximize his utility through time, so that his concern from his portfolio was to supplement his earned income in the best possible manner, we would have found ourselves in a position wherein the investor's portfolio behaviour could have been the consequence of the maximization of a 'utility' function which was dependent upon the return on his portfolio. Thus for a given earned income his utility *in toto*, as a function of current and future consumption could, indeed, have been maximized.

That this standard, straightforward, way of examining asset choice can be stated and explored explicitly is given favour in Professor Shackle's own writings. Thus, in the case where there is no uncertainty about the prospect of returns on assets he has stated consistently that, quite obviously, à la Bernouilli,[1] the investor should choose the asset that promises the highest return; the need to balance return against 'belief in its occurrence' is not a relevant factor. 'Utility' is dependent upon return. Once uncertainty is assumed to be present the picture only alters in that for any specified allocation of wealth, across the available assets, there can exist, in the investor's opinion, numerous returns with associated measures of uncertainty surrounding their realizability. A procedure by which the set of uncertain prospects for any given portfolio can be encapsulated, in some kind of 'index', has to be stipulated.

In the standard approach to choice under uncertainty such a step is accomplished by an extension of the initial hypothesis that the investor is indeed assumed *a priori* to be concerned with maximizing an actual utility function which has as its argument the return on the portfolio/project or on his wealth. Then, for example, to a prescribed portfolio of assets there will be a utility level for each possible (total) return with an accompanying probability of occurrence. The investor's choice under uncertainty becomes one of evaluating for each portfolio, or investment strategy, the *set* of pairs of (utility–probability). *All* of the information on the configuration of expected outcomes on the portfolio or on the investment strategy is utilized. Such a situation, naturally, only arises because all of the information contained in the probability of outcomes on each asset that is a potential component of an optimum portfolio is also used by the investor.

Thus, in essence, the conflation of the set of outcomes that the investor formulates himself and attributes to each asset or investment project does not take place separately. It occurs as a natural implication of the need for the investor to map out the available set of utilities that seem to him, on the basis of his expectations, to be embodied in the various allocations of his wealth, or attainable from the purchase of each of the available types of capital investment. That conflation is not a necessary precursor of the choice of action.

In respect of the Shackle model to circumvent the criticisms which I and others have levelled at the ascendancy function and gambler-preference map, the obvious course to follow is to *convert* the ascendancy function into a choice function and hence rescind the gambler-preference map. The word 'convert' cannot be emphasized too strongly; for what we shall be propounding in the ensuing pages of this chapter does not amount to the same thing, and will not – except in purely fortuitous circumstances – lead to the same choice of portfolio or investment project, as that based on integrating the ascendancy function and the gambler-preference map by resort to a ranking of action-schemes by reference to their net Φ-values. At the moment this must be accepted as an *ex cathedra* statement, as it were; but it can be appreciated from the analysis and discussion of previous chapters that the evaluation of net Φ-values does depend upon maintaining the ascendancy function in exactly the form envisaged for it by Shackle.

Consider once more the first stage of Shackle's framework for choice under uncertainty. For any asset that could be held in a portfolio, or for any kind of investment project, the investor is alleged to be in a position where he can sketch out a series of feasible outcomes, per £1 invested on the asset if it is a financial asset (and the difference between net present value of returns and purchase price if it is an investment project), including a residual hypothesis about those outcomes, if he believes that there is the 'chance' that outcomes other than the set he has thought of could occur over the investment period (which we recall, is of unit length for portfolio choice in keeping with the predominant view in the literature and with Professor Shackle's own chosen time-scale; and, of course, for the economically useful length-of-life for a piece of capital equipment). Now, rather than seek to encapsulate those data into two elements, 'a best to be hoped for' and 'a worst to be feared', we should see the investor as taking all of the potential surprise functions and employing them to construct potential surprise functions for all feasible allocations of wealth; that is for all possible portfolios. It is those aggregate potential surprise functions over which he should be choosing: exactly as in the orthodox approach, with the difference, of course, that probability has been replaced by potential surprise. If the assets hold out the possibility that losses can be made, then if we retain the letter of the Shackle model there is an additional point of divergence from the orthodox approach in that the choice over aggregate potential surprise functions, namely over portfolios, has to be one which requires the investor to balance the gain, or positive returns, branch of any aggregate potential surprise function with its loss, or negative returns, branch. The orthodox approach to choice under uncertainty does, of course, accommodate situations where asset returns are negative: but where, in such cases, the expected return on an asset emerges as positive, there are clearly instances where the distribution of positive/negative returns on the asset are not captured adequately by the mean and the variance. They might only be captured by including some kind of measure of 'skew'.[2] However, the orthodox approach does not always reduce to one wherein the investor considers the mean and the variance of asset returns. As we know, which moments of the distribution are relevant, as the investor sees things, depends upon the form of the investor's utility function over actual returns or wealth and/or upon the nature of the probability distributions of returns themselves. If the utility function is quadratic then no matter what the distributions of asset returns happen to be, the investor will only concern himself with their means and variances. Provided he bases his choice of portfolio on the axioms defined in chapter 1, and maximizes the expected value of his utility in the prescribed conditions, he will be acting rationally. He will be choosing to ignore 'skew' because it is not relevant to his preference ordering. The implication of this is that he does not attach any weight to a situation where for a given portfolio there is only a low probability of high returns but a high probability of small losses; and vice-versa. In effect, he is not a 'strong' risk-averter. Shackle's investors are effectively of that type, since they accord negative gains/losses a separate role in the choice of action. For some investors they dominate the positive returns/gains, their relative role being determined by the weights attached to total standardized focus-losses and gains on the gambler-preference map.

Since we wish to keep as closely as possible to the basic tenets of the Shackle model, in addition to accepting the notion and measurement of potential surprise, we shall also accept the thesis that individual investors are strong risk-averters and attach separate weights to potential gains and losses before deciding on their optimum choice of action. The situation is then that the investor is alleged to form some index for a given portfolio that epitomizes the set of (positive returns/gains, potential surprise) with which he is faced, perhaps the same operation for (negative returns/losses, potential surprise) and weights the two indices to produce a sum index that will be used as the basis for selection of his investment strategy.

To permit such a process the ascendancy function has to be replaced by a preference ordering for the gain and loss branches of the potential surprise function for any allocation of the investor's wealth. The ascendancy function is not adequate for our purposes as a consequence of the fact that it is a conflator, telescoping or 'ϕocusing' mechanism for expectations. It is not necessarily consistent with the axiom of absolute preference, it discards information, and it attributes an increasing stimulatory effect of higher losses, for any specified degree of potential surprise.

To replace the ascendancy function by a proper preference ordering, and so obliterate those weaknesses of the function, it is necessary to axiomatize the ranking of potential surprise functions. In doing so we have two avenues open to us: the one is direct and quite straightforward, since it is predicated on a transformation of potential surprise into subjective probability – so permitting us to mirror the preference-ordering axioms of the orthodox model of action-choice under uncertainty. The other avenue is more difficult and requires us to use the non-additive potential surprise variable. Each of these will be considered in turn and I will investigate their implications, essentially once more for portfolio choice, particularly for the important matter of the permissible degree of asset-diversification that can exist in the portfolio of a rational investor. Note will also be taken of the implications for choice of investment strategy or project for fixed capital investment, as I have done *passim*, despite the fact that the issue and several other decision-making models will be discussed in chapter 6.

As reiterated in the previous paragraphs, as with the traditional approach to the axiomatic treatment of preference over probability distributions of returns, we must state the axioms over portfolio returns, since the choice is over those (total) prospects with their associated degree of uncertainty. Here, however, as just noted, to retain the letter of the first pillar of the Shackle model, we need to distinguish between total positive returns/gains, G, and total negative returns/losses, L. Then we may state, for G first of all:

Axiom 1
Out of a set of actual outcomes:

$$\text{either} \quad G_i \succsim G_j \quad \text{or} \quad G_j \succsim G_i, \quad \text{for all } i, j = 1, \ldots, n$$

Axiom 2
If $P_i \succsim P_j$ and $P_j \succsim P_k$ then $P_i \succsim P_k$, where P_i represents the *portfolio* choice:

$$P_i = [(G_1, W_1), (G_2, W_2), \ldots, (G_n, W_n)]$$

Axiom 3
If $G_1 \succ G_2 \succ G_3 \succ \ldots \succ G_n$, there exists some number U_i where $0 \leqslant U_i \leqslant 1$, for which:

$$G_i \sim [(G_1, U_i), (G_n, 1 - U_i)], \quad \text{for all } i = 1, \ldots, n.$$

Axiom 4
If $G_i \sim Q_i$ then $\lambda_1 \sim \lambda_2$ where:

$$\lambda_1 = [(G_1, W_1), (G_2, W_2), \ldots, (G_i, W_i), \ldots, (G_n, W_n)]$$

$$\lambda_2 = [(G_1, W_1), (G_2, W_2), \ldots, (Q_i, W_i), \ldots, (G_n, W_n)]$$

Axiom 5
If $G_i \succ G_j$ (via axiom 1) and if $P_1 = [(G_i, W_0), (G_j, 1 - W_0)]$ and $P_2 = [(G_i, W_1), (G_n, 1 - W_1)]$ then:

$$P_1 \succsim P_2 \quad \text{iff} \quad W_0 \geqslant W_1$$

Axiom 6
If $P_j = [(G_i, W_{ij}), i = 1, \ldots, n]$ for $j = 1, \ldots, m$, and if $\lambda_1 = [(P_j, \alpha_j), j = 1, \ldots, m]$ then:

$$\lambda_1 \sim \lambda_2 \quad \text{where } \lambda_2 = [(G_i, W_i), i = 1, \ldots, n]$$

$$\text{and} \quad W_i = \sum_{j=1}^{m} W_{ij}\alpha_j, \quad \text{for } i = 1, \ldots, n.$$

The corollary of axiom 5 (axiom 5(a) in chapter 1) is omitted explicitly but it *is* implied by axiom 5. Hence the existence of absolute preference is hypothesized.

W is 'subjective probability' and can be defined as the consequence of transforming potential surprise into W by a mapping such as that set out in chapter 4. It will be remembered that in the latter chapter I put forward the view, as an antidote to the use of such a process in the Shackle model, that psychologically the two concepts of potential surprise and subjective probability are intrinsically different. The point was made that these two concepts represent divergent means of quantifying uncertainty in that if an individual were to be asked to catalogue the degree of subjective probability he feels about the items in a set of feasible outcomes, he is likely to provide a list of answers that conflicts with that provided by the mathematical manipulation of the set of potential surprises he specifies for the outcomes. Being asked to state explicitly the two descriptions of uncertainty seems an entirely different matter. Added to this, of course, are the fundamental objections that Shackle has against the use of probability; especially that it emphasizes belief rather than dis-belief, doubt about outcomes, and that it is a distributional variable.

However, Professor Shackle has less inhibitions about the property of using subjective as opposed to objective probability. Indeed he has conceded on one occasion[3] that he has no quarrel with subjective probability except on the one point that it is a distributional variable, with its attendant limitations. We could then feel reasonably content about using subjective probability.

However, what is now being suggested is that once the potential surprise functions for portfolios or investment strategies have been drawn up those functions can be *translated into another code*. The scalar quantity degree of potential surprise, which has the range zero to $\bar{y}$, is merely represented by another scalar quantity, which has the boundary points zero and unity. When the time is ripe for the investment decision to be made, it is not an illegitimate procedure to translate the measure of uncertainty. At that time, indeed, we have advanced past the point at which the fundamental objection to the transformation of potential surprise into subjective probability is relevant. Even though conceptually that objection is valid, once the investor is satisfied about his potential surprise function for investment in assets, hence for various portfolios, or for investment strategies, no violation is done to the expectations complex set forth by the individual investor by translation of potential surprise into a subjective probability. (That is, he has convinced himself that it does contain all of the expectational elements germane to a particular investment, that there are new elements of information that he should take into account, so that if there are they could be incorporated into the scheme of things without their affecting the degree of potential surprise previously assigned to the already-imagined outcomes). Indeed, the argument is more forceful than that: it is that a mapping of potential surprise into *any* scalar quantity that preserves the properties of the potential surprise functions will be permissible. What we call the resulting quantity does not matter; we can choose to call it 'subjective probability'; but we need not; hence the insertion of the inverted commas. If we give the new code the range zero to unity then, of course, it becomes natural to think of it as a probability measure.

I must now comment on the loss branch of the potential surprise function. The axioms necessary here are identical to those specified in axioms 1–6 above, with the exception that loss/negative returns on the whole portfolio or investment strategy, L, replace G; also, in respect of axiom 3, for a risk-averter/loss-averter, the U_i will he higher for lower values of L_i, because increasing L will now be seen as being less preferable. Thus, in terms of axiom 1, $L_i \succ L_j$ will be the consequence of $L_i < L_j$. Unlike the ordering in the ascendancy function, the higher loss, *ceteris paribus*, is seen as less preferable.

All of the preceding observations lead us to a situation in which the investor can epitomize the two branches of the potential surprise function by the expected 'utility' they bring him. Thus, if there is no loss branch for a particular portfolio allocation of his wealth, the investor should – if he is acting rationally according to the stipulated axioms – regard the expected 'utility' from the gain branch of the potential surprise function ($E[U(G)]$) as epitomizing the (uncertain) prospect of return on that portfolio.

Because, in general, there is likely to exist a loss branch for any portfolio, the investor has to combine the two expected utilities. Since the utility of any certain loss is negative the combination would involve the addition of the two expected utilities, but this would, of course, effectively be the difference between them. We then define the following axiom as the axiom for combining, which produces the action choice index (ACI):

Axiom 7

$$\mathrm{ACI}_i = E[U_i(G_i)] + E[U_i(L_i)]; \quad i = P_i; \quad i = 1, \ldots, n$$

In axiom 7 ACI_i is defined with respect to portfolio i; as with all the axioms here and in chapter 1, of course, they could have been defined more generally with respect to 'a choice i with uncertain outcomes'. A concomitant axiom then is:

Axiom 8

$P_i \succ P_j$ iff $\mathrm{ACI}_i \geqslant \mathrm{ACI}_j$

For portfolio selection it would also be necessary to note that portfolio P_i might be preferred to portfolio P_j but P_i might not be selected because its ACI_i was not greater than the 'do-nothing' portfolio; namely, one in which all wealth is retained in the form of money balances. In a world of no inflation, *ceteris paribus*, the ACI of money balances would be zero.

Risk-aversion enters this Shacklesque model directly via the special attention attached to losses or negative returns. In that sense the model begins to take on a look similar to that advocated by Domar and Musgrave[4] of which I gave a detailed appraisal in chapter 4. The resemblance is only superficial, however. Strictly speaking their model is an attempt to introduce the notion that most investors perhaps have a tendency towards safety-first behaviour, and accordingly lay stress on the potential losses of an investment strategy as representing the risk they face, but it foundered on the representation of that kind of risk by the wider concept of the variance of return. The preference ordering over mean and 'risk' was not derived from an axiomatic treatment of investor behaviour; hence it was not based upon an 'expected utility' approach.

It does not follow automatically, however, that the translation of the Shackle model into a 'probability'-based model, using the axioms of rational behaviour of the orthodox framework, leads to the same choice of portfolio for an individual in a given set of circumstances as the use of that orthodox framework. However, crucially, it does follow that this Shacklesque model will produce situations wherein any individual holds a portfolio diversified over more than two assets.

The exact form of the utility functions of the individual over gain and loss is the key factor here, as we would expect. Thus suppose that these functions assume this form:

$$U(L) = \alpha L; \quad U(G) = \beta G: \quad \alpha < 0; \quad \beta > 0; \quad L > 0 \qquad (5.1)$$

Axioms 1–6 above for gains, and their equivalents for losses, have allowed us to rank the gain side of a portfolio i by $E[U(G_i)]$ and the loss side by $E[U(L_i)]$; whilst axiom 7 tells us that the choice of portfolio depends upon ACI_i, the sum of those two expected utilities. Hence from equation (5.1):

$$\text{ACI}_i = \beta E(G_i) + \alpha E(L_i); \quad i = 1, \ldots, n \tag{5.2}$$

for portfolio i, or project/strategy i as the case might be. From the arguments advanced in chapter 3, it follows that when all portfolios are compared, the one that is chosen will be one which contains at most two assets, except in the analogue of the special case discussed there where for, say, all assets, in a world where money can exist, they all possess the same ratio of $\bar{l}_j$ to $\bar{g}_j$. Here $\bar{l}_j$ is the expected value of loss per unit of investment in asset or project j; similarly, $\bar{g}_j$ is the expected gain per unit of investment in j. Thus, if r denotes the return per unit of investment in any asset:

$$\bar{l} = |E(r \mid r < 0)| \quad \text{and} \quad \bar{g} = E(r \mid r > 0)$$

In accordance with the analysis of chapter 1, however, if $U(L)$ or $U(G)$ (or both) happen to be second-degree polynomials in L and G, respectively, multi-asset portfolios will be feasible, because the investor's maximand (ACI) would be dependent upon the variances of per-unit losses and/or per-unit gains on the individual assets. However, the variances would not be the variance of the whole set of per-unit yields on the assets; because of this the portfolio chosen will not, in general, be identical with that selected, for given prospects of returns on the assets, by a Von Neumann–Morgenstern expected utility-maximizing investor. They will, of course, be exactly the same if the alternative assets promise only gains *and the mapping* of potential surprise into 'subjective probability' produces a probability density function for the unit returns on any asset which is equivalent to that utilized by the Von Neumann–Morgenstern type of investor. Additionally, in view of the fact that the Shacklesque model will be able to accommodate multi-asset diversification, it is also possible to incorporate the holding of money with a risky-asset bundle à la separation theorem of the orthodox probabilistic model.

The validity of these claims can be demonstrated by a simple example. Suppose for the sake of illustration that:

$$U(L) = \alpha L^2; \quad U(G) = \beta G: \quad \alpha = -1 \text{ and } \beta = 1 \tag{5.3}$$

The investor's aim is then to choose, in the case of portfolio selection, that collection of assets (a vector of x's) which given his wealth will maximize ACI. Remembering that since L is now a random variable with a 'probability density function' for any portfolio, $E(L^2)$ will equal the sum of the mean squared and the variance of L. Therefore the investor's aim is to:

$$\max_x \text{ ACI} = -\mu_L^2 - \sigma_L^2 + \mu_G \tag{5.4}$$

$$\text{S.T.} \quad \mu_L^2 = x'Bx \tag{5.5}$$

$$\sigma_L^2 = x'\Omega x \tag{5.6}$$

$$\mu_G = x'\bar{g} = \bar{g}'x \tag{5.7}$$

$$W = x'i = i'x \tag{5.8}$$

where $x' = [x_1 \ldots x_n]$;

$$B = \begin{vmatrix} \bar{l}_1^2 & \bar{l}_1\bar{l}_2 & \ldots & \bar{l}_1\bar{l}_n \\ \bar{l}_2\bar{l}_1 & \bar{l}_2^2 & \ldots & \\ \cdot & & & \\ \cdot & & & \\ \cdot & & & \\ \bar{l}_n\bar{l}_1 & & \ldots & \bar{l}_n^2 \end{vmatrix} \tag{5.9}$$

Ω is the variance–covariance matrix for the losses/negative returns per unit of investment in the available assets; we remind ourselves that $\bar{g}$ is the vector of expected gains/positive returns per unit of investment in the assets, and that the $\bar{l}_j$ denote the per-unit expected losses/negative returns on the assets; in equation (5.8) i is the unit column vector.

If we substitute equations (5.5)–(5.7) into equation (5.4), letting the Lagrangean expression be denoted by L and the Lagrange multiplier on wealth be denoted by λ we have these first-order conditions for that constrained maximization of L (assuming that an interior solution arises, that is $x \geqslant 0$):

$$\frac{\partial \text{L}}{\partial x} = -2(B + \Omega)x + \bar{g} - \lambda i = 0 \tag{5.10}$$

$$\frac{\partial \text{L}}{\partial \lambda} = W - i'x \qquad = 0 \tag{5.11}$$

Thus

$$\begin{pmatrix} x \\ \lambda \end{pmatrix} = \begin{pmatrix} -2(B + \Omega) & -i \\ -i' & 0 \end{pmatrix}^{-1} \begin{pmatrix} -\bar{g} \\ W \end{pmatrix} \tag{5.12}$$

In principle, then, a multi-valued vector of x is feasible; only if $2(B + \Omega)$ is a null-matrix will it be impossible to invert the matrix in equation (5.12). In that instance all aspects of the gain/loss characteristics of all assets, or investment strategies, are identical at zero, and so the choice of portfolio or strategy becomes an empty one. There then exist an infinite number of solutions such that the investor can invest all of his wealth in any asset or any combination of assets, with the same result; and can adopt a 'do-nothing strategy' of holding all of his wealth in money, if he anticipates that there will be zero inflation over his investment period.

The inversion of the matrix in equation (5.12) produces equations which are identical intrinsically with those deduced for the orthodox approach in chapter 1. This is because the only difference now is that the matrix $B + \Omega$ replaces the variance–covariance of returns for assets across all states of nature, thus assimilating the consideration of losses with those of gains. There the Ω was defined, in the usual way, throughout, to embrace the whole gamut of returns per unit of investment in assets. Here, however, B is symmetric, despite the fact that it is not a variance–covariance matrix, whilst Ω is a variance–covariance matrix: thus $B + \Omega$ is symmetric. The asset demand equations are, in effect, as follows:[5]

$$x = \{2^{-1}(B+\Omega)^{-1}[I + i(i'2^{-1}(B+\Omega)^{-1}i)^{-1}i'2^{-1}(B+\Omega)^{-1}]\}\bar{g} \\ - \{2^{-1}(B+\Omega)^{-1}i[i'2^{-1}(B+\Omega)^{-1}i]^{-1}\}W \tag{5.13}$$

As in chapter 1 it is a straightforward matter to demonstrate that the matrix of coefficients on the vector on $\bar{g}$ has column sums of zero, so satisfying the Cournot aggregation condition as it must; also it is a symmetric matrix as in the orthodox model. Likewise, the column vector on W has a sum of unity, so that the Engel aggregation condition is fulfilled, as it too must be.

It is noted in equation (5.13) that the matrix on the x vector is $(B + \Omega)^{-1}$. In deriving the optimal investment frontier for the individual investor we do, in fact, assume that his objective is:

$$\min_{x}: \quad x'(B+\Omega)x \tag{5.14}$$

subject to a prescribed level of μ_G and W; with all variables defined as previously. The x vector is selected so that the dis-utility elements $(B + \Omega)$ are minimized for given values of the mean value of gain and the level of investable resources. The investment frontier is then obtained by the same procedure as noted in chapter

1 and outlined in appendix A. It is:

$$\begin{vmatrix} (\mu_L^2 + \sigma_L^2) & \mu_G & W \\ \mu_G & (\bar{g}'[B+\Omega]^{-1}\bar{g}) & (i'[B+\Omega]^{-1}\bar{g}) \\ W & (\bar{g}'[B+\Omega]^{-1}i) & (i'[B+\Omega]^{-1}i) \end{vmatrix} = 0 \quad (5.15)$$

Furthermore, following the method outlined in appendix B, a riskless asset such as money can be introduced as a possible item in this Shacklesque investor's portfolio; and the optimal trading frontier over money and a bundle of risky assets can be discovered. Thereafter, it can be appreciated that the separation theorem summarized in chapter 1 also holds in the current model, so that there is no need to provide a formal proof.

In general, as maintained, the Shacklesque and the orthodox models will not produce identical portfolios or strategies; even under the assumptions that the probability density functions of asset or strategy outcomes are the same in both cases. Thus, to take a special example that facilitates a comparison between the two models, assume that in the Shacklesque model:

$$U(L) = -L^2; \quad U(G) = G^2 \qquad (5.16)$$

and in the orthodox model:

$$U(R) = R^2 \qquad (5.17)$$

(where, of course, $U''(R) > 0$; so we have a constrained example). Upon forming ACI from equation (5.16) and $E[U(R)]$ from equation (5.17) we see that ACI and $E[U(R)]$ can only be identical for a *given* x-vector if:

$$\mu_R^2 = (\mu_G^2 - \mu_L^2); \quad \sigma_R^2 = (\sigma_G^2 - \sigma_L^2) \qquad (5.18)$$

These relationships cannot hold; and even if we had required $\sigma_R^2 = (\sigma_G^2 + \sigma_L^2)$, for example, this too would have been impossible, *ex definitione*.

The preceding analysis has been developed from a set of axioms that are identical with those which form the basis of the orthodox approach to action-schemes under 'uncertainty'. Those axioms permit us to invoke the Von Neumann–Morgenstern expected utility criterion by which the investor can order strategies. The central features of those axioms, and hence of the theorem itself, is that, *ex hypothesi*, they exclude situations wherein the investor's choice of investment strategy contravenes the absolute preference concept whose importance was emphasized in chapter 4. As an integral part of that acknowledgement of the role of absolute preference, we then have a situation wherein the investor is not casting on one side information – vital information – on the expectational vista of an investment strategy that he has taken the time, effort and trouble himself to compose. The preceding framework has also removed some of the other inconsistencies for which others, and I also, have felt the Shackle schema has suffered.

It cannot be gainsaid, of course, that my framework has brought the Shackle schema to close proximity with that favoured by the orthodox school. In the final analysis there remains only one difference of substance between my framework and the orthodox approach. That is, that I have accepted that Shackle seems to have common sense on his side when he argues that an investor, in seeking to obtain for himself an expectation of the promise of return on an investment strategy, will not average out all the feasible positive and negative returns, or gains and losses. He will keep the positive and negative returns separate from each other and will pay attention to both sets of figures. Potential surprise also still remains in the background; although it could be argued that I have only given it token recognition. However, I have accepted the points made in chapter 4 that if the investor is asked to map out his expectations of prospects on an asset by means of (subjective) probability, he is really being asked to engage in a different activity from one wherein he is asked to portray the information by means of degrees of potential surprise. Once that information has been provided in terms of potential surprise, however, it is legitimate to translate it into another yardstick such as subjective probability.

Nevertheless, it is incumbent upon me to offer some comments on the situation where potential surprise is used explicitly and not translated into 'subjective probability'. Essentially, the axioms listed earlier on in this chapter have to stand, because the foundation of that argument for amending the Shackle schema is that it does not utilize all of the information contained in the potential surprise function and, as a consequence, has to introduce an action-choice selector, in the form of the gambler-preference map which can, at best, be regarded as 'double-counting' on the risk side, but which is likely to be misleading, introducing irrational choices.

To utilize potential surprise as the uncertainty parameter in the combination of the 'indices' derived to encapsulate the gains and the losses on action schemes, however, it is necessary to convert the scale of degrees of potential surprise into one which covers the range of unity (for zero potential surprise, or perfectly possible outcomes) to zero (for those outcomes assigned the maximum degree of potential surprise). This is so because otherwise it is impossible to construct a meaningful version of the continuity axiom (axiom 3 above); it is therefore impossible to state the equivalent of the expected utility theorem, since it cannot be deduced from the set of axioms unless we can detail the axiom of continuity as we have done in axiom 3. The 'weights' that will render a choice of either the best or the worst outcome just equivalent to (that is just indifferent to) any specified outcome have to do so with zero potential in sum; it *represents* the *certainty equivalent*. The requisite transformation of potential surprise can be accomplished quite readily. Such a transformation leaves the essential concept of potential surprise untouched; it preserves its ranking for any investment and it is *not* a probability measure. That transformation is one wherein each degree of potential surprise, y_i, is given a place on a scale equal to $(\bar{y} - y_i)/\bar{y}$. Therefore, all outcomes with zero potential surprise are assigned a value of unity – the maximum value of the scale; and any outcome that would bring forth the maximum degree of potential surprise if it did, in fact, occur, would be set at zero on the scale.

Then, for the gains/positive returns on any specified portfolio, or investment strategy, we can simply invoke the axioms stated previously with the axiom of continuity now being:

Axiom 3(a)

If $G_1 \succ G_2 \succ G_3 \succ \ldots \succ G_n$, there exists some Z_i where $0 \leqslant Z_i \leqslant 1$, for which:

$$G_i \sim [(G_1, Z_i), (G_n, 1 - Z_i)], \text{ for all } i = 1, \ldots, n.$$

It is then possible to define, as was done following Von Neumann and Morgenstern in chapter 1 and implicitly in the preceding discussion in this chapter:

$$U(P) = \sum_{i=1}^{n} \left(\frac{\bar{y} - y_i}{\bar{y}} \right) Z_i = I \qquad (5.19)$$

where P denotes a portfolio, investment strategy, or in general an 'action-choice', available to the investor. Accordingly, in parallel with the expected utility theorem, the investor's behaviour can be described as one whereby, for his given wealth, he chooses that portfolio or investment strategy which maximizes the value of I, the level of his 'utility'. The investor will then only select a portfolio i in preference to a portfolio j if $U(P_i) > U(P_j)$, and this itself can only occur if $P_i \succ P_j$. Those two elements of the expected utility theorem hold with respect to I, given the axioms 1–6 stated earlier, with axiom 3 replaced by axiom 3(a).

Let $y_1 = 0$ in equation (5.19), with $y_j = 0$ for all $j \neq 1$. Axiom 3(a) is predicated on the supposition that the potential surprise attached to G_1 is zero; that is, it is unity on our scale. Thus the investor is given the perfectly possible choice of $G_i = G_1$ alone; there is no other choice available to him. Hence:

$$U(P_1) = U(G_1) = Z_1 \tag{5.20}$$

So the Z_i's in axiom 3(a) denote an index of 'utility' for any outcome, viewed as perfectly possible. Therefore, for any portfolio:

$$P_1 = [(G_1, y_1), (G_2, y_2), \ldots (G_n, y_n)] \tag{5.21}$$

$$U(P_1) = \sum_{i=1}^{n} \left(\frac{\bar{y} - y_i}{\bar{y}}\right) U(G_i) \tag{5.22}$$

A similar process defines the means by which the loss/negative returns branch of the potential surprise function for any portfolio can be conflated into an index summarizing its characteristics. Thereafter, $U(P)$ for G and L are summed to form ACI for any portfolio or investment strategy, and the portfolio that offers the highest value of ACI for given wealth is selected.

In essence, this second variant of the Shacklesque model will produce the same choice of action as the first variant since the weights $(\bar{y} - y_i)/\bar{y}$, say Π_i, in this second variant are related directly to those of the first variant $W_i = (\bar{y} - y_i)/\Sigma(\bar{y} - y_i)$

$$\Pi_i = W_i \sum_i \left(\frac{\bar{y} - y_i}{\bar{y}}\right) = \theta W_i \tag{5.23}$$

where $\theta = \Sigma_i(\bar{y} - y_i)/\bar{y}$ which is a constant.

I have ventured to call the models discussed in this chapter Shacklesque models. Perhaps only the model built on use of potential surprise should be so called. Shackle would no doubt wish to expunge all reference to his type of model. Aside from the fact that we have dispensed with the ascendancy function and the gambler-preference map, his major objection would hinge around the pivotal point of his theory, namely potential surprise. That concept was introduced because it was a non-additive, non-distributional variable, unlike its counterpart in probability. The claim was that it was not sensible to epitomize the prospects on an available investment by a weighted average of the outcomes it promised, since those outcomes are *mutually exclusive*, and hence are *rivals*. The ascendancy function in association with the potential surprise function for any asset or investment was to produce gain/loss elements that epitomized the prospects of returns. The effect of gain, or loss, elements on a potential surprise function were not to be viewed as additive:

> Hopes which are mutually exclusive are not additive; fears which are mutually exclusive are not additive. In each case the greatest prevails, and alone determines the power of the attractive or of the deterrent component of the venture's 'dual personality'. In this last sentence, the word 'greatest' is insufficiently precise. . . . What we mean is the *most powerful element* amongst them.[6]

The Von Neumann–Morgenstern axiomatic framework provides a rigorous justification of the weighted averaging of outcomes in a probabilistic environment, through the expected utility theorem. In that way rational behaviour can be explained with respect to choice over probability distribution (portfolios, investment strategies); and that choice must depend upon weighted averages of outcomes, irrespective of the investor's utility function over returns. For any possible portfolio, or investment strategy, there will be a range of feasible outcomes, in general; all with different probabilities of occurrence. They are mutually exclusive; but for rational behaviour they must be combined. If all information at the disposal of the individual is to be utilized then there is no escaping the fact that an index has to be found through which the quintessence of an action-scheme can be portrayed. Since irrational and contradictory behaviour could occur under the application of the Shackle ascendancy function and gambler-preference map, the roles that they are designed to fill must be covered by one umbrella. The piece of apparatus so devised with the express purpose of using all of the investor's information must be capable of scanning that information and encapsulating it in some index or measure of one kind or another. Hence, the kind of axiomatic approach adopted here, borrowed and developed from that of Von Neumann and Morgenstern, must replace the ascendancy function and the gambler-preference map in Shackle's schema.[7]

6

Uncertainty and Choice: A Wider Perspective

In the preceding discussions the portfolio selection problem has been largely used as the focal point. Reference has been made, *en passant* – when it seemed apposite so to do, to the choice under uncertainty of the optimal project or strategy in regard to fixed capital investment in machinery or 'plant'. In this chapter attention is turned on to an explicit, but necessarily brief, analysis of that issue. To widen our canvas even further, as we mentioned in the introduction, consideration will be given to four other decision-making models that have figured, in one form or another, in the literature and which to date have been analysed by means of the probability calculus. Those models are as follows: a two-period consumption–saving model; a consumer search model; a labour choice model; and an output choice model for an entrepreneur under price uncertainty in a perfectly competitive world. As will be mentioned in the relevant notes, these four models have been covered extensively in the literature. No attempt will be made to survey that literature, and I shall present only sufficient material on each of them to indicate the essence of the method of solution using the probability calculus or the expected utility theorem. The object is essentially to see if the Shackle and/or the Shacklesque model might be able to handle those problems and how it/they would do so. I shall consider investment in real capital first of all, and then proceed to take the four models in the order listed.

INVESTMENT IN REAL CAPITAL

The analysis of choice of investment strategy in the context of Shackle's theory is, indeed, virtually identical to that for choice of financial investment. The outcomes with which the investor is alleged to be concerned are the excess of discounted present value over purchase/construction cost for a piece of machinery/'plant'. Where there is positive excess Shackle refers to this as 'gain', and in the case of negative excess this is simply labelled 'loss'. The investor is assumed to be able to gauge the useful length of life of any piece of capital, and to form expectations of the value of net returns for each of the years, or 'periods', over its life. To each of these he attaches a degree of potential surprise; and he divides the potential surprise function into its two branches.

For each piece of capital equipment or plant there will be, in the usual way, standardized focus-values. Utilizing these focus-values for any item of capital equipment the entrepreneur is assumed to determine not only which capital item he should purchase, but how many; or for a plant, which and what scale of plant should be installed. The opportunities that present themselves to the entrepreneur, such as varying the number of items of equipment or the size of plant, are epitomized in the *scale opportunity line*; this is the counterpart to the efficient investment frontier for asset choice.

How is that line determined? It is necessary, in effect, to make several assumptions concerning the economic environment in three markets; namely: the market for the ancillary factors of production that are needed to operate the machinery or the plant at any scale of activity; the market for the product the entrepreneur is to manufacture with the to-be-newly-acquired capital; and the market for the capital equipment itself.

Let us imagine that each of those three markets is organized on a perfectly competitive basis. In that case it will follow logically that no matter what quantities of machinery, or what size of 'plant', the entrepreneur purchases, the scale opportunity line must indeed be a line; it is linear over standardized focus-values. It will be such that purchasing two machines, say, or doubling the size of plant – as the case might be, will double the standardized focus-values applying to one unit.

This result emerges because all the three variables that influence the 'returns to scale' are assumed to be given to the entrepreneur, and hence are independent of his actions in the product and factor markets (which affect his net return for every period of life of the capital equipment) and in the market for the equipment (which determines its supply price or cost). If we are thinking of investment in a plant rather than in just a machine, then we also require that there are no economies of large-scale production in order to arrive at a linear scale opportunity curve for 'a' plant. Naturally, such economies must be absent if perfect competition *per se* is to remain a viable market form in the long run. Should an entrepreneur be producing in an imperfectly competitive market, or hiring factors in such a market, it is feasible for the scale opportunity line to assume any shape in focus-gain focus-loss space; but Shackle surmises that it will assume the form of the segment BC on figure 6.1, where the segment *OB* is for an entrepreneur operating exclusively in perfectly competitive markets.[1] Should the curve *OBC* be the scale opportunity line for the entrepreneur he will select a scale of plant, or that quantity of machines, consistent with the focus-values at point *A*, where he has attained the highest possible investment-indifference (gambler-preference) curve. If it happens to be the case that the entrepreneur is operating in perfectly competitive markets no matter what type of capital equipment he decides to purchase, it will follow that the type he eventually chooses to buy must be the one that provides him with the promise of the best pair of focus-values from investment in a single machine. Scaling up the focus-values characteristics of the machines cannot influence the decision as to which make of machine the entrepreneur should purchase.

The scale of operations he does decide to select will depend directly upon the resources at his disposal for the purpose of investment, naturally; it will also depend indirectly on those resources since, as Shackle has suggested, they might be a strong influence on his preference ordering over focus-values. In contradistinction to the portfolio choice model, the level of *wealth* does not explicitly enter the analysis (or need not do so) nor does it, or the level of resources, appear as a quantity that has to be allocated

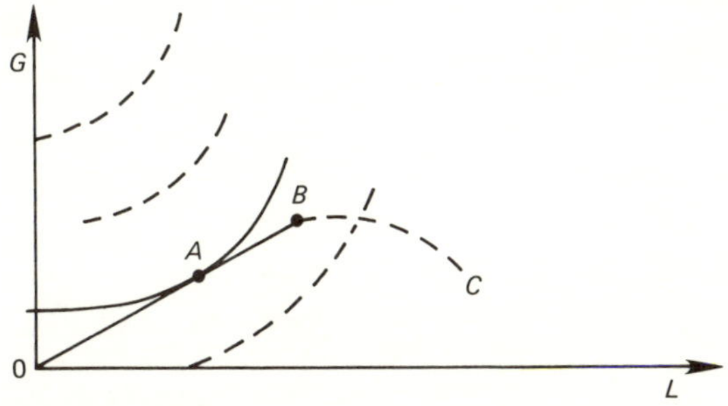

Figure 6.1 *The Shackle scale opportunity line for investment in plant and machinery*

optimally across perhaps a range of items of real capital rather than spent totally on just one such item. However, as noted in the Introduction, it is possible to extend the Shackle paradigm to encompass the possibility of diversification across equipment, but especially over plants in different industries. Since that exercise is extrinsic to our requirements in this book, however, I shall leave the matter here, content with such a bald statement.

Two further points are important. The first is that in respect of the decision to invest in real capital, Shackle does not state explicitly what the entrepreneur's objective function is.[2] The implication is that it can also be formalized in a way identical to that for the individual-cum-financial investor. The second is that in his critique of the probability calculus approach to analysing the real capital investment decision Shackle referred, predominantly, to work which had assumed that the entrepreneur was solely concerned with the maximization of expected returns (or expected value of the difference between discounted net returns over the life of the asset and its supply price).

All of the arguments set out in chapter 2, that Shackle levelled against the applications of the probability calculus, were advanced by him against the background of a standard model which assumed that the entrepreneur was motivated by the desire to maximize the expected value of return. Most of the rebuttals of Shackle's arguments against the use of the probability calculus, naturally, also had to invoke that objective.[3] Yet it might well be argued that such a Bernouillian decision criterion[4] is of limited value and naturally implies risk-neutrality on behalf of the entrepreneur. Nevertheless it can be hypothesized that the entrepreneur possesses a utility function over profit (in the discounted net return sense being employed here) and that, in line with the axiomatic approach of Von Neumann–Morgenstern, in order to make a rational investment decision he maximizes the expected value of his utility function. The probability calculus is then even more firmly an entrenched part of his choice process if his utility function is not linear over return. Naturally, Shackle's arguments against the orthodox dogma still stand.

The consideration of the appropriate kind and extent of investment in real capital that should be entered into by an individual, *per* entrepreneur, is almost identical then to the evaluation of the optimal financial investment the individual should undertake across available assets. The three pillars of the Shackle schema are required.

The critique of the apodictic probabilistic approach retains its prominent place, and for exactly the same reasons as we advanced in discussing asset choice. The difference between the analyses of the two types of investment decisions lie in the way that Shackle himself has chosen to portray the real capital investment decision, in that the role of wealth and the possibility of diversification are pushed into the background, or in the latter instance relegated from consideration. Nevertheless, that divergence can be rescinded if required.

Within its own boundaries, however, the Shackle analysis of the real investment decision will produce very different answers from the standard dogma. This is because in the latter it is largely assumed, as noted previously, that the entrepreneur is preoccupied with the expected value of profit his possible (the to-be-ranked) investments promise him. Even if we were to assert that degrees of potential surprise could be mapped adequately into subjective probability (using say the Krelle-mapping adopted in chapters 4 and 5) utilization of the remainder of the Shackle paradigm will imply that the investor is unlikely, except fortuitously, or in instances where all items of equipment offer no losses (in the sense used here), to select the same piece of capital as the best in which to invest as he would do under the orthodox schema. This result arises, naturally, from the fact that the Shacklesque investor has a special abhorrence for loss ('risk') and so he permits the gains and losses from any feasible investment to have individual impacts upon him. Their effects are not combined as in the orthodox analysis. Again, for example, as in the case of asset choice, if we axiomatize the Shackle model (with or without potential surprise being transferred into subjective probability) we shall not produce the same outcome of the investment decision as that provided by the probabilistic approach – except in special, limiting, situations.

A TWO-PERIOD CONSUMPTION-SAVING MODEL

Out of the many available models we shall utilize the following simple version.[5] An individual possesses a utility (U) function which depends upon his consumption (C) in the current period, C_1, and in the next period, C_2. In period 1 the individual's income consists solely of earned income, Y_1. In period 2 his income will be equal to his earned income, Y_2, plus the yield (r) on his saving undertaken in period 1, S_1. He is assumed to spend all of his income in period 2, hence:

$$C_2 = Y_2 + (Y_1 - C_1)r \qquad (6.1)$$

Now if Y_1, Y_2 and r are all certain, the solution for the level of C_1 that maximizes U is easily obtained.

Assume now that Y_1 and Y_2 are certain but that r is random, with a known probability density function, $f(r)$. Then the conventional solution to the choice of C_1 is that the individual is assumed to maximize the expected value of utility subject to (6.1). Thus:

$$E[U(C_1, C_1)] = \int_a^b U(C_1, Y_2 + (Y_1 - C_1)r)f(r)dr \qquad (6.2)$$

where a to b is the range of the yield on saving. Writing U_i for $(\partial U)/(\partial C_i)$ the first-order condition for a maximum of $E(U)$ with respect to C_1 is:[6]

$$E(U_1 - rU_2) = 0 \qquad (6.3)$$

Implicit differentiation of (6.3) would permit us to evaluate the effect of changes in the budget constraint, including, therefore, an alteration in $E(r)$, on current consumption and saving; but without specifying the exact form of the U-function it would not be possible to sign the partial derivatives $(\partial C_1)/(\partial Y_1)$, . . . Therefore, to avoid a protracted and fruitless exercise, I shall posit straight away the form of the U-function. To be specific, for the sake of illustration then, let:

$$U = C_1^2 C_2 \qquad (6.4)$$

The first-order condition for the maximization of $E(U)$ becomes:

$$2Y_2 + 2Y_1 E(r) - 3C_1 E(r) = 0 \qquad (6.5)$$

$$\therefore \quad C_1 = \frac{2(Y_2 + Y_1\bar{r})}{3\bar{r}} \qquad (6.6)$$

where $\bar{r} = E(r)$; and at the value of C_1 given by (6.6) the second-order condition for a maximum of U obtains, so that C_1 is optimal.[7] From (6.6) we could deduce the effects of changes on income prospects on C_1, S_1 and hence upon C_2; thus, given the form of the U-function we have chosen, we obtain what we might expect to be sensible *a priori* results since:

$$\frac{\partial C_1}{\partial Y_1} > 0; \quad \frac{\partial C_1}{\partial \bar{r}} < 0 \tag{6.7}$$

A *ceteris paribus* increase in current income, at constant opportunity cost of future in terms of current consumption, induces our individual consumer or household to spend some of the increased income on increasing current purchases, since those increased purchases will not reduce future consumption ($\partial C_1/\partial Y_1$ is less than unity).

A *ceteris paribus* increase in the expected yield on saving is seen to reduce current consumption. The substitution effect of the increase has clearly dominated the 'income effect'. An increase in $\bar{r}$, naturally, increases the cost of a unit of C_1 in terms of (forgone) units of C_2. However, to obtain a given level of C_2 it is now not necessary to save as much in period 1 as hitherto; but this 'income effect' is outweighed for our consumer by the substitution effect, and he switches some of his current consumption into saving and, implicitly, into future consumption.

The question now is: would the Shackle schema be able to analyse this simple extension of the Fisherian model? If so, how? Since the model is fundamentally a Fisherian one we may assume that r is the yield on capital-safe investment; so that r is a rate of interest and can be (ignoring inflation) assumed to be positive, although it is uncertain. This assumption makes it easier to see how we might apply the Shackle model to the choice of C_1. The probability density function of r would now be replaced by a 'gain' branch of a potential surprise function. Again, the choice of C_1, and hence of S_1, has to be made before the realization of r in the second period. Since in Shackle's own model there is no role for the expected utility methodology we have to offer a heuristic suggestion as to how such a model would specify the maximand of the consumer.

For this specific analysis the only logical suggestion seems to be that the consumer should seek to maximize the utility he believes he would have from the available range of current consumption. The only unknown is the yield on saving. The 'likely' value of C_2, as the consumer sees things at the present, depends (for any given C_1 and Y_2) upon the 'likely' level of r on S_1. In Shackle's schema that level of r would be provided by the standardized focus-gain (focus-positive return) on saving, rather than by $E(r)$. Let that focus-value be denoted by g. Then applying the Shackle paradigm we would say that the consumer will:

$$\max_{C_1} \quad U = U(C_1, C_2) \tag{6.8}$$

$$\text{S.T.} \quad C_2 = Y_2 + (Y_1 - C_1)g \tag{6.9}$$

Given g, the consumer chooses that value of C_1 that would maximize his U-curve if the *yield on S_1 that did materialize happened to be g*. Such a focus-value would, as shown earlier, occasion zero degree of potential surprise for the consumer. If we assume that the exact form of the U-function is that contained in equation (6.4) the optimal level of C_1 can be discovered and it is similar to that obtained from expected utility approach, namely:

$$C_1 = \frac{2(Y_2 + Y_1 g)}{3g} \tag{6.10}$$

Again we see that if the anticipated opportunity cost of C_1 rises because there is an increase in g, C_1 will be reduced.

It is possible, naturally, for g to turn out equal to $\bar{r}$, in which case two individuals with the same U-function would select – optimally – the same level of current consumption and saving; but the seeming similarity between the expected utility and the Shackle approaches here arises because of the specific form of the U-function used. Consequently only the mean value of the yield affects C_1 in the expected utility framework.

Suppose I postulate that:

$$U = C_1^{\frac{1}{2}} + C_2^{\frac{1}{2}} \tag{6.11}$$

which is a simple additive separable function in C_1 and C_2 with $C_1^{\frac{1}{2}}$ being used rather than, say, C_1 to simplify the results obtained from using equation (6.11).

The expected utility model leads to this optimal value of C_1:

$$C_1 = \frac{Y_2 \bar{r} + Y_1 E(r^2)}{1 + E(r^2)} \tag{6.12}$$

From the Shackle model we generate this outcome:

$$C_1 = \frac{Y_2 g + Y_1 g^2}{1 + g^2} \tag{6.13}$$

which is identical with (6.12) iff $\sigma_r^2 = 0$ and $\bar{r} = \bar{g}$.

Let us now consider the implications of tackling the consumption-saving decision by means of the Shacklesque models developed in chapter 5. The first such model, recall, was one based on the transformation of potential surprise into a 'subjective probability' measure; at least into a series of weights which summed to unity. In the current circumstances we have assumed that the uncertain r only has positive outcomes. It follows, therefore, that applications of this version of the Shacklesque models to the choice of optimal current consumption-saving will be similar to that obtained from use of the orthodox approach. The individual will seek to maximize $E(U)$ in order to act rationally, given the choice of 'probability' distributions in C_2 available to him for given '$f(r)$' and as he allows C_1 to vary. Of course, for any given U-function and $f(r)$ no two individuals will select the same C_1 unless $f(r)$ happens to coincide exactly with the 'probability density function' for r derived from the transformation of potential surprise.

The second version of the Shacklesque model presented in chapter 5 was based upon the translation of potential surprise into an index. In that version of the model the individual would like to maximize $U = U(C_1, C_2)$, but he is confronted by a 'distribution' for C_2 for any given C_1 which is conditioned by the transformed potential surprise function for r, which produces the set of weights $(\bar{y} - y_i/\bar{y})$. Choosing over those distributions and their concomitant C_1, the individual, to act rationally, must maximize the value of the index I:

$$I = \sum_{i=1}^{n} \left(\frac{\bar{y} - y_i}{\bar{y}}\right) U(C_1, C_2) = \sum_{i=1}^{n} \lambda_i U(C_1, C_2) \qquad (6.14)$$

as can be recalled from chapter 5 (but from which I have changed the notation for the weights since later W represents the wage rate). Suppose that $U(.)$ assumes the form given in equation (6.4), then it can be deduced from (6.14) that:

$$C_1 = \frac{2\Sigma\lambda_i Y_2 + 2Y_1\hat{r}}{3\hat{r}} \qquad (6.15)$$

where: $\hat{r} = \Sigma\lambda_i\hat{r}_i$. The equivalent expression to this for the orthodox approach is provided by equation (6.6). These expressions are not as similar as they might seem at first sight: $\hat{r}$ will in general not coincide with $\bar{r}$, not just for the reason advanced for differences that could emerge between the first Shacklesque model and that of the orthodox approach, but also because the sum of the weights $(\Sigma\lambda_i)$ do not sum to unity in the second version of the Shacklesque model. Additionally, although Y_2 is known with certainty, it must be weighted by $\Sigma\lambda_i$ for a consistent rational choice to be made in this model. In the orthodox approach and in the first Shacklesque model Y_2 appears alone, since the sum of the weights does equal unity; but the weights on the r_i and their sum $(\Sigma\lambda_i)$ implicitly reflect the fact that known elements in the U-function have also to be weighted, if a rational choice over 'distribution' of the U's is to be made.

The result portrayed in equation (6.15), however, is exactly the same as that obtained by means of the first variant of the Shacklesque model. This is because, as pointed out in chapter 5, the λ_i are simple functions of the W_i, the 'subjective probability' weights. Thus in the first version of the Shacklesque model the y_i are transformed such that:

$$W_i = \frac{\bar{y} - y_i}{\Sigma(\bar{y} - y_i)} \tag{6.16}$$

Hence, from equation (6.14):

$$\lambda_i = W_i \left[\frac{\Sigma(\bar{y} - y_i)}{\bar{y}} \right] = (\theta) W_i \tag{6.16a}$$

where θ is a constant. Substitution of (6.16a) for λ_i in equation (6.15) reduces that equation to the same format as that given in equation (6.6), where now $\bar{r}$ is to be taken as the expected value of return on saving derived from the transformation of the potential surprise function for r into a 'probability distribution', rather than the expected value of an objective probability density function.

A CONSUMER SEARCH MODEL

In the certainty model of consumer theory it is assumed that the individual has full and accurate information about the variables that affect his purchases of commodities, his sale of his labour services, and hence those that affect his level of utility. Here it is assumed that the individual consumer is indeed certain about all relevant variables except for the prices of the goods he is consuming; and it is assumed further that the consumer is uncertain about the price he will be charged for one type of product. At a cost (by telephoning or by personal visits to various shops) the consumer can gather information about the actual prices being charged. Since the gains from information-gathering are not without cost there must exist an optimal amount of information that should be gathered, or an optimal amount of search-activity that should be undertaken.

Beginning with the seminal paper by Stigler in 1961, on the optimal number of shops an individual should sample, there has grown-up an extensive literature on this consumer search problem which has been extended into search for jobs in the labour market.[8] As indicated already, the object is not to survey that literature, since only an illustrative example of it, based on the probabilistic approach to action-choice, is required.

The example I shall take, since it is the least complex, is that of sequential searching.[9] Thus, suppose that the consumer has been sampling the price (p) charged for the product in a number of shops and he knows the probability density function of the price, $f(p)$, the lowest price he has encountered to date being LP. Assume also that at any stage of the sampling process he is at liberty to choose to buy the product from any shop so far sampled. Thus, in technical language, he can search with recall. The individual is now confronted by this choice: (a) should he stop searching at LP, or (b) should he undertake to sample one more shop and *thereafter* purchase at the lowest price he has found?

The cost involved in (a), C_a, is a known cost equal to the product price at that moment, namely LP. Thus:

$$E(C_a) = LP \tag{6.17}$$

In regard to option (b) the individual must incur a search cost, say c. The latter we may assume is known. However, the total cost of option (b) includes the price that he will have to pay for the product after one more sample. Hence the cost of option (b) is an anticipated cost and, using the probability calculus, will be:

$$E(C_b) = c + LP(1 - F(LP)) + \int_M^{LP} pf(p)dp \tag{6.18}$$

Here, as defined previously, $f(p)$ is the probability density function of p; $F(p)$ is the distribution function of p. Thus $F(LP)$ is the probability that LP will remain the lowest price even after one more search. The third term on the right-hand side of equation (6.18) is the expected price after the next search, given the price after the next search is lower than $LP(M < LP)$; where M is the lowest that could be encountered. The purchase price must be either LP or less, hence the expected price seen before the extra sample is taken is the sum of the second and third terms on the right-hand side of (6.18).

The decision whether to search one more time or to purchase at *LP* depends upon the difference between $E(C_a)$ and $E(C_b)$:

$$E(C_a) - E(C_b) = \Delta(LP) = LP[F(LP)] - \int_M^{LP} pf(p)dp - c \tag{6.19}$$

Using integration by parts to solve the integral in equation (6.19) we have:

$$\Delta(LP) = \int_M^{LP} F(p)dp - c \tag{6.20}$$

On the supposition that $c > 0$, it follows from equation (6.20) that there will be some p, which we label p^*, at which $\Delta(LP)$ is zero, provided, of course, that $p^* > M$. Thus:

$$\Delta(LP) \gtreqless 0 \quad \text{as } LP \gtreqless p^* \tag{6.21}$$

Therefore, given the distribution function for p – hence the minimum price (M) it indicates is available on the market somewhere, and the cost of search – it will pay the consumer to search once more if the last price he was quoted exceeds p^*, which is now his *reservation price*. In fact, in this model the optimal strategy is for the consumer to continue to sample prices until a price less than or equal to p^* is found. Very little of substance is added to the analysis if we do specify the exact form of $f(p)$: for equation (6.20) informs us of the straightforward facts of the situation that when c falls, so that expected costs fall, p^* falls and search activity increases.

The Shackle model would handle this search problem in a simple manner. In that model we would have to envisage a situation in which the consumer maps out a potential surprise function for the prices he thinks he could be quoted for the product in the different shops in the market. Again, since he would clearly only anticipate positive prices there would exist only the analogue of the 'gain' branch of the potential surprise function.

Following the Shackle schema would then mean that the consumer would encapsulate the potential surprise function into one price, a standardized focus-value, with zero potential surprise, which we could label P_f. The situation that the consumer is confronted by is this: should he search once more, at a cost c, given LP and P_f? The no-search option produces a certain cost equal to the lowest price of the product he has been quoted so far, namely LP. Hence:

$$C_a = LP \qquad (6.22)$$

The search once more involves him in the following anticipated cost as he sees things at the present: the cost of search and the cost of the product, which will either be LP or a lower figure. He anticipates that the price at the next search will be P_f. Only if P_f is lower than LP and by an amount equal to the search cost (c) will it be beneficial for him to search. Thus, search will not take place unless $P_f < LP$ *then* the anticipated cost of searching option (b) will be:

$$C_b = c + P_f \qquad (6.23)$$

Therefore:

$$C_a - C_b = \Delta(LP) = (LP - P_f) - c \qquad (6.24)$$

This is merely a restatement of the fact that in the Shackle model no further search can be deemed worthwhile unless $(LP - P_f) > c$. This is exactly the same result in principle as we obtain in the probabilistic version of the model; as it must be from simple intuition. Now P_f has to be the standardized focus-value of P.

It follows at once from equation (6.24) that the consumer will cease to search for a lower price for the product at some P^* which equals $P_f + c$, so that if the lowest price that he has so far been quoted exceeds P^* he should continue to search.

The Shacklesque model that is constructed by mapping potential surprise into a subjective 'probability' variable will produce results similar to those obtained from the conventional approach. Should $f(P)$ happen to coincide with the subjective probability distribution for P then the findings of the models would be identical.

The second variant of the Shacklesque model cannot be utilized to analyse the current decision. This is because its weights do not sum to unity; and it essentially provides no avenue through which we can conflate the 'distribution' of P into an anticipated value.

A LABOUR CHOICE MODEL

In this section I shall consider the standard model of labour supply choice for an individual or a household except that I shall assume that the individual/household is confronted by a situation in which *income is uncertain.* The model I shall utilise is a one-period, static, model.[10] Assume that the individual's (U) utility function is:

$$U = U(L, Y); \quad \frac{\partial U}{\partial L} = U_1 < 0; \quad \frac{\partial U}{\partial Y} = U_2 > 0 \tag{6.25}$$

where: L denotes labour supplied; Y is income; and the partial derivative notation used is that L and Y are defined as variables 1 and 2, respectively. Income can consist of an earned component, which will depend upon w, the wage rate per unit of labour services, and an unearned element, Y_0.

It is obviously possible to permit both or just one or other of the constituents of Y to be stochastic. I shall choose the latter option; so, first of all, I shall assume that w is random. For any given L there will be a probability density function for Y, $f(Y)$. By a simple extension of the axiom system set out in chapter 1 I can state that the individual will be acting rationally in choosing over $(L, f(Y))$ if he maximizes the expected value of his U-function. Thus, with:

$$Y = wL + Y_0 \tag{6.26}$$

he should choose L to maximize:

$$E(U) = \int_a^b U(L, wL + Y_0)f(w)dw \tag{6.27}$$

where $(b–a)$ is the range of w and $f(w)$ its probability density function.

Should w be deterministic but Y random because Y_0 is random then (6.27) becomes:

$$E(U) = \int_\alpha^\beta U(L, wL + Y_0)f(Y_0)dY_0 \tag{6.28}$$

where $(\beta–\alpha)$ is the range of Y_0.

The first-order condition for a maximum value of (6.27) with respect to L is:

$$E[U_1 + wU_2] = 0 \tag{6.29}$$

that is:

$$EU_1 + E(wU_2) = 0 \tag{6.30}$$

since U_2 depends upon w.

Again, in standard fashion, it is possible to deduce some comparative statics results from equation (6.30) by implicit differentiation, such as the sign of the response of L to a change in $E(w)$. Likewise from the first-order condition for a maximum of (6.28) with respect to L:

$$EU_1 + wEU_2 = 0 \tag{6.31}$$

we can deduce the effect of, say, an increase in the mean value of Y_0 on L; it will increase.

Since, in general, the results of those exercises require restrictions to be placed on the U-function, and since for our purposes we wish to deduce the optimal value of L for comparison with the type of outcome generated by a Shackle or Shacklesque model, it is sensible, as done hitherto, to specify a particular form for U. Thus let:

$$U = \alpha L + \beta Y^2; \quad \alpha < 0; \quad \beta > 0 \tag{6.32}$$

Then from equation (6.30):

$$L = \frac{-(\alpha + 2\beta \bar{w} Y_0)}{2\beta E(w^2)}; \quad \bar{w} = E(w) \tag{6.33}$$

From equation (6.31):

$$L = \frac{-(\alpha + 2\beta w \bar{Y}_0)}{2\beta w^2}; \quad \bar{Y}_0 = E(Y_0) \tag{6.34}$$

So, to guarantee $L > 0$ we require $|\alpha| > |2\beta \bar{w} Y_0|$ and $|\alpha| > |2\beta w \bar{Y}_0|$. Under those conditions it can be seen from equation (6.34) that $\partial L / \partial \bar{Y}_0 < 0$; that is as the mean value of unearned income increases, *ceteris paribus*, there is a reduction of labour supplied by the individual. Equation (6.34) also produces a backward-sloping labour supply curve as a function of w. Such a possibility is retained, given our U-function, under wage rate uncertainty since, from equation (6.33):

$$\frac{\partial L}{\partial \bar{w}} \gtreqless 0 \text{ as: } \alpha \bar{w} + \beta Y_0 (\bar{w}^2 - \sigma_w^2) \gtreqless 0 \tag{6.35}$$

How would a Shackle decision-making framework handle the optimal choice of labour supply in the conditions hypothesized? Consider first of all the easier case where only w is uncertain. Here it can be assumed that the expectation is that the wage rate actually received will be positive. Therefore, we are in a position where the Shackle consumer would have to be assumed to map out a potential surprise function for the w he believes he could receive during the working period, to replace $f(w)$. The outcome would be, once more, that having applied his ascendancy function to that potential surprise function the investor has a value of w, in its standardized focus-value, that represents the expectation of w that he will carry forward to the stage where he has to decide on the quantity of labour services he should offer to his employer.

At that stage we cannot imagine any other procedure than that the individual makes his decision by attempting to maximize the level of utility that he would feel if the focus-value w were, in fact, to materialize; so that, in line with Shackle's thinking, the individual maximizes his enjoyment, satisfaction, or utility, by anticipation; a form of expected utility.

If the focus-value of w is assumed to be w_f, then for the Shackle individual/household the choice is to select that value of L which will maximize the value of U subject to:

$$Y = w_f L + Y_0 \tag{6.36}$$

Using equation (6.32) this implies that:

$$L = \frac{-[\alpha + 2\beta w_f Y_0]}{2\beta w_f^2} \tag{6.37}$$

The optimal L can be discovered; but it will differ in general from that obtained for the orthodox model. However, if Y^2 were replaced by Y in the U-function there would again be a similarity between the findings of the two models. From equation (6.37) the usual comparative statics results can be derived. Thus, an increase in w_f, which could be as a consequence of a rightward shift of the potential surprise function for w, has this effect:

$$\frac{\partial L}{\partial w_f} \gtreqless 0 \quad \text{as} \quad \alpha + \beta w_f Y_0 \gtreqless 0 \tag{6.38}$$

Turning now to the situation where Y_0 is uncertain, we can appreciate that the analysis using the Shackle schema is just as straightforward provided Y_0 is always assumed to be positive. In that case all that is entailed in amending the previous analysis is that w_f be replaced by $(Y_0)_f$. It is indeed difficult to imagine a situation where Y_0 could be negative, since it is income and does not include capital value changes; or if it did these would only affect yield if they had to be sold.

For the sake of illustration, since so far we have discussed situations where there has been (or there has been assumed to be) no loss branch to the potential surprise function, there will now be a positive focus-value for Y_0, of say Y_0^g, and a negative focus-value of Y_0^l. Since utility will be zero if Y is zero the individual will decide to supply at least a quantity of labour services equal to L^* where: $L^* > Y_0^l/w$; that is a safety-first choice of labour supply. Thereafter the individual will choose that level of $L > L^*$ which promises the highest value of:

$$U = U(L, wL + Y_0^g) \tag{6.39}$$

L is chosen to maximize $U(.)$ that he can receive by anticipation, as previously.

The Shacklesque models, when both w and Y_0 are assumed to be positive, produce a framework of analysis identical to that based on the Von Neumann–Morgenstern model. However, their actual results, for any given U-function, will not necessarily be identical with those specified in equations (6.33) and (6.34). To achieve that outcome, as previously, the transformation of potential surprise into either of the two indices developed in chapter 5 has to produce a distribution for w and Y_0, respectively, identical to $f(w)$ and $f(Y_0)$.

A MODEL OF CHOICE OF OUTPUT UNDER PRICE UNCERTAINTY

The literature on decision-making under uncertainty has not just taken the standard literature for the consumer or the household and extended it to encompass uncertainty; it has also analysed extensively the introduction of uncertainty into models of the behaviour of business firms.[11] In this section we shall utilize one of the simplest of those models. This is concerned with the optimal output level that an entrepreneur, operating in a perfectly competitive market, should choose if he is confronted by uncertainty, rather than certainty, about the price his product will sell for on the market.

Let us consider a simple static model. The entrepreneur has to choose the output level (x) he will produce, and so hope to sell on the market (since he will have no desire for inventories in this static model), before he knows what the price, p, of his product will be. That prevailing price is determined on the perfectly competitive market. We assume that the firm's cost function, $TC(x)$, is known, and is:

$$TC(x) = A + C(x) \tag{6.40}$$

where A represents fixed costs and $C(x)$ variable costs. The entrepreneur is assumed to possess a utility function over profits, π, where:

$$\pi = px - A - C(x) \tag{6.41}$$

The probability density function for price is assumed to be known by the entrepreneur and is denoted by $f(p)$. Invoking the expected utility theorem the best x to produce in the light of $f(p)$, is found by the entrepreneur's maximizing:

$$E[U(\pi)] = \int_0^\infty U(px - A - C(x))f(p)dp \tag{6.42}$$

where p is assumed to be non-negative.

Differentiation of equation (6.42) with respect to x yields this first-order condition for a maximum value of $E(U)$:

$$E[U'(\pi)(p - C'(x))] = 0; \quad C'(x) > 0 \tag{6.43}$$

It is also instructive in this case to note that the second-order conditions for a maximum are:

$$E[U''(\pi)(p - C'(x))^2 - U'(\pi)C''(x)] < 0 \tag{6.44}$$

These conditions show that under uncertainty it is not necessary for $C''(x) < 0$ for a maximum to be found; under certainty, with the objective being to maximize $U = U(\pi)$, it can be seen that this condition is necessary, as it is in the textbook case where the entrepreneur's objective is just to maximize π; for in the certainty case we find from (6.43) that price must equal marginal cost, as usual. In the uncertainty case, however, $E(p)$ will not necessarily equal $C'(x)$; from (6.44), it is obvious that $C''(x) > 0$ is not necessary for a maximum of $E(U)$ to be obtained.

We can also note two interesting findings that emerge from the uncertainty model. The first is that:

$$E(p) \gtreqless C'(x) \quad \text{if} \quad U''(\pi) \lesseqgtr 0 \tag{6.45}$$

Hence, if $E(p)$ should equal the fixed price that would have ruled in the market under certainty, output would be lower under uncertainty if the entrepreneur is a risk-averter ($U''(\pi) < 0$). If he is risk neutral, so that $U''(\pi) = 0$, output would be identical with the quantity of the good produced under certainty. Should he be a risk-lover, the entrepreneur would produce more under uncertainty.

The relationships in expression (6.45) can be deduced by taking the expectation stipulated in equation (6.43). Thus the latter becomes:

$$E(U'(\pi))[\bar{p} - C'(x)] + \sigma_{p,\, U'(\pi)} - \sigma_{C'(x),\, U'(\pi)} = 0 \qquad (6.46)$$

Here: $\sigma_{i,j}$ is the covariance between i and j; and $\bar{p} = E(p)$. If $U''(\pi) < 0$, the covariance between p and $U'(\pi)$ is negative; and that between $C'(x)$ and $U'(\pi)$ will be positive. Hence, $\bar{p} > C'(x)$ otherwise (6.43) and (6.45) could not be zero. Again, for example, if $U''(\pi) = 0$, then both covariance terms in (6.45) become zero, and so $\bar{p} = C'(x)$.

As with previous discussions in this chapter, let us postulate the precise form that $U(\pi)$ assumes. Thus let:

$$U(\pi) = \alpha\pi + \beta\pi^2; \quad \alpha > 0, \beta < 0 \qquad (6.47)$$

Our representative entrepreneur is a risk-averter. Then (6.43) becomes:

$$\alpha\bar{p} - \alpha C'(x) + 2\beta x E(p^2) - 2\beta\bar{p}C(x) - 2\beta A\bar{p} - 2\beta\bar{p}C'(x)x$$
$$+ 2\beta C(x)C'(x) + 2\beta AC'(x) = 0 \qquad (6.48)$$

Conceptually, if $C(x)$ is specified x can be obtained. But note that if $C(x)$ is defined in any way which renders $C'(x)$ non-constant equation (6.48) becomes a cubic in x. The output equation, in any case, will be dependent upon both the mean and the variance of $f(p)$; unless, of course, we reduce β to zero.

In view of the fact that p can only realistically be positive it will follow that if we use the Shackle model to consider the optimal level of output the possible configuration of market prices for the product will be reduced to one, a standardized focus-value, p_f. Hence, anticipated profit, as seen by the entrepreneur, is:

$$\pi = p_f x - C(x) - A \qquad (6.49)$$

Upon substitution of this figure into (6.47) it is shown that the level of output that will maximize utility by anticipation in the Shackle schema is given by solving:

$$[\alpha + 2\beta(p_f x - C(x) - \beta)](p_f - C'(x)) = 0 \qquad (6.50)$$

The solution for x will be identical with that deduced from equation (6.48) except that $E(p^2)$ will now be replaced by $(p_f)^2$. The solutions will further differ in that $p_f = C'(x)$ for the Shackle model. This is because, in essence in his schema, the entrepreneur is risk-neutral; the sign of β in equation (6.47) has no significance as an indicator of risk-aversion in the Shackle theory. Indeed if, as here, we are solely concerned with the analogue of the gain branch of the potential surprise function and the information contained in it is being used not to effect an investment decision but to be inserted in a utility function, risk-indicators and risk-measures have no meaning in the application of the Shackle schema.

Numerous extensions of the models discussed in the preceding sections of this chapter exist in the literature now. The material presented has deliberately been only a sample of the available literature; but it has been sufficient to illustrate the kind of issues to which decision-making under uncertainty has been applied, and to provide some flavour of the ways in which the probability calculus has been used.

It can be seen that, importantly, the Shackle model can be developed to tackle those issues. Additionally the first Shacklesque model – and often, since they map into each other, its second variant – can be a vehicle for investigating optimal choice of action under a wider set of uncertain circumstances.

7

Summary and Conclusions

In the preceding discussion I have set out: the essence of Professor Shackle's own highly distinctive approach to modelling decision-making under uncertainty; the main elements in his critique of the conventional paradigm that is utilized to analyse such decision-making; a critical appraisal of the literature on Shackle's theory; my own critique of his theory; and an alternative form of model that will rectify the deficiencies in the Shackle theory. These strands of my argument have largely been developed against a background in which an individual is seeking to select the best portfolio of (financial) assets he can at any particular moment, which is to be held for a period of unit-length. However, the argument, just like those of the orthodox school which have provided the backcloth to this whole essay, can be applied to a much wider set of decision-making problems under uncertainty. In effect, the analysis in chapter 6 has demonstrated, even if at times this has had to be heuristically, how the Shackle and Shackle-lesque models can be utilized to tackle questions hitherto regarded as the preserve of the orthodox, probability/expected utility, approach.

For convenience of exposition I shall refer here, largely, to decision-making in regard to investment in financial assets or real capital where examples are needed to fix the observations. There then follows a brief reference to other decision-making problems. Some observations on empirical matters complete the story of this particular volume.

There are three key elements in the Shackle schema: the potential surprise function; ascendancy, stimulus or ϕ-function; and the gambler-preference map. This triad permits the four stages in the Shackle schema to be constructed and locked together. These stages, for any individual investor, in a given set of circumstances – whether he is contemplating the feasibility of investing in this or that piece of machinery or this or that portfolio of assets – are the following.

By the potential surprise function the individual investor sets out the prospects of gains or losses (positive or negative returns, as the case might be) on a given investment, an item of machinery or a named financial claim. He catalogues the range of such gains and losses that he believes could occur, and on occasions he might decide that other outcomes could conceivably materialize that he has not thought of, which are then encapsulated in the 'residual hypotheses'. Often the latter will not enter his mind. To each feasible outcome he is alleged to assign a degree of potential surprise; a degree which is meant to symbolize the surprise he would feel if the particular outcome were to materialize once the consequences of the investment have been permitted to unfold, either in the form of returns from a machine during its working life or from a financial asset once the investment period has ended. That degree of potential surprise is meant to reflect his dis-belief in an hypothesis.

The individual is designated to be a loss- or 'risk'-averter, so that he does keep the gain/loss branches of the potential surprise function separate in his thinking. The information on expectational elements contained in those two branches is then reduced to one element for each branch.

That telescoping is achieved by use of the ascendancy, stimulus or ϕ-function. From each branch the individual selects that expectational element, consisting as it does of a money value and a degree of potential surprise, which most catches his attention. On the gain side the element so selected is alleged to represent, epitomize, 'the best that can be hoped for'; whilst on the loss side it is designed to indicate 'the worst that has to be feared'. These two resultant elements, the primary focus-values, characterize the particular investment under consideration.

When a comparison is being effected between two investments – which can be purchases of capital equipment, or the holding of wealth in one asset or another – by means of their two expectational elements, a problem of non-comparability emerges. This is because although it is a cardinal measure, potential surprise is said to be non-additive, because it is not a distributional variable. Evaluation of combinations of investments is not then possible; so potential surprise has to be eliminated from the two expectational elements for a given investment. This standardization – by placing all expectational elements on the same, money value, footing – is achieved by selecting, for example, the gain that will provide the same ascendancy value as the primary focus elements but without their attendant degrees of potential surprise.

Thus two stages of the decision-making process are accomplished by utilization of the ascendancy function. The fourth stage requires the gambler preference-map by which the investor orders the derived standardized focus-values on the investments or investment strategies. He balances gain against loss; often bearing in mind the resources constraint upon him (in his capacity as an entrepreneur) or the level of wealth he stands to lose (as a financial investor).

The criticisms that have been voiced against Shackle's theory have concerned all three of its supporting pillars. The most vehement arguments have been those levelled at the ascendancy function and the gambler-preference map; there, the emphasis has been to question the existence of the gambler-preference map. Comparatively less attention has been devoted to the concept of potential surprise which is the notion underlying the Shackle theory.

The general view is, though, that the Shacklesque concept of potential surprise is not an operationally useful concept. It cannot make the distinction between 'perfectly possible' and 'perfectly likely' outcomes. Additionally, it is nothing other than subjective probability in another guise. It has been shown in previous chapters that these are not claims that have been acceded to by Shackle and, indeed, they are not necessarily valid.[1] Yet we have maintained that once the investor has set out his potential surprise function for any investment, and he is satisfied that it does contain all of the information (including, as necessary, a residual hypothesis) about the investment's prospects, it does no violence to the function to translate it into a 'subjective probability' function. Nevertheless, using such a transformed function within the Shackle schema *per se* does not affect the outcome in respect of the optimal action-scheme.

The difficulty with the ascendancy function in my view is that it is supposed to be a conflator function but has been explained and described in a manner such as to imply that it is also a device for ranking investment projects, an implication conveyed, indeed, by the word ascendancy itself. The extreme ambivalence over its part in the scheme of things is probably one of the major reasons why the contention has been advanced that we can dispense with the gambler-preference map. Net ϕ-values, or net ascendancy values, should be the variable by which a particular investment project is assessed.

My objections against such a procedure – a procedure, as shown earlier, much favoured, in the critical literature on the Shackle model – are these. If the ϕ-function is retained in exactly the same format as that advocated by Professor Shackle, this has two important implications. The first is that, for given degree of potential surprise, the higher is the prospective loss on an asset, project, or whatever, the greater is its power of ascendancy. If the 'loss ϕ-value' is to be subtracted from the 'gain ϕ-value' for an asset to arrive at an indicator of the attraction of the asset or investment per asset or per investment, the function that epitomizes the prospects contained in the loss branch of the potential surprise function should assign a lower 'degree of attractiveness', for given degree of potential surprise, to an asset or project the greater is the prospective loss; for the attractiveness or desirability of the asset or the project is what is now being evaluated. Secondly, and of more importance, is the fact that the use of the ascendancy function à la Shackle means that the investor does not use all of the information he has accumulated on the expectational elements in either branch of the potential surprise function. The choice over those functions *per se*, and hence over the feasible set of investment strategies, requires that the ranking of potential surprise functions be axiomatized.

These two objections are naturally related since they necessitate a change in the conception of the ascendancy function and its rationalization. The second objection has been raised several times in the literature, as shown in previous chapters, but no attempt (apart from that of Professor W. Krelle) has been made to replace the ascendancy function by a preference ordering for a rational individual, over the prospects for particular investment strategies, be they in one or several financial assets or in real capital projects. This I have endeavoured to accomplish in a standard fashion in chapter 5 and to investigate its consequences in chapters 5 and 6, for action-choice compared with the findings for the Shackle schema.

That kind of approach removes the third pillar of that schema, namely the gambler preference-map. In essence the role designated to it, to enable choice of action to be accomplished, is subsumed in the axiomatic preference ordering over potential surprise functions.

In the literature the view has often been propounded, as have noted in chapter 4, that the gambler-preference map cannot express any other aspect of the individual's temperament, and hence attitude to 'risk', than those aspects that are implied in the ascendancy function. Professor Shackle was unable to accept that standpoint. Indeed, if we could just rename the ascendancy function it could be accepted as a conflator function, or more straightfowardly if the investor's expectation in respect of a particular investment consisted solely of two money values, then the gambler-preference map would be indispensable.

One of the other worries we expressed about the gambler preference-map was that it does not make allowance for uncertainty, or potential surprise – the very essence of the Shackle model. This situation arises, it may be recalled, because of the major deficiencies with the Shackle model *per se*; namely that the ascendancy function should not be used to standardize focus-values. This statement accepts the ascendancy function as a conflator or telescoping function for expectations. Its message is that the conflation exercise will produce a money value and an attendant degree of potential surprise, in general, for the primary focus-values, and those degrees of potential surprise cannot be discounted. The standardized focus-values – which are designed to be the 'certainty equivalents' of the primary focus-values – will, in general, be figments. The individual will be surprised if they do occur!!

The primary focus-values should be ranked by means of a gambler-preference map. It has been shown, however, that because potential surprise is non-additive (and on this occasion this attribute of potential surprise *is* relevant), for the analysis of portfolio selection at least, although the gambler-preference map could be amended so that it does incorporate potential surprise, this would be of no assistance to us, because we cannot embody potential surprise in the efficient investment frontier.

An interesting question arises at this juncture concerning the feasibility of using primary focus-values for analysis of the choice of investment in real capital. If we make the assumption that the entrepreneur operates totally in perfectly competitive markets, it must follow that we can utilize the primary focus-outcomes for a specified item of real capital in constructing its scale opportunity line. This is because increasing the quantity of the equipment purchased will scale up the money values of the primary focus-outcomes by the same factor, but it must leave their associated degrees of potential surprise unaffected.[2] It would then be possible to derive the four-dimensional scale opportunity curve, over scaled-up focus-values, and their (constant) associated degrees of potential surprise. Should the entrepreneur also be operating in a perfectly competitive environment in regard to alternative items of capital equipment he is considering for purchase, however, the comparison between the alternative items can be effected by a straight ranking of their primary focus-outcomes and their degrees of potential surprise, via the amended gambler-preference map.

The Shackle schema is designed so that the probability distribution of outcomes on an investtment which is the basis of the orthodox framework can be replaced by the potential surprise function. It is argued that the probability calculus is only applicable to 'experiments' that are infinitely repeatable in unchanging conditions. If decisions are based on that calculus, however, there can be no uncertainty, since *ex definitione* the result of the *whole* 'experiment' is known and must also be for the individual, since he must be assuming that he will be ranking an infinitely repeatable experiment – otherwise he should not use relative frequencies at all in his decision-making process. Investment decisions, decisions made in an economic context, are unique, non-seriable decisions. Additionally, probability is a distributional variable with all the implications that entails.

The Shackle schema is also an attempt to avoid choice over probability distribution of returns being made by reference to the whole distribution for an investment project. Since all the outcomes are mutually exclusive, and hence rivals, they should not be combined together to form, say, an expected value of the outcome. Neither should the gains and losses be considered together. In the application of the probability calculus they are, and the choice of action is made by comparison of the various probability distributions of outcomes for the alternative investment strategies. The comparison is effected by telescoping each probability distribution into an 'index', namely the expected value of utility it yields. That telescoping encompasses both the conflation of the expectational elements for investments and the choice of action; tasks which are accomplished in the Shackle model by the ascendancy function, and the gambler-preference map.

In sum, the position in which we find ourselves is one wherein we have doubts about two of the pillars of the Shackle construct, namely the ascendancy function and the gambler-preference map. The upshot of the analysis and discussions in chapters 4 and 5, especially, is that the attempt to replace the one mechanism in the orthodox model by means of two pieces of apparatus, the ascendancy function and the gambler-preference map, although well-intentioned, is, ultimately, an unsuccessful and inappropriate procedure. The ideas that underlie the concept of potential surprise seem entirely reasonable and acceptable; especially if we bear in mind the point that the use of relative frequencies provides us with no information about the consequences of a single 'experiment'.

Having conceded all that, and bearing in mind that the concepts of potential surprise and (subjective) probability are intrinsically different, once an investor has mapped out his expectational vista for any investment in terms of potential surprise it is legitimate to convert the (cardinal) concept of potential surprise into a 'subjective probability' measure. At that stage the essential differences between the two ideas adumbrated in earlier chapters count for nothing.

In specifying a Shacklesque model in chapter 5, which also makes it apparent explicitly what the individual investor's (entrepreneur's) objective is, the only idea retained without emendation is that which underlies the notion that the potential surprise function should have two branches. The investor will pay special attention to the possibility of loss. Acceptance of that viewpoint provides, ultimately, the only divergence between the Shacklesque model and the current orthodoxy.

However, the Shacklesque model developed in chapter 5 does circumvent all of the objections that I and others have levelled at the Shackle schema *per se*. It does also produce results for portfolio selection that differ from those derivable from the orthodox model; and although in the analysis of some decision-making situations it will inevitably produce the same outcome as the orthodox model, it will not always do so and so it offers an alternative approach that is at least Shacklesque in spirit.

It was also observed in chapter 6 that the Shackle schema, *per se*, can be applied to decision-making models that have up to now been tackled by the orthodox approach, despite the deficiencies seen in the schema. On occasions it will produce results for the optimal choice of action by the individual (per individual, household or producer) that are really indistinguishable from those that can be derived from the traditional model. Such is the case with the decision to invest in capital equipment, so that in sum, the Shackle schema *per se* seems to produce different, and counter-intuitive, results only for financial investment. Yet the fact that it can only predict that an individual investor will hold merely two financial assets at most, is not of itself a valid criticism of the schema. Investors who have been observed to possess multi-asset portfolios in the real world might indeed be behaving irrationally; if the Shackle schema is correct then this must be the case, unless there exist objective constraints on their asset holdings which force them to diversify.

Indeed, should we desire to subject the Shackle model to empirical evaluation, with regard to the portfolio behaviour of individuals or individual units (such as banks, discount houses, insurance companies, and so on) it is perfectly possible for it to perform at least as well in explaining that behaviour as the models derived from the orthodox approach. For example, suppose that the latter produces a situation where a bank (or group of banks assumed to have identical utility functions over profit) seeks to maximize the expected utility from profit, its actual utility function being a quadratic over profit. The demand equations, for the items it can choose, will assume the kind of format taken on by the demand equations for the x's given in chapter 1. The only difference now is that those equations will have to be amended to incorporate exogenous or non-choice items (perhaps total deposits)[3] and the fact that the budget constraint for the bank, since it possesses assets and liabilities, is the balance sheet constraint that net worth (assets less liabilities) should be zero. Additionally, the structure of the equations for asset holdings will have to incorporate any binding and effective constraints imposed by the monetary authorities.

In that respect let us suppose that there is a constraint on the holding of cash ('pure' money) to the effect that it must at least equal some proportion, α, of total deposits (equal total liabilities); and that the bank adheres to this constraint. We could assume further that its utility function is likely to be such that we can regard this constraint as effective. Thus the bank's holding of cash can be explained wholly by total deposits, which for the sake of argument we can assume are exogenous (see note 3). Furthermore, the monetary authorities are likely to impose a liquid assets ratio; that is, they will stipulate that liquid assets (such as cash, call loans, treasury bills and commercial bills) should be at least a fraction, β, of total deposits. In the U.K. in the past, up to the publication of *Competition and Credit Control* (1970) by the Bank of England and the introduction of new reserve asset controls on banks in 1971, the liquid assets of the banks were defined as above and had to have at least a fraction (0.28) of deposits. The historical data can be interpreted as suggesting that, up to the change of regime in 1971, the liquid assets ratio was also binding and effective.[4]

The earning assets of each bank would include Government bonds and advances in addition to the non-money liquid assets. The imposition of the binding and effective cash and liquid assets constraints, in conjunction with the balance sheet constraint, would – under a 'mean variance' representation of the portfolio behaviour of each bank and all banks collectively – mean that the banks' portfolio could be segmented into three separate portfolios. Thus cash would be explained solely by α times deposits, there would be no expected returns, no variances of return and no other exogenous scalar variables that could affect the value of the holding of cash; call loans, treasury bills and commercial bills would be explained by $(\beta-\alpha)$ of deposits, any exogenous scalar variable, plus the expected returns and variances of returns (as in chapter 1) on those three assets *alone*; and Government bonds and advances, assumed to be endogenous here, would be explained by the scalar variables $(1-\beta)$ of deposits, any other scalar variable, the expected return and variance of return on the two assets themselves and on no others.

These emendations of the asset demand equations deduced in chapter 1 accommodate the special conditions in which banks have to operate. Although the Cournot and Engel conditions must still apply, and the equations are essentially the same as those given in chapter 1, the emendations have produced, as it were, three separate portfolios where, within those for non-money liquid assets and for 'earning assets', the equations do have the same structure as those presented in chapter 1. The only difference is the nature of the exogenous scalar variables.

The point of this brief statement of the consequences of applying the analysis of chapter 1 to the portfolio behaviour of a financial firm, such as a bank or banks (seen as banks, by aggregation over all banks, on the supposition that they all behave in the same manner and have identical probability distributions of return on assets) is to compare it, by way of a simple illustration, with use of the Shackle schema.

Under the assumed conditions the Shackle schema could explain the holding of cash, *ex hypothesi*. It could also offer an explanation of the holding of bonds and advances because to do so requires an allocation of, as it were, $(1-\beta)$ of deposits to either bonds or advances. As far as non-money liquid assets are concerned there is a minor problem because to explain them necessitates accounting for a three-asset portfolio; but at least the Shackle schema could explain the shares of two of the assets in (β–α) of deposits; and, under the conditions delineated in chapter 4, it is possible for the schema to explain the holding of some of all three assets.

As far as the actual empirical evaluation of the resultant equations is concerned also, there is not likely to be any way by which we can decide between the two models. Why is this? The reason is simple. To test the models *a priori*, the investigator himself has to form some opinion as to how the banks arrive at their estimates of the characteristics of the returns on the assets. In the 'mean variance' version of the expected utility analysis, if the equations are to be tested as demand equations, then it is necessary to assume that at least the risks on asset returns are constant over the data sample period. That constancy, together with the assumed constancy of the utility function, provides the constant parameters needed in the econometric analysis. As shown in chapter 1, the independent variables in the equation thereby are the expected asset returns and the scalar variables.

In the Shackle model, given the type of equations we have seen from chapter 3 that it can produce, the constants are provided by the properties of the gambler-preference function. The independent variables are the focus-values on the assets plus any appropriate scalar variable. Again, to estimate the model it is necessary to construct data on those independent variables – especially, of course, on focus-values.

It is now perfectly apparent that various *a priori* methods employed to generate the data required by the econometric estimation of the two models can be such that they produce the same empirical results. That is to say, they both have the same level of success in explaining portfolio behaviour; likewise it is self-evident that it would be possible to construct (or, if we like, manufacture) a set of focus-values that would permit the Shackle schema to outperform the orthodox model.

In sum, as we are all too well aware, it is not feasible in econometric research to obtain 'a knock-down answer'. A move away from *a priori* modelling by, for example, questionnaire work to ascertain information from investors themselves about their motives, the data they consider relevant to their decisions, the methods they use to form any expectation, would all be of assistance in reducing the degree of scepticism about the empirical findings and permit a more reliable assessment of the opposing models.

Whilst there has been a vast quantity of empirical research surrounding the orthodox model, in one form or another (as noted in chapter 1), there has been no such research carried out for the Shackle theory on similar topics. Indeed, there is a dearth of empirical work on the Shackle theory in any context.[5] Professor Shackle himself has proposed that work be undertaken, and implied that he would indicate it, largely of a questionnaire/interview variety, to ascertain the correctness of his basic approach itself.[6] Obviously any such information would be a means by which pilot studies of its value in accounting for specified economic decisions could be made; since the information will be provided by individuals and businessmen in the context of particular decision, investment or otherwise, that they have had to make. No such research effort has been forthcoming, however. As also intimated in chapter 4, such pilot studies might be used to gather impressions as to whether or not, and to what extent, there was any relationship between 'subjective probability' and potential surprise. One fact that is likely to emerge from any such detailed investigation is that individuals and businessmen have a strong desire to simplify, to narrow down the situations they have to consider and the choices they have to make. Shackle is probably correct in his surmise here that we all sift out a problem requiring us to choose some course of action in the face of uncertainty by reducing it to manageable proportions. In that way there could be something of great importance in a device such as the ϕ-function. Choices too are frequently unique.

Here lies a paradox: if the underlying motivation for Shackle's schema is correct, and he is on the right lines, the logic of his schema means that the individual is capable of producing minute details on, and assessment of, the outcomes with which he could be confronted. He performs an intricate procedure to encapsulate and to utilize those details, but then to not do so rationally. The logic, in sum, produces an elaborate and inconsistent analysis. There is here a basic conflict between logic and choice.[7]

Notes

INTRODUCTION

1. Noted by M. Lachmann in his distinguished philosophical paper, 'Professor Shackle on the economic significance of time', *Metroeconomica*, April–August 1959, pp. 64–73.
2. Cambridge: Cambridge University Press, 1972.
3. See, for example: A. Coddington, 'Keynesian Economics: the search for first principles', *Journal of Economic Literature*, No. 4, 1976, pp. 1258–73; L. M. Lachmann, 'From Mises to Shackle: an essay on Austrian economics and the Kaleidic Society', *Journal of Economic Literature*, March 1976, pp. 54–62; H. Guiton, 'Causalité et imagination', *Revue d'Economique Politique*, January–February 1980, pp. 56–60; and P. Beaugrand, 'Le temps, l'imagination, l'incertitude, dans la théorie du Professor G. L. S. Shackle', *Revue Economique*, March 1982, pp. 297–322.
4. Cambridge University Press, and Edinburgh University Press, respectively.
5. Most of the contributions of a philosophical nature are contained in the special symposium on Professor Shackle's theory in *Metroeconomica*, April–August 1959. An exhaustive bibliography of books and articles that appeared on his theory up to 1960 can be found in the Bibliography to his *Decision, Order and Time in Human Affairs*, Cambridge: Cambridge University Press, 1st edition, 1961. For relevant publications in the period since 1960 see the 2nd edition of *Decision, Order and Time in Human Affairs* (1969), *Epistemics and Economics*, and *Imagination and Choice*.
6. C. F. Carter and J. L. Ford (eds), *Expectations and Uncertainty in Economics: Essays in Honour of G. L. S. Shackle*, Oxford: Basil Blackwell, 1972.
7. G. L. S. Shackle, *Time in Economics*, Amsterdam: North Holland Publishing Company, 1957, p. 107. This is the second in the series of de Vries Lectures in Economic Theory.
8. See, for example, the Symposium in *Metroeconomica*, April–August 1959; C. F. Carter, G. P. Meredith and G. L. Shackle (eds), *Uncertainty and Business Decisions*, Liverpool: Liverpool University Press, 1954; and

R. A. D. Egerton, *Investment Decisions Under Uncertainty*, Liverpool: Liverpool University Press, 1960.

9. It is, however, accorded a separate mention in some books specifically on the theme of expectations and uncertainty in economics. In at least one book it is set aside for separate consideration: see S. Ozga, *Expectations in Economic Theory*, London: Wiedenfeld & Nicolson, 1965.
10. R. A. D. Egerton, *op. cit.*
11. 'A study in expectations: reflections on Shackle's "Expectations in Economics", Part I', *Yorkshire Bulletin of Economic and Social Research*, vol. 2, no. 2, July 1950, pp. 63–98.
12. *Ibid.*, p. 96.
13. *Critical Essays in Monetary Theory*, Oxford: The Clarendon Press, 1967; pp. 103–104.
14. The empirical work on the application of the expected utility theorem, usually ultimately via a mean–variance representation of it (these issues are considered in chapter 1), is now voluminous. That work has taken three forms essentially: the first is an evaluation of the existing portfolios of individuals, usually business or financial firms, to see if they are optimum portfolios prescribed by theory; the second arises from the additional supposition that all participants on financial markets possess the same utility function, and accordingly a model of capital asset pricing, hence market phenomena can be investigated; and the third type of research has been concerned with the direct testing of the theory for individuals (again usually individual units such as business or financial firms) by an empirical evaluation of the reliability of the asset demand equations the theory predicts the individuals will have.

    It is this last kind of investigation which is most pertinent to the contents of this volume; so I might be permitted to refrain from providing indicative references for anything other than such research. Even here, though, I shall just note one or two papers by way of example. These are for the U.K.; further work on the U.K. and the U.S.A. can be found referenced in them: J. M. Parkin, M. R. Gray and R. J. Barratt, 'The portfolio behaviour of commercial banks', in D. Heathfield and K. Hilton (eds), *The Econometric Study of the United Kingdom*, London: Macmillan, 1970; W. R. White, 'Some econometric models and deposit bank portfolio behaviour in the U.K. 1963–1970', in G. Renton (ed.), *Modelling the Economy*, London: Heinemann, 1975; and G. Clayton, J. C. Dodds, M. J. Driscoll and J. L. Ford, *The Portfolio and Debt Behaviour of British Building Societies*, SUERF Pamphlet 16A, 1975.
15. For example, on military strategy (and strategy in sport) and Shackle's theory see, for example: B. S. Kierstead, 'Decision-taking and the theory of games', in Carter and Ford, *op. cit.*, pp. 160–174; M. B. Nicholson, 'Uncertainty and crisis behaviour: an illustration of conflict and peace research', *ibid.*, pp. 237–265. On bargaining strategy in general see: A. Coddington, 'On the theory of bargaining', *ibid.*, pp. 43–57.

16. This is perhaps a convenient place to comment on a point that Professor Shackle has made persistently in his writings on expectations and uncertainty in economics, and no more so than in *Epistemics and Economics*. This concerns the definition of rationality. He has stated, for example, that rationality is:

    > . . . the claim of a chosen action to be based on full relevant information and to be demonstrably superior in its results to any other available . . . (*op. cit*., p. 85)

    His argument, to paraphrase him, has often been put like this: man cannot apply reason to his circumstances unless he has full information, therefore he cannot act rationally. We would accept that man can act rationally if, in a defined set of circumstances, he chose what he regarded as the best option. Whether his information is accurate, and hence whether *ex post* his decision turns out to have been the correct one, is not relevant.

CHAPTER 1

1. See, for example, J. H. Dreze and F. Modigliani, 'Consumption decisions under uncertainty', *Journal of Economic Theory*, vol. 5, 1972, pp. 308–335; D. H. Neane, 'Multiperiod consumption–investment decisions and risk preference', *Journal of Economic Theory*, vol. 3, 1971, pp. 40–53; and P. A. Samuelson, 'Lifetime portfolio selection by dynamic stochastic programming', *Review of Economics and Statistics*, vol. 51, 1969, pp. 239–246.
2. 'A suggestion for simplifying the theory of money', *Economica*, February 1935, reprinted as chapter 4 in *Critical Essays in Monetary Theory*, Oxford: Oxford University Press, 1967.
3. See, for example, J. M. Keynes, *Treatise on Probability*, London: Macmillan, 1921.
4. *The Theory of Games and Economic Behaviour*, 2nd edition, Princeton: Princeton University Press, 1947, chapter 1 and appendix.
5. For excellent expositions of the expected utility theorem and of their axioms, and upon which my treatment is largely based, see: D. R. Luce and H. Raiffa, *Games and Decisions*, New York: John Wiley & Sons, 1957, chapter 2; and J. D. Hey, *Uncertainty in Microeconomics*, Oxford: Martin Robertson, 1979.
6. The importance of *absolute preference* has been accorded most prominence in the literature by Maurice Allais; see, for example, 'Le comportement de l'homme rationnel devant le risque: critique des postulates et axiomes de l'Ecole Americaine', *Econometrica*, October 1953, pp. 503–546. The concept has been employed by Karl Borch to demonstrate the inconsistencies, that is the irrational choices, that can materialize if the investor's selection of portfolio or investment strategy is carried out by his attempting to maximize some 'index' which is posited to be dependent

upon moments of the probability distribution of portfolio returns, such as the mean and variance. Unless the choice of portfolio is made explicitly by the maximization of the expected utility of the investor then there will be no guarantee that the portfolio chosen via reference to mean and variance, will satisfy the axiom of absolute preference.

Thus, to anticipate part of the ensuing text, consider a situation in which it is hypothesized that the investor endeavours to maximize $I = I(\mu, \sigma^2)$, where μ and σ^2 are, respectively, the mean and the variance of return from the investor's given value of wealth, over a specified investment period. Suppose the investor can only hold one or both of two assets. Two out of the many feasible investment strategies that present themselves, of course, are the two polar cases, namely hold all of wealth in the one asset (asset 1) or the other asset (asset 2). Now, let us further hypothesize that returns on asset 2 are always twice the returns on asset 1 for any state of the world. Then both the mean and the variance of total return from investing all of wealth in asset 2 will be higher than when all of wealth is held in asset 1. It would then be legitimate to state that (with $\partial I/\partial\mu > 0$ and $\partial I/\partial\sigma^2 < 0$) they lie on the same I-indifference curve. By the stochastic dominance axiom, however, the investor must prefer a portfolio consisting solely of asset 2 to one consisting only of asset 1. If the investor's actual utility function (in the returns from the portfolio) had been used to deduce his expected utility function, and his utility function had been a quadratic in the portfolio return, the weights on μ and σ^2 would have been such that his expected utility indifference curves over μ, σ^2 would have indicated a preference for asset 2 over asset 1.

Borch's emphasis on the need to invoke the Von Neumann–Morgenstern absolute preference axiom is, in effect, a criticism of the recent work of Sir John Hicks on portfolio selection as he works in terms of an Index I. See: K. Borch, 'A note on uncertainty and indifference curves', *Review of Economic Studies*, January 1969, pp. 1–4, and 'The rationale of the mean–standard deviation analysis: comment', *American Economic Review*, June 1974, pp. 428–430; and J. R. Hicks, 'Portfolio Selection', *Critical Essays*, chapter 6.

7. J. Tobin, 'Liquidity preference as behaviour towards risk', *Review of Economic Studies*, February 1958, pp. 65–86.
8. The expected value of utility is:

$$E(U) = \alpha - cE(e^{-\beta R}) \tag{i}$$

We can re-write equation (i) by noting that $E(e^{-\beta R})$ is the moment-generating function of the random variable R, $(M_R(-\beta))$, and that for a normal distribution:

$$M_R(-\beta) = e^{-\beta\mu_R + (1/2)\beta^2\sigma_R^2} \tag{ii}$$

This follows from the fact that the moment-generating function for any random variable x is written as $M_x(t) = E(e^{tx})$ where t is an undefined constant. Thus:

$$M_x(t) = e^{t\mu_R + (1/2)t^2\sigma_R^2} \quad \text{for } R \sim N(\mu_R, \sigma_R^2) \tag{iii}$$

Thus, making use of (ii) in (i) we have:

$$E(U) = a - ce^{-\beta[\mu_R - (\beta/2)\sigma_R^2]} = U^o \tag{iv}$$

Now let:

$$dU^o = \frac{\partial U^o}{\partial \mu} d\mu_R + \frac{\partial U^o}{\partial \sigma^2} d\sigma_R^2 \tag{v}$$

equal zero and we have the equation for any constant expected utility indifference curve. We then deduce that the slope of the latter is:

$$\frac{\partial \mu_R}{\partial \sigma_R^2} = \frac{\beta}{2} > 0 \tag{vi}$$

and thus it is constant.

In effect, we can see this from equation (iv) which informs us that the investor need only maximize $\mu_R - (\beta/2)\sigma_R^2$ and he will maximize his expected utility. That maximization produces linear indifference curves in μ_R and σ_R^2.

For normally distributed returns, for a given set of expectations about them and for given wealth, the investor will face the same investment opportunity frontier with the quadratic and exponential utility functions. However, the optimum portfolio selected by the investor will almost certainly differ if the one utility function is relevant rather than the other. As noted in the text, the two utility functions differ in their risk-aversion properties and also $E(U)$ has an upper bound of α so there is no need to place a limit on R to guarantee that marginal utility is positive, as is the case with the quadratic utility function.

9. However, despite the vast literature that exists on these concepts (see, for example, J. W. Pratt, 'Risk-aversion in the large and the small', *Econometrica*, vol. 32, 1964, pp. 122–136; K. J. Arrow, *Essays in the Theory of Risk-Bearing*, Amsterdam: North-Holland, 1971; J. E. Stiglitz, 'The effects of income, wealth and capital gains taxation on risk-taking', *Quarterly Journal of Economics*, vol. 83, 1967, pp. 263–283) they provide little that is of value in predicting the portfolio behaviour of investors, with respect to the effect of changes in wealth or returns, in a world other than one in which only a riskless and a risky asset exist. On the latter see, for example, D. Cass and J. E. Stiglitz, 'Risk aversion and separability and wealth effects on portfolios with many assets', *Review of Economic Studies*, July 1972, pp. 331–354 and O. D. Hart, 'Some negative results on the existence of comparative statics results in portfolio theory', *Review of Economic Studies*, November, 1975, p. 615–621.
10. This result is proved by setting the partial derivatives of σ_R^2 (equation (1.21)) with respect to x_1 and x_2 equal to zero and solving for x_1/x_2 when $\sigma_{12} = -\sigma_1\sigma_2$.

11. Setting the partial derivatives of the variance with respect to x_1 and x_2 equal to zero reveals that when $\rho_{12} = 0, x_1/x_2 = (\sigma_2/\sigma_1)^2$. That information, together with the wealth constraint $w = x_1 + x_2$, enables us to write minimum total risk, as in the text. The result points to the conclusion that asset diversification can be beneficial since it can indeed permit 'risk' to be diversified away, should favourable returns on the one asset be accompanied by unfavourable returns on the other asset.
12. Again taking the partial derivatives of σ_R^2 with respect to x_1 and x_2 allows us to deduce this result.
13. Thus in equation (1.26) ρ_{12} is set at zero, and the value of σ_R^2 for that correlation is inserted into the equation. When the same procedure has been carried out for $\rho_{12} = 0$ the two equations are set equal to each other (since each equals zero); then the condition in the text can be deduced.
14. This statement will hold true provided $\sigma_1/\sigma_2 > \rho_{12}$. Then it is valid for $-1 < \rho_{12} \leqslant 0$, possibly for $\rho_{12} > 0$, but not for $\rho_{12} = +1$. This can be seen by taking the partial derivative of the slope of the frontier (derived from equation (1.26)) with respect to e_2.
15. This result is based on the standard formula for block inversion of a matrix. Thus if we let an $n \times n$ matrix M be partitioned as follows:

$$M = \begin{bmatrix} A & B \\ C & D \end{bmatrix}$$

A is $n_1 \times n_1$; B is $n_1 \times n_2$; C is $n_2 \times n_1$; D is $n_2 \times n_2$.

Suppose A and $E = D - CA^{-1}B$ are non-singular. Then

$$M^{-1} = \begin{bmatrix} A^{-1}(I + BE^{-1}CA^{-1}) & -A^{-1}BE^{-1} \\ -E^{-1}CA^{-1} & E^{-1} \end{bmatrix}$$

where I is the $n_1 \times n_1$ identity matrix.
16. To prove this, we recall that $-(i'[(\partial u/\partial v)\Omega]^{-1}i)$ is a scalar, and that $[(\partial u/\partial v)\Omega]^{-1}$ is symmetric since $(\partial u/\partial v)$ is a scalar and Ω is symmetric. The transpose of a symmetric matrix is equal to the matrix itself and likewise the transpose of the scalar is equal to the scalar itself.
17. We recall from note 8, above, that the ratio of $\partial U/\partial \mu$ to $\partial U/\partial V$ remains constant for the exponential utility function (R being assumed to be normally distributed, of course).
18. See J. Tobin, *op. cit.*; J. R, Hicks, *Critical Essays*, J. Lintner, 'The valuation of risk assets and the selection of risky investments in stock portfolios and capital budgets', *Review of Economics and Statistics*, vol. 47, 1965, pp. 13–37; and W. F. Sharpe, 'Capital asset prices: a theory of market equilibrium under conditions of risk', *Journal of Finance*, 1964, pp. 435–442.
19. How the investor arrives at the frontier *OZB*, in effect how he selects *Z*, is demonstrated in appendix B.

20. J. R. Hicks, *Critical Essays*; and A. D. Roy, 'Safety-first and the holding of assets', *Econometrica*, vol. xx, July, 1952, pp. 431–449.
21. On the literature that has been developed for these kinds of circumstances (such as the 'maximin' principle) see, for example, S. Ozga, *Expectations in Economics*, London: Weidenfeld & Nicolson, 1965, where detailed references to all original sources will also be found.

    An axiomatic theory based on the probability calculus for a situation of ignorance, defined to be one where there is not 'a fixed list of states of nature' is provided by: K. J. Arrow and L. Hurwicz, 'An optimality criterion for decision-making under ignorance', in C. F. Carter and J. L. Ford (eds), *Expectations and Uncertainty in Economics*, Oxford: Basil Blackwell, 1972, pp. 1–11.
22. I think here especially of the work of Ramsey, De Finetti and Savage: F. P. Ramsey, 'Truth and probability', in F. P. Ramsey, *The Foundations of Mathematics and Other Logical Essays*, London: Kegan Paul, Trench, Trubner & Co., 1931, pp. 156–198; B. DeFinetti, 'La prévision: ses lois logiques, ses sources subjectives', *Annales de l'Institut Henri Poincaré*, 1937, pp. 1–68, translated by H. E. Kyburg in H. E. Kyburg, Jr and H. E. Smokler (eds), *Studies in Subjective Probability*, New York: Wiley, 1964, pp. 95–158; and L. J. Savage, *The Foundations of Statistics*, New York: Wiley, 1954. These seminal publications have spawned a vast literature consisting of both journal papers and monographs which is being added to continually.

CHAPTER 2

1. G. L. S. Shackle, *Decision, Order and Time in Human Affairs*, p. 59 (italics in original).
2. *Ibid*., p. 60 (italics in original).
3. Though, as will be appreciated after the ensuing discussion of the ascendancy function, such as assumption is necessary if we wish to guarantee that the global and total maxima of that function coincide.
4. G. L. S. Shackle, *Expectation in Economics*, Cambridge, Cambridge University Press, 1952.
5. *Ibid*., p. 10.
6. *Ibid*., pp. 10–11 (italics in original).
7. *Decision, Order and Time*, p. 70.
8. *Review of Economics and Statistics*, vol. XXXVII, August 1955, p. 45, being a review of *Uncertainty and Business Decisions*, C. F. Carter, G. P. Meredith and G. L. S. Shackle (eds), Liverpool: Liverpool University Press, 1954.
9. These axioms were originally contained in the appendix to *Expectation in Economics*, pp. 128–132. They are reprinted with an alternative form of Axiom 7 in *Decision, Order and Time*, Chapter X, pp. 80–81.
10. *Decision, Order and Time*, p. 71.

11. *Ibid*., p. 73 (italics in original).
12. The objections, however, mainly manifested themselves over the distinction between *possibility* (whether represented by belief or dis-belief) and *probability* which, according to Professor Shackle himself, places the stress on *belief* in particular outcomes. Whether or not Professor Shackle had felt able to retain his original measure of potential surprise as indicating dis-belief in an outcome, as an explicit antidote and contrast to the probabilistic conception, the question of the relationship between possibility and probability was bound to arise.

    The most difficult issue of interpretation has occurred, naturally, over the situation where more than one outcome, for an asset or investment strategy, is assigned zero potential surprise. Remember that by the last of the nine axioms that set out the notion of potential surprise, at least one member of an exhaustive set of rival hypotheses has to carry zero potential surprise. Such a member then becomes 'perfectly possible'. Should several outcomes be awarded that status then it has been contended, most frequently and persuasively by Dr C. F. Carter, that stating that several hypotheses are equally possible does not dispose of the overriding question as to whether or not some of these outcomes might be more likely than others. See his review of Shackle's *Time in Economics* (Amsterdam: North-Holland Publishing Company, 1958) in the *Economic Journal*, vol. LXVIII, no. 271, September 1958. Prior to that in, for example, "A revised theory of expectations", *Economic Journal*, vol. LXIII, no. 252, December 1953, pp. 811–20, Dr Carter had developed the view that for all outcomes that had been assigned the same degree of potential surprise, whether or not that degree was zero, there existed a problem over assesing the relative likelihood of the competing outcomes. This led Dr Carter to propose his own variant of Professor Shackle's theory; and in a sense it re-introduces probability (likelihood) and belief. I shall comment on his viewpoint in chapter 4.
13. *Decision, Order and Time*, pp. 87–8.
14. *Ibid*., p. 114 (italics in original).
15. *Ibid*., pp. 151–2.
16. *Ibid*., p. 147 (italics in original).
17. *Ibid*., pp. 163–4.
18. *Ibid*., p. 164.
19. *Expectation in Economics*, p. 31.

CHAPTER 3

1. *Investment Decisions Under Uncertainty*, Liverpool: Liverpool University Press, 1960, p. 22. See also R. A. D. Egerton, 'Safety-first or gambler preference and the holding of assets', *Oxford Economic Papers*, February 1956, pp. 51–9.

2. The augmented matrix of the system (3.11), is the matrix formed by the addition to the matrix on the left-hand side, as a sixth column, of the column vector on the right-hand side.
3. K. Lancaster, 'A new approach to consumer theory', *Journal of Political Economy*, vol. 74, 1966, pp. 132–57; see also R. G. Lipsey and G. Rosenbluth, "A contribution to the new theory of demand: a rehabilitation of the Giffen good", *Canadian Journal of Economics*, May 1971, pp. 131–163.
4. Professor Shackle has offered some comments on the place of money in his model in *Expectation in Economics*, chapter IV; and, especially, in 'Expectation and liquidity', in M. J. Bowman (ed.), *Uncertainty and Business Decisions*, New York: Social Science Research Council, 1958, pp. 30–44. In the latter he explains the holding of liquid assets in a situation to enable the investor to obtain more information about investment prospects. A shortage of immediate information will not, of course, always mean that an investor will play for safety with some of his assets, and it requires an analysis based on at least a two-unit investment period.

CHAPTER 4

1. *Expectation in Economics*, p. 25 (italics in the original).
2. These points were first advanced, it would appear, by J. de V. Graaf and W. J. Baumol in 'Three notes on expectations in economics', *Economica*, November 1949; and they have been developed most of all by R. A. D. Egerton, in *Investment Decisions Under Uncertainty*, Liverpool: Liverpool University Press, 1960.
3. Given in R. A. D. Egerton, *op. cit.*, p. 13, figure II.i as an illustration of the points made in Graaf-Baumol, *op. cit.*
4. *Decision, Order and Time in Human Affairs*, pp. 176–7 (italics in original).
5. The strongest advocates of this position are perhaps J. Mars and especially B. R. Williams. See, for example: J. Mars, 'A study in expectations', *Yorkshire Bulletin of Economic and Social Research*, July 1950 (this is an extensive review article of *Expectation in Economics*); and B. R. Williams, 'Shackle's ϕ-function and gambler-indifference map', in C. F. Carter, G. P. Meredith and G. L. S. Shackle (eds), *Uncertainty and Business Decisions*, Liverpool: Liverpool University Press, 1954, pp. 122–133.
6. *Expectation in Economics*, pp. 14–16 (italics in original).
7. *Decision, Order and Time in Human Affairs*, pp. 156–7 (emphasis added).
8. By J. Mars, *op. cit.*
9. 'Three versions of the ϕ surface: some notes for a comparison', *Review of Economic Studies*, 1950–51, pp. 119–122; reprinted in G. L. S. Shackle, *Uncertainty in Economics and Other Reflections*, Cambridge University Press, 1954.

   It is apparent from the presentation so far in this book that I have not allowed the gambler-indifference curves the independence from each other Professor Shackle is arguing that they should possess. What I have done, in fact, is to refer continually to a gambler-preference ordering by means of a gambler-preference function. Having implicitly assumed that the latter was continuous and twice differentiable we could always produce a *set* of smooth gambler-indifference curves that were necessarily related. For our part we can see no (valid) reason to take exception to such a procedure. The gambler-indifference curves and their relationships with one another can reflect the temperament of the investor: they can, for example, show increasing 'risk-aversion'; they are able to make allowances for the latter to be influenced by the level of wealth the investor has, and in particular by the potential losses from investment relative to his total wealth (thus reflecting his 'safety-first' attitude, for example). With an appropriately defined preference function gambler-indifference curves can indeed be produced that assume the shape, and the relationships linking one with the other, that Professor Shackle seems to express a preference for as 'best' representing his own conception of gambler-preference. Those sort of gambler-indifference curves, which Professor Shackle uses in all his writings, have been illustrated in the figures in chapter 2.

10. See Professor Shackle's own diagrammatical proof of this; *Review of Economic Studies*, 1950–1, pp. 119–22.
11. *Expectation in Economics*, p. 35.
12. *Ibid.*, p. 90.
13. R. A. D. Egerton, *Investment Decisions Under Uncertainty*, p. 22 (italics in original).
14. C. F. Carter, 'A revised theory of Expectations', *Economic Journal*, December 1953, pp. 811–820.
15. *Ibid.*, pp. 814–818 (italics in the original).
16. *Ibid.*, p. 819.
17. *R. A. D. Egerton, op. cit.*, pp. 23–24.
18. 'Proportional income taxation and risk-taking', *Quarterly Journal of Economics*, 1944, pp. 388–422.
19. *Ibid.*, pp. 393–6.
20. *Ibid.*, pp. 396–7 (italics in original).
21. *Ibid.*, pp. 399–400.
22. See, as an example, P. P. Streeten, 'The effects of taxation on risk-taking', *Oxford Economic Papers*, October 1953, pp. 271–287.
23. Domar and Musgrave, *op cit.* (see note 10), pp. 395–396. We have not discussed the question of taxation in the Shackle model, but taxation can readily be assimilated into the model, as it can in the probabilistic model; the only consequence is that the returns on assets are now to be viewed as net of tax. It makes no difference to the mechanics of the exercise if there happen to be separate taxes on asset interest returns and on asset capital gains. However, whatever type of tax option is envisaged, the introduction of taxation cannot increase the optimum degree of asset diversification within the Shackle model *per se*.

24. *Expectation in Economics*, 2nd edn., p. 93.
25. Dr R. A. D. Egerton, *op. cit.*, pp. 25–33 accepted this point but he contended that the Shackle model could be regarded as equivalent to the Roy model in the special case where asset returns are perfectly positively correlated. He attempted to establish the equivalence by arguing that the indifference curves in the Roy model (defined by the index h, where h is the slope of the straight lines radiating from the mean–axis at the disaster rate of portfolio return (d) on the mean–standard deviation diagram; see appendix B) can be transformed into Shackle gambler-preference indifference curves. Such a transformation and comparison is contrived, however; it has no meaning; and in any case it is unable to increase the degree of asset diversification, for in the situation of perfectly positive asset return correlation there is no advantage to be gained from diversification at all; furthermore, the transformation of the Roy indifference curves into Shackle gambler-preference indifference curves means, inevitably, that choice of portfolio is by reference to the Shacklesque investment frontier.
26. This is the procedure by which Sir John Hicks, in fact, has introduced the Roy idea of a disaster level of return into the expected utility analysis of portfolio selection: see his *Economic Perspectives*, Oxford: The Clarendon Press, 1977, chapter VIII.
27. On constraints and rationing see, for example, P. A. Samuelson, *Foundation of Economic Analysis*, Cambridge: Harvard University Press, 1947; and J. Tobin, *Essays in Economics*, vol. 2, Amsterdam: North-Holland, 1975, chapter 3.
28. See, for example, W. Edwards, 'Note on potential surprise and non-additive subjective probability', *Expectations, Uncertainty and Business Behaviour*, M. J. Bowman (ed.), New York: Social Science Research Council, 1958, p. 45: see also S. A. Ozga, *Expectations in Economics*, London: Weidenfeld & Nicolson, 1965, chapter 3; W. Krelle, *Econometrica*, October 1957, pp. 618–619; and for an application of subjective probability to Shackle's model, see W. Krelle, 'A theory of rational behaviour under uncertainty', *Metroeconomica*, 1958, pp. 51–63. Essentially all that Krelle achieves in this paper is an amalgamation of the ϕ-function and the gambler-preference map which he sees as being completely interdependent. Subjective probability replaces potential surprise but two branches are still maintained within the spirit of the Shackle schema. However, the means by which the individual encapsulates the information in each branch of the 'new ϕ-function' seems to imply that only one asset can be held. The analysis presented here, of a Shacklesque model in chapter 5, is similar to that of Krelle but is not identical since the axiom system I shall use is based on that of Von Neumann–Morgenstern, whereas Krelle's is not. Consequently, although I shall use a probabilistic interpretation of potential surprise, keep 'gains' separate from 'losses', and hence have to employ an index that epitomizes the combined influences on action-choice of gains and losses, I have a different representation of the deci-

sion problem than Krelle and can demonstrate, for example, that multi-asset portfolios can exist.

29. *Econometrica*, October 1957, pp. 618–19.
30. *Decision, Order and Time in Human Affairs*, p. 92 (italics in original).
31. Though what follows was developed before I came across the paper by Professor M. McManus, his work on transformations of functions in economics, which used the ϕ-function as a major example, implicitly proves my result. See his paper: 'Transformations in economic theories', *Review of Economic Studies*, February 1958, pp. 97–108.

CHAPTER 5

1. See D. Bernouilli, 'Exposition of a new theory on the measurement of risk', *Econometrica*, 1954, pp. 23–36; originally published in 1738.
2. J. R. Hicks, *Critical Essays in Monetary Theory*, Oxford: The Clarendon Press, 1967, chapter 6; S. C. Tsiang, 'The rationale of the mean–standard deviation analysis, skewness preference and the demand for money', *American Economic Review*, June 1972, pp. 354–71; and K. Borch, 'The rationale of the mean–standard deviation analysis', *American Economic Review*, June 1974, pp. 428–50.
3. See his *Expectations, Enterprise and Profit*, London: George Allen & Unwin, 1970, p. 111.
4. E. D. Domar and R. A. Musgrave, 'Proportional income taxation and risk-taking', *Quarterly Journal of Economics*, May 1944, pp. 388–422.
5. The formula for partitioned inversion of the matrix in equation (5.12) is stated in note 15, chapter 1. Note that I am assuming here, as always, that there is an interior solution for the x's, i.e. $x \geqslant 0$, since I am excluding consideration of liabilities; strictly if that condition is not satisfied and I am ruling out the possibility that any x can be a liability I would need to use a programming approach to obtain the solution for x. Also, note that I am assuming that the requisite second-order conditions are satisfied for a maximum.
6. *Expectation in Economics*, p. 38.
7. The only other work that treats the Shackle model in the way we have done here is that of W. Krelle, 'A theory of rational behaviour under uncertainty', *Metroeconomica*, April–August, 1959, pp. 51–63. In that paper Professor Krelle converts potential surprise into subjective probability using his mapping function (adopted here) and he then utilizes an axiomatic analysis that results in the investor's having a preference ordering over gains with attendant probabilities of occurrence and over losses with attendant probabilities. For any possible action-choice the values of these two preference orderings were netted-out, producing a magnitude similar to a net Φ-value. It was professor Krelle's contention, in effect, that the gambler-preference map could be dispensed with.

Professor Krelle's analysis is not at all transparent. However, we may venture to suggest, as we did in note 28, chapter 4, that our Shacklesque model differs significantly from his, because although Krelle does utilize a subjective probability and an axiomative approach he has not, as he could have done, produced a set of axioms which lead to the Von Neumann–Morgenstern expected utility theorem. Krelle's ideas as to how choice under uncertainty (à la modification of Shackle's work) should be made, are reiterated and developed further in his *Price Theory*, Zurich: Polygraphieseher Verlag A.G., 1961. That work is criticized in, for example, S. A. Ozga, *Expectations in Economic Theory*, London: Weidenfeld & Nicolson, 1965.

CHAPTER 6

1. G. L. S. Shackle, *Expectations, Enterprise and Profit*, London: George Allen & Unwin, 1970, chapter 5.
2. One of the comments (as described in the Introduction), made by Dr J. Mars about the Shackle framework. See his 'A study in expectations: reflections on Shackle's "expectation in economics", Part I', *Yorkshire Bulletin of Economic and Social Research*, vol. 2, no. 2, July 1950, pp. 63–98.
3. See the symposium on Professor Shackle's theory in *Metroeconomica*, April–August 1959.
4. D. Bernouilli, 'Exposition of a new theory on the measurement of risk', *Econometrica*, 1954, pp. 23–36 (first published in 1738).
5. The model utilized here is based on that of A. Sandmo, 'The effect of uncertainty on saving decisions', *Review of Economic Studies*, vol. 37, 1970, pp. 353–360. The most general, and sophisticated, model is contained in J. H. Dreze and F. Modigliani, 'Consumption decisions under uncertainty', *Journal of Economic Theory*, December 1972, pp. 308–335. Full bibliographical detail is available in J. D. Hey, *Uncertainty in Microeconomics*, Oxford: Martin Robertson, 1974.
6. The second-order conditions are simple in this case (since there is only one choice variable):

   $$E(U_{11} - 2rU_{12} + r^2 U_{22}) < 0; \quad (U_{12} \equiv U_{21})$$

7. From equation (6.4) and note 6 we have this as the second-order condition:

   $$2E[C_2 - 2rC_1] = -\tfrac{2}{3}[Y_2 + Y_1\bar{r}] < 0 \text{ if } \bar{r} > 0$$

8. As noted the first paper on this subject was G. J. Stigler, 'The economics of information', *Journal of Political Economy*, June 1961, pp. 213–225. For further detailed references on consumer and labour search models, see J. D. Hey, *op. cit.*

9. The framework employed here is based on M. H. Degroot, *Optimal Statistical Decisions*, New York: McGraw-Hill, 1970. See also J. D. Hey, *op. cit.*, where full references on the literature can be found.
10. This section is derived from the paper by M. K. Block and J. M. Heineke, 'The allocation of effort under uncertainty: the case of risk averse behaviour', *Journal of Political Economy*, March/April 1973, pp. 376–385.
11. This analysis is based on A. Sandmo, 'On the theory of the competitive firm under price uncertainty', *American Economic Review*, March 1971, pp. 65–73. For extensions see J. D. Hey, *op. cit.*

CHAPTER 7

1. From chapter 2, and especially from chapter 4, recall that several commentators have not been prepared to accept that Shackle is right; because in their opinion an individual can say that two outcomes are both judged by him to be perfectly possible, and with zero degree of potential surprise (hence they both have attached to them the minimum degree of *dis-belief* in their occurrence), yet the individual can assign a higher degree of probability of occurrence to the one outcome than to the other. One of those who challenged Shackle on this point, Sir Charles Carter, remains convinced that he is right. In kindly commenting on the manuscript of this book he has argued that, in regard to real world investment decisions:

   > The states of nature which *are* considered are generally unsurprising: they are of the nature of 'Conservative victory at the next election/ Labour victory/Hung parliament', any of which I could regard as having zero potential surprise at the moment. But this does not mean that they are treated as the *same*. In correspondence with Shackle on this issue, it seems to me that the difficulty is semantic: he says (in effect) that if I regard a Thatcher victory as more likely than a Foot victory, I must attach positive potential surprise to a Foot victory. I think this distorts the meaning of 'surprise', and that consequently it is better to go back to a concept of 'degree of belief'.

   Note that Sir Charles has had wide experience of making and observing investment decisions, both of a financial and a physical nature, as a director of major companies and as a professional economist studying the physical investment decisions of many firms over the years. His observation on the types of states of nature considered is a most interesting one. Additionally, from his business experience he has made counter-observations to our critique of his development of the Shackle model considered in chapter 4. This will be referred to in note 7.
2. On this issue reference can be made to the comments made in chapter 4

and to the views expressed in correspondence by Professor Shackle which are recorded there.

3. References to models of banks' portfolio behaviour have been made in chapter 1. If we think of the form of model employed by Parkin *et al.*, then if the banks set the rate of interest on deposits and there is an excess supply of deposits by the banks at the rate of interest (remember that deposits are liabilities to banks so they are supplied by them in the terminology of financial theory) then deposits are determined by the non bank sector and are endogenous to it. This is the line of argument favoured by Parkin *et al.*, supplemented by the fact that, at various times, the monetary authorities have set effective limits on the banks' level of advances. See: J. M. Parkin, M. R. Gray and R. J. Barrett, 'The portfolio behaviour of commercial banks', in D. Heathfield and K. Hilton (eds), *The Econometric Study of the U.K.*, London: Macmillan (1970).
4. The empirical data for the U.K. suggest that the liquid assets constraint was binding and effective. We do not possess explicit knowledge of the banks' utility function and the facts indicate that the holdings of liquid assets stand on average at 30 per cent rather than at 28 per cent of deposits. However, that figure has been a consistent one, indicating that in order to guarantee meeting the legal constraint (or perhaps for, additional, precautionary reasons) the banks are influenced by the 28 per cent ratio. Indeed, after 1971 when the constraint was reduced, the liquid assets ratio of the banks fell *pari passu* with that reduction.
5. M. Wray has made a limited use of the theory. See her book *The Women's Outwear Industry*, London: Duckworth & Co., 1957.
6. Some general observations on testing theories of uncertainty, paying special attention to Shackle's theory, can be found in A. D. Roy, 'The empirical testing of alternative theories of uncertainty', in C. F. Carter *et al.* (eds), *Uncertainty and Business Decisions*, Liverpool: Liverpool University Press, 1957, pp. 75–88.
7. From his experience in, and his observations of, the taking of business decisions, Sir Charles Carter still holds to the opinion he had in the early 1950s that Shackle is on the right lines, that the orthodox approach is wrong (because of its emphasis on seriable experiments and hence risk), but that Shackle has not gone far enough. His view is that Shackle should have referred to degrees of belief and that decisions are simplified but they are made malleable by the process we considered in chapter 4. Thus in correspondence (30 August 1982) he has reiterated his position:

    > The *order* of the decision-making process is to think of states of nature which ought to be considered first, and *then* of actions appropriate to each state, before reaching the final decision on an overall set of actions. This is very clearly seen in portfolio decisions about overseas investment. Here Shackle is, I think, wrong: the problem is not one of reaching focus-gains for a particular investment over a range of states, but of deciding between investments

for a particular state and then finding some way of dealing with the multiplicity of states.

Accordingly, he stands by his theory based on the above ideas which are outlined and criticized in chapter 4. He does so on the grounds that real decisions are made that way; and that, as part of the decision-making process, ultimate indecision (his views upon which I commented in chapter 4) is a common phenomenon.

Bibliography

Allais, M. 'Le comportement de l'homme rationnel devant le risque: critique des postulates et axiomes de l'école Americaine', *Econometrica*, October 1953, pp. 503–46.

Arrow, K. J. and Hurwicz, L. 'An optimality criterion for decision making under ignorance', in C. F. Carter and J. L. Ford (eds), *Expectations and Uncertainty in Economics*, Oxford: Basil Blackwell, 1972, pp. 1–11.

Arrow, K. J. *Essays in the Theory of Risk-Bearing*, Amsterdam: North-Holland, 1971.

Beaugrand, P. 'Le temps, l'imagination, l'incertitude, dans la théorie du Professor G. L. S. Shackle', *Revue Economique*, March, 1982, pp. 297–322.

Bernouilli, D. 'Exposition of a new theory on the measurement of risk', *Econometrica*, 1954, pp. 23–36.

Block, M. K. and Heineke, J. M. 'The allocation of effort under uncertainty: the case of risk averse behaviour', *Journal of Political Economy*, March/April, 1973, pp. 376–85.

Borch, K. 'A note on uncertainty and indifference curves', *Review of Economic Studies*, January, 1969, pp. 1–4.

Borch, K. 'The rationale of the mean-standard deviation analysis: comment', *American Economic Review*, June, 1974, pp. 428–50.

Carter, C. F. 'A revised theory of expectations', *Economic Journal*, Vol. LXIII, No. 252, December, 1953, pp. 811–20.

Carter, C. F., Meredith, G. P. and Shackle, G. L. S. (eds) *Uncertainty and Business Decisions*, Liverpool: Liverpool University Press, 1954.

Carter, C. F. Review of 'Time in Economics', *Economic Journal*, Vol. LXVIII, No. 271, September, 1958.

Carter, C. F. and Ford, J. L. (eds) *Expectations and Uncertainty in Economics: Essays in Honour of G. L. S. Shackle*, Oxford: Basil Blackwell, 1972.

Cass, D. and Stiglitz, J. E. 'Risk aversion and separability and wealth effects on portfolios with many assets', *Review of Economic Studies*, July, 1972, pp. 331–54.

Clayton, G., Dodds, J. C., Driscoll, M. J. and Ford, J. L. *The Portfolio and Debt Behaviour of British Building Societies*, SUERF Pamphlet 16A, 1975.

Coddington, A. 'On the theory of bargaining', in C. F. Carter and J. L. Ford (eds), *Expectations and Uncertainty in Economics*, Oxford: Basil Blackwell, 1972, pp. 43–57.

Coddington, 'Keynesian economics: the search for first principles', *Journal of Economic Literature*, Vol. XIV, No. 4, 1976, pp. 1258–73.

De Finetti, B. 'La prévision: ses lois logiques, ses sources subjectives', *Annales de l'Institut Henri Poincaré*, 1937, pp. 1–68; reprinted in: H. E. Kyburg, Jnr. and H. E. Smokler (eds), *Studies in Subjective Probability*, New York: John Wiley & Sons, 1964, pp. 95–158.

Degroot, M. H. *Optimal Statistical Decisions*, New York: McGraw-Hill, 1970.

Domar, E. D. and Musgrave, R. A. 'Proportional income taxation and risk-taking', *Quarterly Journal of Economics*, 1944, pp. 388–422.

Dorfman, R. Review of *Uncertainty and Business Decisions*, C. F. Carter, G. P. Meredith and G. L. S. Shackle (eds), Liverpool: Liverpool University Press, 1954, in *Review of Economics and Statistics*, Vol. XXXVII, August, 1955.

Dreze, J. H. and Modigliani, F. 'Consumption decisions under uncertainty', *Journal of Economic Theory*, Vol. 5, 1972, pp. 308–35.

Egerton, R. A. D. 'Safety-first or gambler preference and the holding of assets', *Oxford Economic Papers*, February, 1956, pp. 51–9.

Egerton, R. A. D. *Investment Decisions Under Uncertainty*, Liverpool: Liverpool University Press, 1960.

Edwards, W. 'Note on potential surprise and non-additive subjective probability', in *Uncertainty and Business Decisions*, M. J. Bowman (ed), New York: Social Science Research Council, 1958, p. 45.

Graaf, J. de V. and Baumol, W. J. 'Three notes on expectations in economics', *Economica*, November, 1949, pp. 338–42.

Guiton, H. 'Causalité et imagination', *Revue d'Economique Politique*, January–February, 1980, pp. 56–60.

Hart, O. D. 'Some negative results on the existence of comparative statics results in portfolio theory', *Review of Economic Studies*, December, 1975, pp. 615–21.

Hey, J. D. *Uncertainty in Microeconomics*, Oxford: Martin Robertson, 1979.

Hicks, J. R. 'A suggestion for simplifying the theory of money', *Economica*, February, 1935.

Hicks, J. R. *Critical Essays in Monetary Theory*, Oxford: The Clarendon Press, 1967.

Hicks, J. R. *Economic Perspectives*, Oxford: The Clarendon Press, 1977.

Jeffreys, H. *Theory of Probability*, Cambridge: Cambridge University Press, 1939.

Keynes, J. M. *Treatise on Probability*, London: Macmillan, 1921.

Kierstead, B. S. 'Decision-taking and the theory of games', in C. F. Carter and J. L. Ford (eds), *Expectations and Uncertainty in Economics*, Oxford: Basil Blackwell, 1972, pp. 160–74.

Krelle, W. Review of G. L. S. Shackle, *Uncertainty in Economics*, Liverpool:

Liverpool University Press, 1954, in *Econometrica*, October, 1957, pp. 618–19.

Krelle, W. 'A theory of rational behaviour under uncertainty', *Metroeconomica*, April–August, 1959, pp. 51–63.

Krelle, W. *Price Theory*, Zurich: Polygraphieseher Verlag, A. G., 1961.

Lachmann, L. M. 'Professor Shackle on the economic significance of time', *Metroeconomica*, April–August, 1959, pp. 64–73.

Lachmann, L. M. 'From Mises to Shackle: an essay on Austrian economics and the Kaleidic Society', *Journal of Economic Literature*, March, 1976, pp. 54–62.

Lancaster, K. 'A new approach to consumer theory', *Journal of Political Economy*, 74, 1966, pp. 132–57.

Lintner, J. 'The valuation of risk assets and the selection of risky investments in stock portfolios and capital budgets', *Review of Economics and Statistics*, Vol. 47, 1965, pp. 13–37.

Lipsey, R. G. and Rosenbluth, G. 'A contribution to the new theory of demand: a rehabilitation of the Giffen good', *Canadian Journal of Economics*, May, 1971, pp. 131–63.

Luce, D. R. and Raiffa, H. *Games and Decisions*, New York: John Wiley & Sons, 1957.

Mars, J. 'A study in expectations: reflections on Shackle's "Expectation in Economics", Part I', *Yorkshire Bulletin of Economic and Social Research*, Vol. 2, No. 2, July, 1950, pp. 63–98.

McManus, M. 'Transformations in economic theories', *Review of Economic Studies*, February, 1958, pp. 97–108.

Neane, D. H. 'Multiperiod consumption-investment decisions and risk preference', *Journal of Economic Theory*, Vol. 3, 1971, pp. 40–53.

von Neumann, J. and Morgenstern, O. *The Theory of Games and Economic Behaviour*, Princeton: Princeton University Press, 2nd edition, 1947.

Nicholson, M. B. 'Uncertainty and crisis behaviour: an illustration of conflict and peace research', in C. F. Carter and J. L. Ford (eds) *Expectations and Uncertainty in Economics: Essays in Honour of G. L. Shackle* Oxford: Basil Blackwell, 1972, pp. 237–65.

Ozga, S. *Expectations in Economic Theory*, London: Wiedenfeld and Nicolson, 1965.

Parkin, J. M. Gray, M. R. and Barratt, R. J. 'The portfolio behaviour of commercial banks', in D. Heathfield and K. Hilton (eds), *The Econometric Study of the United Kingdom*, London: Macmillan, 1970.

Pratt, J. W. 'Risk-aversion in the large and the small', *Econometrica*, Vol. 32, 1964, pp. 122–36.

Pyle, D. H. and Turnovsky, S. J. 'Safety-first and expected utility maximisation in mean-standard deviation portfolio analysis', *Review of Econmics and Statistics*, Vol. 52, 1970, pp. 75–81.

Ramsey, F. P. 'Truth and probability', in F. P. Ramsey, *The Foundations of*

Mathematics and Other Logical Essays, London: K. Paul, Trench, Trubner and Company, 1931, pp. 156–98.

Roy, A. D. 'Safety-first and the holding of assets', *Econometrica*, Vol. XX, July, 1952, pp. 431–49.

Roy, A. D. 'The empirical testing of alternative theories of uncertainty', in C. F. Carter, G. P. Meredith and G. L. S. Shackle (eds), *Uncertainty and Business Decisions*, Liverpool: Liperpool University Press, 1957, pp. 75–88.

Samuelson, P. A. *Foundations of Economic Analysis*, Cambridge: Harvard University Press, 1947.

Samuelson, P. A. 'Lifetime portfolio selection by dynamic stochastic programming', *Review of Economics and Statistics*, Vol. 51, 1969, pp. 239–46.

Sandmo, A. 'The effect of uncertainty on saving decisions', *Review of Economic Studies*, Vol. 37, 1970, pp. 353–60.

Sandmo, A. 'On the theory of the competitive firm under price uncertainty', *American Economic Review*, March, 1971, pp. 65–73.

Savage, L. J. *The Foundations of Statistics*, New York: John Wiley and Sons, 1954.

Shackle, G. L. S. 'Three versions of the ϕ surface: some notes for a comparison', *Review of Economic Studies*, 1950–1, pp. 119–22.

Shackle, G. L. S. *Expectation in Economics*, Cambridge: Cambridge University Press, 2nd edition, 1952 (1st edition, 1949).

Shackle, G. L. S. *Uncertainty in Economics and Other Reflections*, Cambridge: Cambridge University Press, 1954.

Shackle, G. L. S. *Time in Economics*, Amsterdam: North Holland Publishing Company, 1957.

Shackle, G. L. S. 'Expectation and liquidity', in M. J. Bowman (ed), *Uncertainty and Business Decisions*, New York: Social Science Research Council, 1958, pp. 30–44.

Shackle, G. L. S. *Decision, Order and Time in Human Affairs*, Cambridge: Cambridge University Press, 1st edition, 1961; 2nd edition, 1969.

Shackle, G. L. S. *Expectations, Enterprise and Profit*, London: George Allen and Unwin, 1970.

Shackle, G. L. S. *Epistemics and Economics*, Cambridge: Cambridge University Press, 1972.

Shackle, G. L. S. *Imagination and the Nature of Choice*, Edinburgh: Edinburgh University Press, 1979.

Sharpe, W. F. 'Capital asset prices: a theory of market equilibrium under conditions of risk', *Journal of Finance*, 1964, pp. 425–42.

Stiglitz, J. E. 'The effects of income, wealth and capital gains taxation on risk-taking', *Quarterly Journal of Economics*, Vol. 83, 1967, pp. 263–83.

Stigler, G. J. 'The economics of information', *Journal of Political Economy*, June, 1961, pp. 213–25.

Streeten, P. P. 'The effects of taxation on risk-taking', *Oxford Economic Papers*, October 1953, pp. 271–87.

Tobin, J. 'Liquidity preference as behaviour towards risk', *Review of Economic Studies*, February, 1958, pp. 65–86.

Tobin, J. *Essays in Economics*, Vol. 2, *Econometrics and Consumption*, Amsterdam: North-Holland, 1975.

Tsiang, S. C. 'The rationale of the mean-standard deviation analysis, skewness preference and the demand for money', *American Economic Review*, June, 1972, pp. 345–71.

Venn, J. *The Logic of Chance*, London: Methuen, 3rd edition, 1880.

White, W. R. 'Some econometric models and deposit bank portfolio behaviour in the U.K. 1963–1970', in G. Renton (ed), *Modelling the Economy*, London: Heinemann, 1975.

Williams, B. R. 'Shackle's ϕ-function and gambler-indifference map', in C. F. Carter, G. P. Meredith and G. L. Shackle (eds), *Uncertainty and Business Decisions*, Liverpool: Liverpool University Press, 1954, pp. 122–33.

Wray, M. *The Women's Outwear Industry*, London: Duckworth & Co., 1957.

Index

ϕ function, *see* ascendancy function

absolute preference, *see* axiom of combining
action choice index (ACI), 147–8
aggregation conditions (Cournot *and* Engel), 31, 93
aggregative economics, *see* macroeconomics
Arrow, K. J., 24
ascendancy function, 59, 60–2, 65, 72–5, 77, 98–103, 104–5, 178–80
  as utility function, 107
  conversion into choice function, 142
  critique, 137–40
  replacement with preference ordering, 144, 180
  role of, 105–12
axiom of combining (stochastic dominance or absolute preference), 20–1, 59, 139, 145, 147, 152–3
axiomatic treatment of Shackle's model, 144–55

Bernouilli, D., 141

capital investment decision, 11, 56, 57–8, 99–100, 103
  application of Shackle's theory, 157–61, 177–83
  market forces and, 158–9
Carter, C. F., 'A revised theory of expectations', 114–18
Carter, C. F. and Ford, J. L., *Expectations and Uncertainty in Economics*, 7
certainty model of consumer theory, 166
choice of output under price uncertainty, model of, 173–6
consumer search model, 166–9
continuity, 19, 154

decision making
  construction of models, 4–5, 10, 64–5, 134
  in general, 11, 116, 136, 138–9, 183–7
  uniqueness of, 7–8, 54, 123, 182
diversification
  of capital investment, 11, 160
  of financial assets, 10, 35–9, 41–5, 82–7, 102–3, 113–29, 148–9
Domar, Professor E. D. and Musgrave, Professor R. A., 123–7, 148
Dorfman, Robert, 70

Egerton, Dr R. A. D., 8, 81, 121
  Investment Decisions under Uncertainty, 113–14, 117–19
expectations and uncertainty, Shackle's theory of, 7–12, 54–78
  application to portfolio selection, 79–95
  axiomatic treatment, 144–55
  critique, 96–134, 135–44, 155–6
  lack of empirical research, 187
  reasons disregarded, 10–11, 96–7
  summary and conclusions, 177–87
  wider applications, 157–76
expected utility theorem, 12, 18–22, 58–9, 116, 147, 152, 154
  money plus *n* risky assets, 41–5
  money plus one risky asset, 39–41
  n risky assets, 35–9
  two risky assets, 23–35
expected value of returns, 56–8, 157–8, 160

Fisherian model, 161–3

gambler-preference map, 63–4, 65, 75–7, 102–3, 104–5, 179–81
  critique, 140
  role of, 105–12
general equilibrium (GE) theory, 2

Hicks, Professor Sir John R., 10, 16, 44

independence of irrelevant alternatives, *see* monotonicity
individual utility function, 78, 80–2, 140–1, 147, 148–9, 154–5, 160
  in consumption contexts, 161–5, 166
  in labour context, 170–3
institutional investment, application of Shackle's theory, 87, 129, 184–5
investment opportunities frontier, 24–5, 80–1, 113–27
  mean–variance frontier, derivation, 46–8

Jeffreys, H., *Theory of Probability*, 54

Keynes, John Maynard, 3–4, 6
  The General Theory of Employment, Interest and Money, 15
  Treatise on Probability, 54

Knight, Frank, 10
Krelle, Professor, W., 129, 180

labour choice model, 169–73
Lancaster, Professor Kelvin, 86
Lintner, J., 44

macroeconomics (Keynesian), 3–4, 6
Mars, Dr J., 9–10
money, role of, *see* riskless assets
monotonicity (independence of irrelevant alternatives), 19

net present value criterion, 11–12
non-divisible, non-seriable experiments, 55–6

ordering of the outcomes, 18

portfolio choice (individual), 8–9, 45, 58–9, 142–4
  application of Shackle's theory, 79–95, 177–83
  constraints on, 87, 129, 184
  critique of Shackle's theory, 96–134
  equations, 88–93
  general economic situation, as factor, 117–18, 121
  hedging, 116–19
  orthodox approach, 15–45, 143
  safety-first models, 45, 47, 48–53, 87, 127–8
potential surprise function, 8, 55, 59–60, 64–5, 68–72, 98–105, 178
  critique, 114–19, 135–7
  in terms of subjective probability, 129–34, 145–7, 153, 179
  non-distributional nature, 105, 178
  residual hypothesis, 70, 178
Pratt, J. W., 24
primary focus-values, 62, 65, 98–9, 108, 139, 178, 182–3
probability-based theories, 6, 7–8, 12, 15–53
  and unique decisions, 54–6, 123–7
  subjective probability and potential surprise, 129–34, 145–7, 153, 179
  see also expected utility theorem; states of nature approach
Pyle, D. H. and Turnovsky, S. J., 53

rational expectations hypothesis, 6, 18, 21, 82–3, 142–3
risk-preference, measurement of, 76–7, 138
riskless assets, 39, 93–5
  as delaying strategy, 116
  liquid assets ratio, 184–5
  Shackle's theory and, 185–6
  speculative demand for money, 41
Roy, A. D., safety-first models of asset choice, 45, 46–7, 48–53, 127–8

scale opportunity line, 158–9, 181–2
separation theorem, 44–5
Shackle, Professor, G. L. S.
  Decision, Order and Time, 71, 74
  Epistemics and Economics, 2, 4, 7
  Expectation in Economics, 9, 71, 74, 80, 106, 113, 127
  Imagination and the Nature of Choice, 7
  see also expectations and uncertainty
Sharpe, W. F., 44
speculative investment, *see* portfolio choice
standardized focus-values, 62–3, 65, 98–103, 105, 110–12, 113–14, 158, 181
states of nature approach, 16–22, 60, 115
Stigler, G. J., 167
stimulus function, *see* ascendancy function
stochastic dominance or absolute preference, *see* axion of combining
substitutability of outcomes and portfolios, 19
substitution effect, 31–3, 163

time, role of, 1, 5–6, 12
Tobin, J., 44
  Tobinesque utility function, 23, 24, 28, 30, 40–1, 95
transitivity of portfolios, 19
two-period consumption-saving model, 161–6

uncertainty, certainty of, 1–2, 5
  see also expectations and uncertainty
utility functions, *see* expected utility theorem; individual utility function; Tobinesque utility function *under* Tobin, J.

Venn, J., *The Logic of Chance*, 54–5
Von Neumann, J. and Morgenstern, O., 12, 18, 149, 152, 154, 156, 173

Index by Ann Edwards